Statistics for Business and Economics

Problems, Exercises, and Case Studies

Fifth Edition

Statistics for Business and Economics

Problems, Exercises, and Case Studies

Fifth Edition

EDWIN MANSFIELD

DIRECTOR, CENTER FOR ECONOMICS AND TECHNOLOGY
UNIVERSITY OF PENNSYLVANIA

W. W. Norton & Company • New York • London

Composition by Roberta Flechner Graphics.

ISBN 0-393-96488-4

W. W. Norton & Company, Inc., 500 Fifth Avenue, New York, N.Y. 10110
W. W. Norton & Company Ltd., 10 Coptic Street, London WC1A 1PU

1 2 3 4 5 6 7 8 9 0

Contents

Preface

This study guide is designed to accompany my textbook, *Statistics for Business and Economics: Methods and Applications,* Fifth Edition. As in the text, there is an emphasis on actual cases in which statistical methods have been used.

A new feature of this study guide is the inclusion of the following five full-length cases:

1. Faulty Inspection of Industrial Output, by W. Edwards Deming

2. Estimates of Unmeasured Television Viewing, by Network Television Association

3. The Louisiana State Museum, by Caroline M. Fisher and Claire J. Anderson

4. U.S. Consumer Demand for Dairy Products, by R. Haidacher, J. Blaylock, and L. Myers

5. How Large Are Economic Forecast Errors? by Stephen K. McNees

In addition, each chapter of the study guide contains six parts:

1. A *Chapter Profile,* which provides a brief overview of the highlights of the corresponding chapter in the text. This profile, which is more informal and self-contained than the chapter summary in the text, helps to orient students by summarizing the highlights of the text discussion.

2. A list of *Behavioral Objectives,* which contains the key concepts that students must master, as well as specific tasks that students should be able to do. The list indicates in detail exactly what students should make sure they understand and can do.

3. A brief *Case Study,* which generally is based on an actual case (and which uses real or realistic numbers) and illustrates how statistical techniques are used to solve real-world problems. To answer the questions regarding each case study, students must decide which techniques are relevant and how to apply them.

4. *Multiple-Choice Questions,* which probe students' ability to apply statistical concepts and to understand the theory underlying statistical techniques. They help students test their understanding of the basic concepts and methods taken up in the chapter.

5. *Problems and Problem Sets,* which are based on actual business and economic situations and which test students' ability to apply the statistical methods presented in the chapter. An attempt has been made to keep the problems and problem sets to a reasonable length, since the amount of time that students can devote to such problems is limited. An important feature of this book is the inclusion of some problems utilizing computer packages. Of course, if such packages are not available to the student, these problems can be worked by hand.

6. *Answers* to the Case Study questions, the Multiple-Choice Questions, and the Problems and Problem Sets are given. These answers show, step by step, how each question or problem is solved. They should provide sufficient feedback to

students to enable them to gauge their own progress and to see where they may have gone astray.

I am indebted to my wife, Lucile, for help in preparing this study guide and in reading and correcting proofs.

Philadelphia, 1993   E.M.

PART I

Descriptive Statistics

Summary and Description of Data

Chapter Profile

A *frequency distribution* is a table showing the number of cases that fall into each of a number of classes. To establish a frequency distribution, one must set up a number of well-defined classes, each class being defined by a lower limit and an upper limit. Then one determines how many cases fall into each class.

Frequency distributions are often presented in graphical as well as tabular form. A *histogram* is composed of a series of bars or rectangles; the bottom of each bar is the line segment on the horizontal axis that corresponds to the interval from the lower limit of the class to its upper limit. The area of each bar is proportional to the number of cases in the class. A *frequency polygon* is another type of graphical representation of a frequency distribution.

There are several frequently used measures of location, or central tendency: the mean, median, and mode. The *mean* is the sum of the numbers contained in the frequency distribution divided by how many numbers there are in the distribution. The *median* is a figure that is chosen so that one-half of the numbers in the frequency distribution are below (or equal to) it and one-half are above (or equal to) it. The *mode* is the number in the frequency distribution that occurs most often. These three measures of central tendency may differ substantially from one another.

Measures of variability, or dispersion, have been devised to indicate the extent to which the individual cases included in a frequency distribution depart from the average. The simplest measure of variability is the *range,* which is defined as the difference between the highest and lowest value in the frequency distribution. A more frequently used measure is the *standard deviation,* which is defined as the square root of the mean of the squared deviations of the observations from their mean.

A frequency distribution with a relatively long tail to the right is said to be *skewed to the right,* while a frequency distribution with a relatively long tail to the left is said to be *skewed to the left.* A *symmetrical* frequency distribution, one with symmetrical tails, is said to have no skewness.

Behavioral Objectives

A. You should be able to define the following key concepts from Chapters 1 and 2:

frequency distribution	median
lower class limit	mode
upper class limit	central tendency
class interval	variability
histogram	range
frequency polygon	standard deviation
mean	variance

skewed to the left	skewed to the right
symmetrical	bimodal frequency distribution
stem-and-leaf diagram	coefficient of variation
Pareto diagram	run chart

B. Make sure that you can do each of the following:
1. Construct a frequency distribution from a set of numbers.
2. Draw a histogram to represent a frequency distribution.
3. Construct a frequency polygon to represent a frequency distribution.
4. Calculate the mean of a set of numbers, given (a) the set of numbers and (b) a frequency distribution of the numbers.
5. Compute the median of a set of numbers, given (a) the set of numbers and (b) a frequency distribution of the numbers.
6. Calculate the mode of a set of numbers.
7. Compute the standard deviation of a set of numbers, given (a) the set of numbers and (b) a frequency distribution of the numbers.
8. Calculate the range of a set of numbers.
9. Determine whether a frequency distribution is skewed to the left, skewed to the right, or symmetrical.
10. Determine whether a frequency distribution has more than one mode.

Telechron Clock Gears: A Case Study[1]

A manufacturing firm was interested some years ago in the diameters of the Telechron clock gears it was producing. A sample of 50 of the gears was drawn, and it was found that their diameters (in inches) were as follows:

.4160	.4159	.4158	.4157	.4155
.4148	.4149	.4156	.4148	.4130
.4160	.4143	.4158	.4155	.4152
.4148	.4159	.4135	.4152	.4157
.4143	.4153	.4154	.4150	.4152
.4160	.4153	.4150	.4157	.4146
.4141	.4156	.4152	.4156	.4149
.4156	.4145	.4155	.4147	.4150
.4140	.4152	.4149	.4150	.4146
.4150	.4150	.4148	.4155	.4149

(a) Construct a frequency distribution of the diameters.
(b) What is the median of this frequency distribution?
(c) What is the mode of the frequency polygon?
(d) If the firm wanted the diameters to be less than or equal to .4165 and greater than or equal to .4155 inch, to what extent was this objective realized?

After analyzing the results of the sample described above, the firm built adjustments and attachments into the machine which cut the gear. Then a sample of 30 of the gears was drawn, and it was found that their diameters (in inches) were as follows:

1. This case is taken from Theodore H. Brown's article on "Quality Control" in the *Harvard Business Review*.

.4166	.4165	.4160	.4164	.4163
.4154	.4160	.4164	.4160	.4161
.4165	.4163	.4159	.4162	.4162
.4162	.4159	.4163	.4161	.4161
.4157	.4164	.4162	.4161	.4164
.4164	.4161	.4161	.4161	.4161

(e) Construct a frequency distribution of the diameters in this second sample.
(f) Compare the median and range of the diameters in the second sample with those in the first sample.
(g) Assuming that the firm wanted the diameters to be less than or equal to .4165 and greater than or equal to .4155 inch, write a one-paragraph report describing your findings.

Multiple-Choice Questions

1. The frequency distribution of the hourly wage rate of 100 employees of a paper mill is as follows:

Wage rate	Number of Workers
$4 to under $6	40
$6 to under $8	20
$8 to under $10	20
$10 to under $12	10
$12 to under $14	10

The mean wage rate is approximately

(a) $8.60.
(b) $8.00.
(c) $7.60.
(d) $7.10.
(e) $6.10.

2. In question 1, the median wage rate is approximately

(a) $5.00.
(b) $6.00.
(c) $7.00.
(d) $8.00.
(e) $9.00.

3. In Delaware, suppose that the following 12 cities had 5,000 or more inhabitants in the year in which your boss is interested.

City	Population	City	Population
Brookside	15,255	Newark	25,247
Claymont	10,022	Seaford	5,256
Dover	23,507	Stanton	5,495
Edgemoor	7,397	Talleyville	6,880
Elsmere	6,493	Wilmington	70,195
Milford	5,366	Wilmington Manor	9,233

Source: *World Almanac.*

Suppose that your boss asks you to construct a frequency distribution of the populations of Delaware cities in this year, where the class intervals are 5,000 to 9,999, 10,000 to 25,000, and over 25,000. The class containing the most cities contains

(a) 5 cities.
(b) 6 cities.
(c) 7 cities.
(d) 8 cities.
(e) 9 cities.

4. In the circumstances described in question 3, none of the classes contains less than

(a) 1 city.
(b) 2 cities.
(c) 3 cities.
(d) 4 cities.
(e) 5 cities.

5. Based on the data given in question 3, the median population of these Delaware cities was

(a) 6,493.
(b) 9,233.
(c) 8,315.
(d) 7,397.
(e) 6,880.

6. From the data in question 3, the range of the population of these Delaware cities was

(a) 80,386.
(b) 74,849.
(c) 73,802.
(d) 64,939.
(e) 5,314.

7. Based on the date in question 3, the frequency distribution of the population of these Delaware cities is

   (a) skewed to the right.
   (b) skewed to the left.
   (c) symmetrical.
   (d) all of the above.
   (e) none of the above.

8. Using the data in question 3, the mean population of Delaware cities (with 5,000 or more inhabitants) is

   (a) greater than 15,000.
   (b) more than 50 percent greater than the median.
   (c) larger than the median.
   (d) larger than the populations of nine of the cities.
   (e) all of the above.

9. A frequency distribution of the heights of buildings of 500 ft. or more in New York City is given below:

Height (ft.)	Number of buildings
1,300 to under 1,400	1
1,200 to under 1,300	1
1,100 to under 1,200	0
1,000 to under 1,100	1
900 to under 1,000	3
800 to under 900	3
700 to under 800	10
600 to under 700	23
500 to under 600	53

   The median of this distribution is

   (a) between 500 and 520 ft.
   (b) between 520 and 540 ft.
   (c) between 540 and 560 ft.
   (d) between 560 and 580 ft.
   (e) between 580 and 600 ft.

10. If we confine our attention only to buildings of 900 ft. or more, the mean height of such buildings in New York City is

    (a) between 900 and 999 ft.
    (b) over 1,100 ft.
    (c) less than the median.
    (d) equal to the median.
    (e) about 1,083 ft.

11. An automobile manufacturer obtains data concerning the sales of five of its dealers in the last week of 1993. The results indicate that the standard deviation of their sales equals 5 autos. If this is so, the variance of their sales equals

   (a) $\sqrt{5}$ autos.
   (b) 5 autos.
   (c) 25 (autos)^2.
   (d) $1/\sqrt{5}$ autos.
   (e) none of the above.

12. In the situation in question 11, the automobile manufacturer finds that the median sales of the five dealers equals 6 autos during this period. Based on the information in question 11,

   (a) the median is less than the mean sales of these dealers.
   (b) the median equals the mean sales of these dealers.
   (c) the median is greater than the mean sales of the dealers.
   (d) the median is greater than the range of the sales of the dealers.
   (e) we cannot be sure that any of the above are true.

Problems and Problem Sets

1. Bank A draws a sample of eight checks written by the Jones Manufacturing Company in 1993. These checks are for the following amounts (in dollars):

96	1,400	18	96
128	142	103	2,998

   For this sample, what is the value of (a) $\sum_{i=1}^{n} X_i$, (b) $\sum_{i=1}^{n} X_i^2$, (c) the variance, and (d) the standard deviation?

2. The following are the numbers of years that 50 employees of the Acme Corporation have worked for the firm:

5.4	2.3	11.0	4.8	1.4
6.8	0.4	9.3	2.2	3.2
6.9	1.3	8.6	10.9	2.4
7.1	4.9	2.3	5.7	4.6
8.6	7.6	4.4	3.9	0.6
8.4	8.2	0.7	13.8	9.8
3.2	9.3	0.8	11.6	5.1
2.1	10.8	3.9	10.1	3.9
10.6	14.4	5.7	0.9	4.1
11.3	15.0	6.2	0.7	2.7

Use these numbers to construct a frequency distribution having the following classes: 0 to under 2.0; 2.0 to under 4.0; 4.0 to under 6.0; and so on.

3. Based on the frequency distribution you constructed in problem 2, estimate the *mean* years of service of the 50 employees. Compare this result with the mean you would have obtained if you had used the original array of data in problem 2 rather than the frequency distribution you constructed.

4. Based on the frequency distribution you constructed in problem 2, estimate the *median* years of service of the 50 employees. Compare this result with the median you would have obtained if you had used the original array of data in problem 2 rather than the frequency distribution you constructed.

5. Based on the frequency distribution you constructed in problem 2, estimate the *standard deviation* of the years of service of the 50 employees. Compare this result with the standard deviation you would have obtained if you had used the original array of data in problem 2 rather than your own frequency distribution.

6. In the graph below, draw a *histogram* of the frequency distribution you constructed in problem 2.

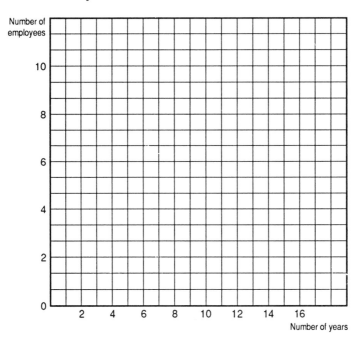

7. In the graph below, draw a *frequency polygon* of the frequency distribution you constructed in problem 2.

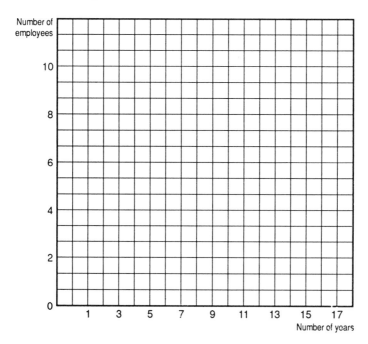

8. The sales of the IBM Corporation in 1966–76 are shown below:

Year	Sales (billions of dollars)
1966	4.2
1967	5.3
1968	6.9
1969	7.2
1970	7.5
1971	8.3
1972	9.5
1973	11.0
1974	12.7
1975	14.4
1976	16.3

A financial writer publishes a newspaper story saying that IBM's average sales during 1966–76 were $8.3 billion. What kind of average is the writer using?

9. A reader writes to the editor of the newspaper in problem 8 saying that the article on IBM was misleading since the average sales of the firm during 1966–76 were $9.39 billion, not $8.3 billion. Who is right—the financial writer or the reader? If both are right, what are the relative advantages and disadvantages of the figures furnished by each?

10. The *geometric mean* of a set of n numbers (all of which must be positive) is the nth root of their product. For example, the geometric mean of the three numbers 1, 2, and 4 is $\sqrt[3]{1 \times 2 \times 4} = 2$. The geometric mean is used primarily to average index numbers, ratios, and rates of change. One simple way of computing the geometric mean is to recognize that the logarithm of the geometric mean equals the arithmetic mean of the logarithms of the set of n numbers. That is, the logarithm of the geometric mean equals $\frac{1}{n} \sum_{i=1}^{n} \log x_i$, where x_i is the ith number in the set.

Calculate the geometric mean of the following three numbers: (1) the ratio of IBM's sales in 1967 to its sales in 1966, (2) the ratio of IBM's sales in 1968 to its sales in 1967, and (3) the ratio of IBM's sales in 1969 to its sales in 1968. (Can you see a shortcut to the answer?)

11. Given that y_t is defined as IBM's sales in billions of dollars in year t, evaluate each of the following expressions (use the data in problem 8):

(a) $\sum_{t=1966}^{1971} y_t$

(b) $\displaystyle\sum_{t=1967}^{1970} (y_t - 3)$

(c) $\displaystyle\sum_{t=1968}^{1970} (y_t - 2)^2$

(d) $\displaystyle\sum_{t=1969}^{1973} 2y_t^2$

12. Prove that $\sum_{i=1}^{N} (x_i - \mu)^2 = \sum_{i=1}^{n} x_i^2 - N\mu^2$. Indicate how this result can be used to simplify statistical calculations.

13. The financial writer in problem 8 claims that IBM's sales were more variable during 1966–71 than during 1972–76. Is this true if variation is measured by (a) the range and (b) the standard deviation? (Regard the data as samples, not populations.)

14. If the coefficient of variation is used as the relevant measure, is the financial writer correct in saying that IBM's sales were more variable during 1966–71 than during 1972–76?

15. Another frequently used measure of absolute variation is the *interquartile range*, which equals $Q_3 - Q_1$, where Q_3 is a number such that 75 percent of the observations fall below it (and 25 percent fall above it) and Q_1 is a number such that 25 percent of the observations fall below it (and 75 percent fall above it). Q_1 is called the *first quartile*, and Q_3 the *third quartile*. Thus, the interquartile range is the width of the interval that includes the middle one-half of the observations.

   (a) Is the first quartile of the observations in problem 2 less than two years?

   (b) Is the third quartile of these observations equal to eight or more years?

   (c) A statistics student claims that the interquartile range exceeds 12 years. Is this true?

16. A measure of relative variation that is sometimes used is the *coefficient of quartile variation,* which equals

$$\frac{Q_3 - Q_1}{Q_1 + Q_3}.$$

Indicate why this is a reasonable measure of relative variation, and prove that it is independent of the units in which the observations are measured. (For example, its value is the same, whether IBM's sales are measured in billions of dollars, millions of dollars, or dollars.)

17. The following quotation describes the results of a test of a polio vaccine carried out a number of years ago: ". . . 450 children were vaccinated in a community and 680 were left unvaccinated, as controls. Shortly thereafter the community was visited by an epidemic. Not one of the vaccinated children contracted a recognizable case of polio."[2] Can one conclude from these results that the vaccine was effective? Why, or why not?

18. The following statement was published in 1952 by the American Civil Liberties Union (ACLU) after the Chicago police banned the showing of an Italian film *The Miracle:* "In the past few months, the Chicago Division [of the ACLU] has shown 'The Miracle' at several private meetings. Of those filling out questionnaires after seeing the film, less than 1 percent felt it should be banned. 'It thus seems,' said Sanford I. Wolff, Chairman of the Chicago Division's Censorship Committee, and Edward H. Meyerding, the Chicago ACLU's Executive Director, 'that the five members of the Censorship Board do not

2. D. Huff, *How to Lie with Statistics* (New York: Norton, 1954).

represent the thinking of the majority of Chicago citizens.'"[3] Do you agree with this conclusion? Why, or why not?

19. A study showed that the alumni of a college's school of business who had grades that were close to the average tended to have higher incomes than either the poor or very good students who graduated at the same time. Does this mean that very good grades are a handicap for those seeking high incomes? What other factors might cause this result?

20. In 1937 the number of deaths per thousand in Arizona was about 17, whereas in 1943 it was about 8. Does this indicate that Arizona became a healthier place during 1937–43? Why, or why not?

3. *Civil Liberties* (American Civil Liberties Union, 1952).

21. According to Oskar Morgenstern,[4] there are many more mental cases per 100,000 of population in Sweden than in Yugoslavia. Do you think this is related to the fact that the Swedes put mental patients in hospitals whereas the Yugoslavs are much less likely to do so? Why, or why not?

22. An advertising executive finds that the circulation (in millions of people) of the 20 leading American magazines is as follows:[5]

Reader's Digest	17.9	Ladies' Home Journal	5.3
TV Guide	17.1	National Enquirer	4.7
National Geographic	10.6	Time	4.6
Modern Maturity	9.3	Playboy	4.2
AARP News Bulletin	8.8	Redbook	4.0
Better Homes and Gardens	8.0	The Star	3.7
Family Circle	7.2	Penthouse	3.5
Woman's Day	7.0	Newsweek	3.0
McCall's	6.4	Cosmopolitan	3.0
Good Housekeeping	5.4	People Weekly	2.8

(a) Use Minitab (or some other computer package) to construct a histogram of these data. If no such package is available, do so by hand.

(b) Use Minitab (or some other computer package) to construct a stem-and-leaf diagram for the circulation of the magazines that are ranked third to twentieth on this list.

---

4. O. Morgenstern, *On the Accuracy of Economic Observations* (Princeton, N.J.: Princeton University Press, 1963).

5. These data come from the *World Almanac*.

Answers

Telechron Clock Gears: A Case Study

(a) One possible answer is:

Diameters (inches)	Number of gears
.4130 to under .4135	1
.4135 to under .4140	1
.4140 to under .4145	4
.4145 to under .4150	12
.4150 to under .4155	14
.4155 to under .4160	15
.4160 to under .4165	3
Total	50

(b) Based on the frequency distribution, the median equals

$$\left(\frac{50/2 - 18}{14}\right).0005 + .4150 = .41525 \text{ inch.}$$

(c) .41575 inches.

(d) In only 18 of the 50 cases was this objective realized.

(e) One possible answer is:

Diameters (inches)	Number of gears
.4154 to under .4157	1
.4157 to under .4160	3
.4160 to under .4163	14
.4163 to under .4166	11
.4166 to under .4169	1
Total	30

(f) Based on the frequency distribution, the median equals

$$\left(\frac{30/2 - 4}{14}\right).0003 + .4160 = .41624 \text{ inch.}$$

This is about .001 inch higher than the median of the first sample. The range of this sample is .4166 − .4154 = .0012 inch. In the first sample the range was .4160 − .4130 = .0030 inch.

(g) Based on the second sample, the diameters of 28 of the 30 gears met this objective. That is, in 93 percent of the cases, the objective was met. This contrasts with the first sample, where only 18 out of 50 (or 36 percent) of the gears met this objective. (The remainder had diameters that were undesirably small.) The adjustments and attachments built into the machine that cuts the gear apparently have increased markedly the percent of gears that meet this objective.

Multiple-Choice Questions

1. (c) 2. (c) 3. (c) 4. (b) 5. (c) 6. (d) 7. (a) 8. (e) 9. (e) 10. (e)
11. (c) 12. (e)

Problems

1. (a) $\Sigma X_i = 4,981$.
   (b) $\Sigma X_i^2 = 11,013,917$.
   (c) $s^2 = 1,130,375$.
   (d) $s = 1,063$.

2.

Number of years	Number of employees
0 to under 2.0	8
2.0 to under 4.0	11
4.0 to under 6.0	9
6.0 to under 8.0	5
8.0 to under 10.0	7
10.0 to under 12.0	7
12.0 to under 14.0	1
14.0 to under 16.0	2
Total	50

3. Based on the frequency distribution, the mean is
   $(1/50)[8(1) + 11(3) + 9(5) + 5(7) + 7(9) + 7(11) + 1(13) + 2(15)]$
   $= 304/50 = 6.08$ years.
   Using the original observations, the mean is $299.9/50 = 6.00$ years.

4. Based on the frequency distribution, the median is

$$\left(\frac{50/2 - 19}{9}\right)2 + 4.0 = 4/3 + 4.0 = 5\frac{1}{3} \text{ years.}$$

   Using the original observations, the median is 5.25 years.

5. In the following calculations, it is assumed that the 50 observations are a sample, not the entire population. Based on the frequency distribution, the variance is
   $[8(1)^2 + 11(3)^2 + 9(5)^2 + 5(7)^2 + 7(9)^2 + 7(11)^2 + 1(13)^2 + 2(15)^2$
   $- 50(6.08)^2] \div 49 = (8 + 99 + 225 + 245 + 567 + 847 + 169 + 450$
   $- 1848.32) \div 49 = (2610 - 1848.32) \div 49 = 761.68 \div 49 = 15.54$.

   Thus, the standard deviation is $\sqrt{15.54}$, or 3.94 years.
   Using the original observations, the variance is
   $[5.4^2 + 6.8^2 + 6.9^2 + 7.1^2 + 8.6^2 + 8.4^2 + 3.2^2 + 2.1^2 + 10.6^2 +$
   $11.3^2 + 2.3^2 + 0.4^2 + 1.3^2 + 4.9^2 + 7.6^2 + 8.2^2 + 9.3^2 + 10.8^2 +$
   $14.4^2 + 15.0^2 + 11.0^2 + 9.3^2 + 8.6^2 + 2.3^2 + 4.4^2 + 0.7^2 + 0.8^2 +$
   $3.9^2 + 5.7^2 + 6.2^2 + 4.8^2 + 2.2^2 + 10.9^2 + 5.7^2 + 3.9^2 + 13.8^2 +$
   $11.6^2 + 10.1^2 + 0.9^2 + 0.7^2 + 1.4^2 + 3.2^2 + 2.4^2 + 4.6^2 + 0.6^2 + 9.8^2 +$
   $5.1^2 + 3.9^2 + 4.1^2 + 2.7^2 - 50(6.00)^2] \div 49$
   $= [29.16 + 46.24 + 47.61 + 50.41 + 73.96 + 70.56 + 10.24 + 4.41 +$
   $112.36 + 127.69 + 5.29 + 0.16 + 1.69 + 24.01 + 57.76 + 67.24 +$
   $86.49 + 116.64 + 207.36 + 225.00 + 121.00 + 86.49 + 73.96 + 5.29 +$
   $19.36 + 0.49 + 0.64 + 15.21 + 32.49 + 38.44 + 23.04 + 4.84 +$

118.81 + 32.49 + 15.21 + 190.44 + 134.56 + 102.01 + 0.81 + 0.49 + 1.96 + 10.24 + 5.76 + 21.16 + 0.36 + 96.04 + 26.01 + 15.21 + 16.81 + 7.29 − 50(36)] ÷ 49

= 781.19/49 = 15.94.

Thus, the standard deviation is 3.99 years.

6.

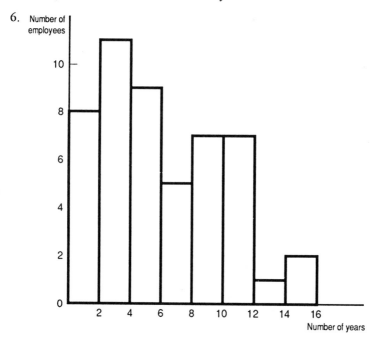

7.

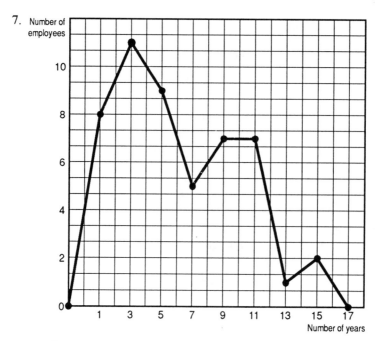

8. Median.

9. Both are right. They are using different kinds of averages. The reader is using the mean. The relative advantages and disadvantages of the mean and median are given in the text.

10. Let S_{66} be IBM's sales in 1966, S_{67} be its sales in 1967, and so on. Then

$$\sqrt[3]{\left(\frac{S_{67}}{S_{66}}\right)\left(\frac{S_{68}}{S_{67}}\right)\left(\frac{S_{69}}{S_{68}}\right)} = \sqrt[3]{\frac{S_{69}}{S_{66}}} = \sqrt[3]{\frac{7.2}{4.2}} = \sqrt[3]{1.71} = 1.20.$$

11. (a) $4.2 + 5.3 + 6.9 + 7.2 + 7.5 + 8.3 = 39.4$.
    (b) $2.3 + 3.9 \div 4.2 + 4.5 = 14.9$.
    (c) $4.9^2 + 5.2^2 + 5.5^2 = 24.01 + 27.04 + 30.25 = 81.3$.
    (d) $2(7.2^2 + 7.5^2 + 8.3^2 + 9.5^2 + 11.0^2)$
        $= 2(51.84 + 56.25 + 68.89 + 90.25 + 121.00)$
        $= 2(388.23) = 776.46.$

12. $\displaystyle\sum_{i=1}^{N}(x_i - \mu)^2 = \sum_{i=1}^{N}(x_i^2 - 2\mu x_i + \mu^2)$

$$= \sum_{i=1}^{N} x_i^2 - \sum_{i=1}^{N} 2\mu x_i + \sum_{i=1}^{N} \mu^2$$

$$= \sum_{i=1}^{N} x_i^2 - 2\mu \sum_{i=1}^{N} x_i + N\mu^2$$

$$= \sum_{i=1}^{N} x_i^2 - 2N\mu^2 + N\mu^2$$

since $\displaystyle\sum_{i=1}^{N} x_i = N\mu$. Thus, it follows that

$$\sum_{i=1}^{N}(x_i - \mu)^2 = \sum_{i=1}^{N} x_i^2 - N\mu^2.$$

In calculating the population standard deviation, it is necessary to evaluate

$\displaystyle\sum_{i=1}^{N}(x_i - \mu)^2$. It may be more convenient to evaluate this expression by

calculating $\displaystyle\sum_{i=1}^{N} x_i^2 - N\mu^2$.

13. (a) The range was $8.3 - 4.2 = 4.1$ billions of dollars in 1966–71, whereas it was $16.3 - 9.5 = 6.8$ billions of dollars in 1972–76.

(b) We are told to regard the 1966–71 and 1972–76 data as samples, not populations. Thus, we must calculate the standard deviation based on $(n-1)$, not N. The results are the following:

Time period	s
1966–71	1.52
1972–76	2.69

Based on the range and the standard deviation, it does not appear that the absolute variability of IBM's sales was greater in 1966–71 than in 1972–76.

14. The mean and coefficient of variation of IBM's sales in each time period were the following:

Time period	$\bar{x}$	$s/\bar{x}$
1966–71	6.567	.23
1972–76	12.78	.21

The coefficient of variation was somewhat higher in 1966–71 than in 1972–76.

15. (a) No.
    (b) Yes.
    (c) No. The first quartile is at least 2 years. The third quartile is less than 10 years. Thus, the interquartile range must be less than 8 years.

16. The numerator, which equals the interquartile range, is a measure of absolute variation. The denominator, which is the sum of the first and third quartiles, is proportional to the *midquartile,* which is defined as $(Q_1 + Q_3) \div 2$. The midquartile is sometimes used as a measure of central tendency instead of the median or mean. Thus, the coefficient of quartile variation equals one-half of the interquartile range divided by the midquartile. This is a measure of relative variation.

    To see that it is independent of units, note that if IBM's sales are measured in millions of dollars rather than in billions, the values of Q_1, Q_2, and Q_3 would all be multiplied by 1,000, with the result that the coefficient of quartile variation would be unaffected.

17. No, because it turned out that none of the children in the control group got polio either.

18. The people attending the private meetings sponsored by the American Civil Liberties Union are likely to be different in many relevant respects from Chicago citizens as a whole. Thus, these results may be quite biased. Also, those who filled out the questionnaire may not be representative of those who attended.

19. No. Many of the very good students may have gone into teaching or research, where the earnings are not very high.

20. No. A major reason was the establishment of a large number of military posts there. The military personnel, because of their age and physical condition, had very low death rates.

21. Yes. For this reason, it seems likely that more Swedish mental cases are identified and counted in the data.

22. (a) MTB> SET In C1
DATA>   17.9 17.1   10.6   9.3   8.8   8.0   7.2   7.0   6.4   5.4
DATA>   5.3   4.7   4.6   4.2   4.0   3.7   3.5   3.0   3.0   2.8
DATA>   END
MTB>   HISTOGRAM OF C1

Histogram of C1   N = 20

Midpoint	Count	
2	1	★
4	8	★★★★★★★★
6	3	★★★
8	4	★★★★
10	2	★★
12	0	
14	0	
16	0	
18	2	★★

(b)

2	8
3	0057
4	0267
5	34
6	4
7	02
8	08
9	3
10	6

CASE ONE

Faulty Inspection of Industrial Output*

W. Edwards Deming

The histogram in Figure 1 shouts a message. It tells us that the inspector distorted the data. One may encounter this histogram almost any day anywhere. Measurements pile up just inside the specification, followed by a gap. Possible reasons for the distortion are obvious:

1. The inspector is trying to protect the people that make the part.
2. He is afraid of his instrument—afraid that it may reject a part unjustly; that if it were in good order it might accept the part.
3. He is afraid of his own use of the instrument, which is of course confounded with No. 2.

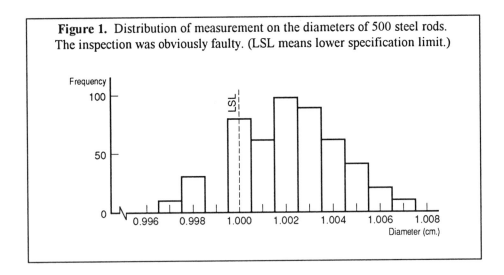

Figure 1. Distribution of measurement on the diameters of 500 steel rods. The inspection was obviously faulty. (LSL means lower specification limit.)

Figure 2 shows a distribution of measured values during production. The lower specification limit was 6.2 mils; no upper limit. No part was recorded a failure. . . . Were there any failures? No one will ever know.

No one wishes to be a bearer of bad news.

The peaks at 6.5 and 7.0 may arise from rounding. . . .

*This excerpt comes from W. Edwards Deming, *Out of the Crisis* (Cambridge, Mass.: Massachusetts Institute of Technology, 1986), pp. 266–71.

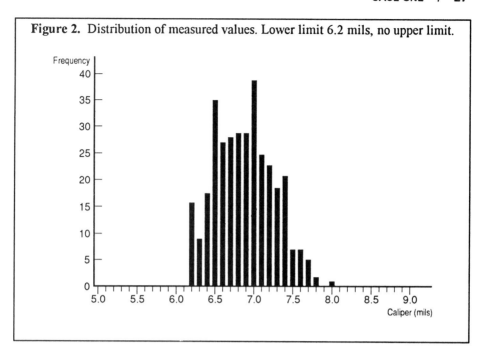

Figure 2. Distribution of measured values. Lower limit 6.2 mils, no upper limit.

This actual dialogue was reported to me by Kate McKeown.

Millwright (to his foreman): That bearing [in a blast machine] is about to go out, and it will ruin the shaft along with it when it goes if we don't take care of it now.

Foreman: This load of castings must be on its way today.

He is thinking of his production record, and says to the man: "We can't take care of it now." The foreman, for fear of his job, could not protect the best interests of the company. He is judged by numbers only, not for avoiding shutdowns. Can anyone blame him for doing his job?

Before they get the load out, the bearing freezes, as the millwright predicted. In the repair job, the millwright finds, sure enough, that the shaft is badly grooved: four days lost to get a new shaft from Baltimore and replace it. . . .

Statistical investigation usually discovers within a few weeks that:

1. Few workers know what the job is.
2. Few inspectors know, either. Production worker and inspector do not agree on what is right and what is wrong. Right yesterday; wrong today.
3. The electronic testing equipment is not doing the job. It passes an item one minute, rejects it the next, and the converse.
4. Electronic testing machines do not agree with each other.
5. Vendor and purchaser do not agree: no wonder, the testing equipment used by the purchaser does not agree with itself. The vendor has the same problem. Neither one knows it.

Few people in supervisory positions and in management are aware how important reliable inspection is for morale of production workers.

Figure 3. Results of eight testing machines over the course of a week.

Testing machine	Yield	40%	50%	60%
0	66.2			×
7	66.3			×
8	54.1		×	
9	56.0		×	
10	56.9		×	
11	54.1		×	
12	66.5			×
13	57.3		×	
All	59.7			

Example. There are eight testing machines at the end of the line to separate good product from bad in order to protect customers. Around 3000 items run through this inspection every day. The compilation and chart (plotted by machine) shown in Figure 3 shows the results for a week. The rule was to rotate the test machine with the product as the pieces come off the line.

The eight testing machines obviously fall into two groups. The difference between their means is around 11 per cent. A serious problem exists. What the customer gets depends on what machine does the testing—an alarming condition. It is vital to find out the reason for the existence of two groups and for the difference between them.

One can imagine the frustration of the production workers, seeing apparent and unexplainable variation from day to day, unaware that much of the trouble lies in the testing equipment.

One might look first, in such a problem, for confounding of the operator with the machine. A machine does not work by itself. It has no characteristic of its own. The machine and the operator form a team. Change of operator may give different results. In this case, the machines worked three shifts. It would be well to enquire whether the same operators worked all week on any one machine.

Questions

1. What message does the histogram in Figure 1 shout?

2. Why does the author say that no one will ever know whether there were any failures in Figure 2?

3. In what sense is the foreman's incorrect decision a result of the firm's use of improper statistical methods?

4. In Figure 3, what role did measures of central tendency play in leading the author to the conclusions he states?

5. In Figure 3, what role might measures of variation play in sharpening the author's conclusions?

6. In Figure 3, why does the author stress that the effects of the operator may be confounded with those of the machines? If such confounding can be shown to exist, why might it be important to the firm's management?

PART II

Probability, Probability Distributions, and Sampling

CHAPTER 3

Probability

Chapter Profile

The set of all possible outcomes of an experiment is called the *sample space*. There are two principal definitions of probability—the *frequency* concept and the *subjective* concept. Regardless of which concepts are used, three *axioms* must hold: (1) the probability of any event must be greater than or equal to zero; (2) the probability that some event in the sample space occurs is 1; and (3) if two events are mutually exclusive, the probability that either of them occurs is equal to the sum of their probabilities.

The *addition rule* states that if $P(A)$ is the probability that event A occurs and if $P(B)$ is the probability that event B occurs, then the probability that either A or B (or both) occurs equals $P(A) + P(B) - P(A \text{ and } B)$. Of course, if A and B are mutually exclusive, it follows that $P(A \text{ or } B) = P(A) + P(B)$.

The *multiplication rule* states that the probability that both A and B occur—that is, $P(A \text{ and } B)$—equals $P(A|B) \times P(B)$, where $P(A|B)$ is the conditional probability that event A occurs, given that event B occurs. If A and B are independent events, $P(A|B) = P(A)$, with the result that $P(A \text{ and } B) = P(A) \times P(B)$.

To begin with, one frequently has an initial estimate of the probability (a *prior* probability) of whatever event is of interest. Then, based on new information generated by a survey, test, or other source, one revises this probability; the result is a *posterior* probability. *Bayes' theorem* is used to carry out this revision. According to Bayes' theorem,

$$P(H_1|E) = \frac{P(E|H_1)P(H_1)}{P(E|H_1)P(H_1) + P(E|H_2)P(H_2) + \cdots + P(E|H_m)P(H_m)},$$

where $P(H_1|E)$ is the probability of event H_1 given that some piece of information E turns up. The other events (besides H_1) that can take place are $H_2, H_3, \ldots, H_m$.

Appendix Profile

If there are m kinds of items—n_1 items of the first kind, n_2 items of the second kind, . . . , and n_m items of the mth kind—the number of ways we can select one of each of the m kinds of items is $n_1 \times n_2 \times \cdots \times n_m$. If x items are selected from n items, any particular sequence of these x items is called a *permutation*. The number of permutations of x items that one can select from a set of n items is $n(n-1)(n-2) \cdots (n-x+1)$.

In contrast to a permutation, where the order of the items matters, a *combination* is a selection of items where the order does not matter. The number of combinations of x items that one can select from a set of n items is

$$\frac{n(n-1) \cdots (n-x+1)}{x(x-1) \cdots (2)(1)} = \frac{n!}{(n-x)!x!}.$$

Behavioral Objectives

A. You should be able to define the following key concepts in this chapter:

experiment   *combination
outcome   *permutation
event   conditional probability
frequency definition of probability   multiplication rule
subjective definition of probability   independent events
sample space   Bayes' theorem
mutually exclusive events   prior probability
exhaustive events   state of nature
addition rule

B. Make sure that you can do each of the following:
  1. Present the frequency and subjective concepts of probability.
  2. State, prove, and apply the addition rule for probabilities.
  3. State and apply the concepts of conditional probability and independence.
  4. State, prove, and apply the multiplication rule for probabilities.
  5. Use Bayes' theorem to calculate the probabilities that various events occur, given that some piece of information turns up.
  6. Discuss the assumptions underlying Bayes' theorem and its usefulness in business and economics.
  *7. Calculate the number of ways we can choose one of each of m kinds of items.
  *8. Compute the number of permutations of x items that one can select from n items.
  *9. Calculate the number of combinations of x items that one can select from n items.

Breakfast Food: A Case Study

Experts in marketing have devoted considerable study during the past 20 years to the way in which the probability that a consumer will purchase a given brand of a product depends on what brands he or she has purchased in the past.[1] As a very simple illustration, suppose that it has been determined that a consumer, if he or she purchases breakfast food, has a 20 percent chance of purchasing a particular brand of breakfast food if he or she has purchased this brand once before, and a 10 percent chance of purchasing it if he or she has never purchased it before.

(a) Suppose that this consumer has not tried this brand at the beginning of April and that he or she purchased breakfast food once in April and once in May. What is the probability that he or she did not purchase this brand either time?
(b) What is the probability that he or she purchased this brand in April but not in May?
(c) What is the probability that he or she purchased this brand in May but not in April?

---

* Material pertaining to the chapter appendix.
1. For example, see F. Bass, C. King, and E. Pessemier, *Applications of the Sciences in Marketing Management* (New York: Wiley, 1968).

(d) What is the probability that he or she purchased this brand in both April and May?

(e) What is the probability that he or she purchased this brand once during April or May?

(f) What is the probability that he or she purchased this brand at least once during April and May?

(g) Would you expect that the probability that the consumer would purchase this brand will always increase as he or she has purchased it more and more often in the past? Why, or why not?

Multiple-Choice Questions

1. Suppose that $P(A) = .5$, $P(B) = .2$, and $P(A \text{ and } B) = .2$. Which of the following is true?

   (a) A and B are mutually exclusive and statistically independent events.
   (b) A and B are mutually exclusive but not statistically independent events.
   (c) A and B are statistically independent but not mutually exclusive events.
   (d) A and B are neither statistically independent nor mutually exclusive events.
   (e) None of the above.

2. An economic model is used to forecast the Acme Corporation's sales for next year. The possible outcomes of this forecast can be classified 0 (which means sales are expected to decline from this year's level), 1 (which means that sales are expected to equal this year's level), or 2 (which means that sales are expected to exceed this year's level). In a diagram these outcomes can be plotted along the horizontal axis. Along the vertical axis we can plot 0 if sales *actually* decline from this year's level, 1 if sales *actually* equal this year's level, or 2 if sales *actually* exceed this year's level. The coordinates of the point corresponding to sales being expected to decline from this year's level, and actually declining from this year's level are

   (a) 2,2.
   (b) 1,1.
   (c) 0,0.
   (d) 0,1.
   (e) 0,2.

3. In question 2 a point with coordinates 1,1 means that

   (a) sales were forecasted to decline from this year's level, and did so.
   (b) sales were forecasted to increase over this year's level, and did so.
   (c) sales were forecasted to equal this year's level, and did so.
   (d) sales were forecasted to equal this year's level, and did not do so.
   (e) none of the above are true.

4. In question 2 the subset of the sample space corresponding to the forecast being no lower than this year's sales level is

    (a) all points with vertical coordinates of 1 or 2.
    (b) all points with a vertical coordinate of 2.
    (c) all points with horizontal coordinates of 1 or 2.
    (d) all points with a horizontal coordinate of 2.
    (e) none of the above.

5. The probability that the Jones Company will go bankrupt in 1996 is .1. The probability that it will lose money in 1996 is .2. The probability that it will both go bankrupt and lose money in 1996 is .1. The probability that it will either go bankrupt or lose money (or both) in 1996 equals

    (a) less than .1.
    (b) .1.
    (c) .2.
    (d) more than .2.
    (e) none of the above.

6. In the preceding question, whether the Jones Company will go bankrupt in 1996

    (a) is not statistically independent of whether it loses money in 1996.
    (b) is statistically independent of whether it loses money in 1996.
    (c) cannot be represented by a probability.
    (d) cannot be represented by a subjective probability.
    (e) cannot be analyzed by statistical methods.

7. Based on question 5, the probability that the Jones Company will not lose money in 1996 equals

    (a) zero.
    (b) .1.
    (c) .2.
    (d) .8.
    (e) .9.

8. If $P(A) = .3$ and $P(B) = .6$, what is P (not A and not B) if A and B are statistically independent?

    (a) .18
    (b) .28
    (c) .30
    (d) .60
    (e) None of the above

*9. The number of different five-card hands that could occur by dealing the top five cards from a full deck is

(a) 52! ÷ 47!.
(b) 52! ÷ (47!5!).
(c) less than 1 million.
(d) 47! ÷ 52!.
(e) none of the above.

10. A publisher is considering compiling an anthology containing two of Joseph Conrad's works. The candidates for inclusion are *Typhoon, Heart of Darkness, The Nigger of the "Narcissus,"* and *Lord Jim.* How many different books can be formed from these, if two anthologies are considered different if they contain the same works but in different order?

(a) 16
(b) 12
(c) 6
(d) 8
(e) None of the above

11. Under the circumstances in question 10, how many different books can be formed, if two books containing the same stories are considered the same regardless of the order in which the stories appear?

(a) 16
(b) 12
(c) 6
(d) 8
(e) None of the above

Problems and Problem Sets

1. Richard Feynman, a Nobel prize winner at the California Institute of Technology, was a member of the presidential commission that investigated the 1986 accident of the space shuttle. According to his estimates, the probability of failure of the shuttle was about .01 to .02. (See *Science,* June 27, 1986, p. 1596.) If this was true, what was the probability of no failures in three launches of the shuttle?

---

* Material pertaining to the chapter appendix.

2. Suppose that $P(C) = .5$ and $P(D) = .4$. If C and D are statistically independent events, what is $P(C \text{ and } D)$?

3. Mary Moroney believes that if she is to be admitted to a particular graduate school, she must get an A in statistics, in economics, and in money and banking. If she does this, she will be admitted. If the probability of her getting less than an A in any one of these subjects is 2/3, and if her grade in one of these subjects is statistically independent of her grade in any of the other subjects, what is the probability that she will be admitted to this graduate school?

4. An automobile manufacturer makes four different models, each of which comes in two sizes. Any of these cars can be obtained in any one of five colors. How many different kinds of cars does the firm produce? That is, how many different combinations of model, size, and color are there?

*5. A firm's personnel manager wants to fill three openings in its training program with two people with engineering degrees and one with an M.B.A. In how many ways can these openings be filled if eight engineering graduates and four M.B.A.'s applied for the job?

---

* Material pertaining to the chapter appendix.

6. If the president of Merrill Lynch feels that 7 to 3 are fair odds that the price of IBM's common stock will go up next week, what is his subjective probability that it will go up then? What is his subjective probability that it will not go up then?

7. The director of engineering of an aerospace firm says that the probability that a new airplane will be ready for deployment in one year or less is .2, that it will be ready for deployment in less than five years is .6 and that it will take five years or more for it to be ready for deployment is .5. Comment on the logic of this statement.

8. The director of engineering in Problem 7 says that the probability that both the new airplane discussed there and a similar German airplane will be ready for deployment in one year or less is .3. Comment on the logic of this statement (in combination with the director's statement in problem 7).

9. A marketing director feels that the probability is 1/4 that a competing firm will come out with an improved product in 1996 and 1/4 that the competitor will come out with an improved product in 1997. Also the director feels that the probability is .6 that the competitor will come out with an improved product in either 1996 or 1997 or both. Comment on the consistency of these probabilities.

10. Given that A and B are independent events and that $P(A) = .25$ and $P(B) = .52$, calculate P (not A), that is, the probability that A does not occur. Calculate P (A and B), P (A or B), and P (not A and not B).

11. If each card in a standard 52-card deck of playing cards has the same probability of being drawn, state the probability that a single card that is drawn will be

    (a) a black 10.
    (b) a red ace.
    (c) a red card.
    (d) neither a black card nor a king.
    (e) a jack, queen, or king.

12. The probability that an accountant will find an error in the Adams Corporation's accounts in a particular month is .05, and the probability that the accountant will find an error in the Jones Corporation's accounts in the same month is .1. The two events are independent.

    (a) What is the probability that the accountant will find an error in Adams's accounts, but not in Jones's accounts in this month?

    (b) What is the probability that the accountant will find an error in the accounts of either Adams or Jones, or possibly both, during this month?

(c) What is the probability that the accountant will find an error in either Adams's accounts or Jones's accounts, but not both, during this month?

(d) What is the probability that the accountant will find an error in neither Adams's nor Jones's accounts during this month?

13. If A is the event that the Adams Corporation will hire John Brown as president, B is the event that the Adams Corporation will go bankrupt, and C is the event that John Brown will make a million dollars, state *in words* what probability is expressed by each of the following expressions:

(a) $P(B|A)$

(b) *P(C|B)*

(c) *P(A|not C)*

(d) *P(A and C|B)*

(e) *P(not B|A and C)*

14. The Adams Corporation stores spare parts at two warehouses, one in Baltimore and one in Plattsburgh. The number of defective and acceptable spare parts at each warehouse is given below:

Warehouse	Number of spare parts		
	Defective	*Acceptable*	*Total*
Baltimore	28	272	300
Plattsburgh	10	190	200

If one of the 500 spare parts kept by the firm is chosen at random (i.e., if each spare part has a 1/500 chance of being chosen), D and A denote the events that the spare part is defective or acceptable, while B and G denote the events that it comes from Baltimore or Plattsburgh. Calculate each of the following probabilities:

(a) $P(D)$

(b) $P(A$ or $B)$

(c) $P(A$ and $B)$

(d) $P(B|A)$

(e) $P(D|G)$

(f) $P(A|\text{not } G)$

15. Let's again take the situation in problem 14.

(a) Is the event denoted by D independent of the event denoted by G? Why, or why not?

(b) Is the event denoted by A independent of the event denoted by G? Why, or why not?

(c) Suppose that someone flips a coin to decide whether to obtain a spare part from Baltimore or Plattsburgh and then randomly chooses a spare part from whichever warehouse is picked. If the spare part chosen is defective, what is the probability that it came from Plattsburgh?

16. The Adams Corporation knows from past experience that its three sales representatives, A, B, and C, differ markedly in their attitudes toward alcohol. Given that representative A takes client X out for an evening on the town, the probability is .1 that representative A will need assistance home, whereas the probability is .05 that this will be true of representative B, and only .005 that it will be true of representative C (who moonlights as a bartender).

(a) Given that it is equally likely that each of these representatives will entertain client X this time, what is the probability that it is representative A, if afterward it is reported that the Adams Corporation's representative needed assistance home?

(b) What is the probability that representative C entertained client X this time, given that it is reported that the Adams Corporation's representative did not need assistance home?

17. The Adams Corporation receives telephone calls from its three sales representatives, A, B, and C. Representative A makes 40 percent of the calls, whereas representatives B and C each make 30 percent of the calls. If representative A calls, there is a 10 percent chance that A will ask the company's sales manager for assistance, whereas if representatives B or C call, there is only a 5 percent chance that either of them will ask the company's sales manager for assistance. One of the three representatives telephones and asks the sales manager for assistance, but the sales manager is away from her office, and no one can remember which sales representative called.

   (a) What is the probability that representative A called?

   (b) What is the probability that it was not representative C who called?

Answers

Breakfast Food: A Case Study

(a) The probability of not purchasing it in April is .9. The probability of not purchasing it in May (given that it was not purchased in April) is also .9. Thus, the probability of not purchasing it in both months is $(.9)(.9) = .81$.

(b) The probability of purchasing it in April is .1. The probability of not purchasing it in May (given that it was purchased in April) is .8. Thus, the desired probability is $(.1)(.8) = .08$.

(c) The probability of not purchasing it in April is .9. The probability of purchasing it in May (given that it was not purchased in April) is .1. Thus, the desired probability is $(.9)(.1) = .09$.

(d) The probability of purchasing it in April is .1. The probability of purchasing it in May (given that it was purchased in April) is .2. Thus, the desired probability is $(.1)(.2) = .02$.

(e) There are two mutually exclusive possibilities: (1) the consumer purchased it in April but not May, and (2) the consumer purchased it in May but not April. The probability of the first is .08; the probability of the second is .09. Thus, the desired probability is $.08 + .09 = .17$.

(f) The desired probability equals 1 minus the probability that the consumer did not purchase it at all during April and May. Thus, it equals $1 - .81 = .19$.

(g) No. Beyond a point, the consumer may become tired of the product and may turn to something different.

Multiple-Choice Questions

1. (d)   2. (c)   3. (c)   4. (c)   5. (c)   6. (a)   7. (d)   8. (b)   9. (b)   10. (b)
11. (c)

Problems

1. $.98^3$ to $.99^3$, or .94 to .97.
2. $.5 + .4 - .2 = .7$.
3. $(1/3)^3 = 1/27$.
4. $(4)(2)(5) = 40$.
5. There are $8!/(6!2!)$ different pairs of engineering graduates that can be chosen, and 4 different people with M.B.A.s who can be chosen, so the total number of triads meeting the conditions are

$$\frac{8!}{6!2!}(4) = \frac{(8)(7)(4)}{2} = 112.$$

6. .7.
   .3.
7. The probability that it will take less than five years plus the probability that it will take five or more years must equal 1. According to the engineering director's statement, they sum to 1.1, which is incorrect.
8. Let $P(A \text{ and } B)$ be the probability that both this airplane and the German airplane will be ready for deployment in one year or less. Let $P(A)$ be the probability that this airplane will be ready in one year or less. Let $P(B|A)$ be the probability that the German airplane will be ready in one year or less, given that this airplane is ready in one year or less. Then,

$$P(A \text{ and } B) = P(A)P(B|A).$$

Since $P(B|A) \leq 1$, it follows that $P(A \text{ and } B)$ must be less than or equal to $P(A)$. But the director of engineering says that $P(A) = .2$ and $P(A \text{ and } B) = .3$. This must be wrong.

9. Let $P(C)$ be the probability that the competitor will come out with an improved product in 1996 and $P(D)$ be the probability that it will come out with one in 1997. Let $P(C \text{ and } D)$ be the probability that it will come out with one in both years. Then,

$$P(C \text{ or } D) = P(C) + P(D) - P(C \text{ and } D),$$

where $P(C \text{ or } D)$ is the probability that it will come out with one in 1996 or 1997, or both. According to the marketing manager, $P(C \text{ or } D) = .6$, $P(C) = 1/4$, and $P(D) = 1/4$. This is impossible. Since $P(C \text{ and } D) \geq 0$, $P(C) + P(D)$ must be greater than or equal to $P(C \text{ or } D)$. But this is not true of the marketing manager's probabilities.

10. $P(\text{not } A) = 1 - P(A) = .75$.
    $P(A \text{ and } B) = P(A)P(B) = (.25)(.52) = .13$, since A and B are independent.
    $P(A \text{ or } B) = P(A) + P(B) - P(A \text{ and } B) = .25 + .52 - .13 = .64$.
    $P(\text{not } A \text{ and not } B) = P(\text{not } A)P(\text{not } B|\text{not } A) = (.75)(.48) = .36$.

11. (a) $2/52 = 1/26$.
    (b) $2/52 = 1/26$.
    (c) $26/52 = 1/2$.
    (d) The probability of a black card is $1/2$. The probability of a king is $1/13$. The probability that either a black card or a king will be drawn is $1/2 + 1/13 - 1/26$, or $14/26$, since there are 2 black kings. Thus, the probability that neither a black card nor a king will be drawn equals $1 - 14/26 = 6/13$.
    (e) $3/13$.

12. (a) Let A be an error in the Adams Corporation's accounts, and B be an error in the Jones Corporation's accounts. We want the probability that both A and not B occur. $P(A \text{ and not } B) = P(A)P(\text{not } B|A)$. Since not B is independent of A, $P(\text{not } B|A) = P(\text{not } B)$. Thus, $P(A \text{ and not } B) = P(A)P(\text{not } B) = (.05)(.90) = .045$.
    (b) $P(A \text{ or } B) = P(A) + P(B) - P(A \text{ and } B) = .05 + .10 - .005 = .145$.
    (c) $P(A \text{ or } B)$ is the probability of A or B, or both. It is the probability of (1) either A or B, but not both, or (2) both A and B. They are mutually exclusive events. Thus, the probability of either A or B, but not both, equals $P(A \text{ or } B) - P(A \text{ and } B) = .145 - .005 = .140$.
    (d) $P(\text{not } A \text{ and not } B) = (.95)(.90) = .855$.

13. (a) $P(B|A)$ is the probability that the Adams Corporation will go bankrupt, given that it hires John Brown as president.
    (b) $P(C|B)$ is the probability that John Brown will make a million dollars, given that the Adams Corporation goes bankrupt.
    (c) $P(A|\text{not } C)$ is the probability that the Adams Corporation will hire John Brown as president, given that he does not make a million dollars.
    (d) $P(A \text{ and } C|B)$ is the probability that both the Adams Corporation hires John Brown as president and he makes a million dollars, given that the corporation goes bankrupt.
    (e) $P(\text{not } B|A \text{ and } C)$ is the probability that the Adams Corporation will not go bankrupt, given both that the corporation hires Brown as president and he makes a million dollars.

14. (a) $P(D) = 38/500$.
    (b) $P(A \text{ or } B) = 490/500$.
    (c) $P(A \text{ and } B) = 272/500$.
    (d) $P(B|A) = 272/462$.
    (e) $P(D|G) = 10/200$.
    (f) $P(A|\text{not } G) = 272/300$.

15. (a) No, because $P(D|G) \neq P(D|\text{not } G)$. $P(D|G) = 10/200$, while $P(D|\text{not } G) = 28/300$.

    (b) No, because $P(A|G) \neq P(A|\text{not } G)$. $P(A|G) = 190/200$, while $P(A|\text{not } G) = 272/300$.

    (c) $P(G|D) = \dfrac{P(D|G)P(G)}{P(D|G)P(G) + P(D|B)P(B)}$

    $= \dfrac{(10/200)(1/2)}{(10/200)(1/2) + (28/300)(1/2)}$

    $= \dfrac{.025}{.025 + .047} = .35$.

16. (a) This probability equals

    $\dfrac{(.1)(1/3)}{(.1)(1/3) + (.05)(1/3) + (.005)(1/3)} = \dfrac{.0333}{.0333 + .0167 + .0017} = .64$.

    (b) This probability equals

    $\dfrac{(.995)(1/3)}{(.9)(1/3) + (.95)(1/3) + (.995)(1/3)} = \dfrac{.3317}{.3000 + .3167 + .3317}$

    $= \dfrac{.3317}{.9484} = .35$.

17. (a) This probability equals

    $\dfrac{(.10)(.40)}{(.10)(.40) + (.05)(.30) + (.05)(.30)} = \dfrac{.04}{.04 + 015 + .015} = \dfrac{.04}{.07} = .57$.

    (b) This probability equals

    $1 - \dfrac{(.05)(.30)}{(.10)(.40) + (.05)(.30) + (.05)(.30)} = 1 - \dfrac{.015}{.04 + .015 + .015}$

    $= 1 - \dfrac{.015}{.070} = 1 - .21 = .79$.

CHAPTER 4

Probability Distributions and Expected Values

Chapter Profile

A *random variable* is a quantity whose value is determined by an experiment; in other words, its value is determined by chance. A random variable must assume numerical values, and its value must be defined for all possible outcomes of the experiment in question. Random variables are of two types: discrete and continuous.

A table which provides the probability of each possible value of a random variable is called the *probability distribution* of that random variable. If $P(x)$ is the probability that x is the value of the random variable, the sum of $P(x)$ for all values of x must be 1. Probability distributions may be represented by graphs and equations as well as by tables.

If $x_1, x_2, \ldots, x_n$ are the possible values of a random variable, and if $P(x_1)$ is the probability that x_1 occurs, $P(x_2)$ is the probability that x_2 occurs, and so on, then the expected value of this random variable, denoted by E(X), is $\sum_{i=1}^{n} x_i P(x_i)$. In other words, the expected value is the weighted average of the values that the random variable can assume, each value being weighted by the probability that it occurs. The variance of a random variable X, denoted by $\sigma^2(X)$, is the expected value of the squared deviation of the random variable from its expected value.

Behavioral Objectives

A. You should be able to define the following key concepts in this chapter:
    random variable   continuous random variable
    probability distribution   Chebyshev's inequality
    variance of a random variable   discrete random variable
    expected value of a random variable

B. Be sure that you can do each of the following:
    1. Represent a probability distribution by a table or a graph.
    2. Calculate a random variable's expected value from its probability distribution.
    3. Calculate a random variable's variance and standard deviation.
    4. State and apply Chebyshev's inequality.

The Overall Rate of Return: A Case Study

Investors generally hold more than a single financial asset; they seldom invest in only a single asset. Consequently, they tend to be more interested in the overall rate of return from their portfolio of assets than in the rate of return from any single asset they hold. Moreover, the rate of return from each of the assets they hold is generally uncertain because it depends on future events that cannot be predicted with certainty. Thus, the overall rate of return from a particular portfolio of assets is generally uncertain as well.

Mary Tobin has invested in two stocks, the amount of the investment being the same in each stock. The rate of return from each of these stocks has the probability distribution shown below:

Rate of return (percent)	Probability
−10	1/3
0	1/3
+10	1/3

The rate of return from one stock is statistically independent of the rate of return from the other stock.

(a) The overall rate of return from her portfolio can assume five possible values: −10, −5, 0, +5, and +10 percent. What is the probability that it will equal −10 percent?

(b) What is the probability that the overall rate of return will equal +10 percent?

(c) What is the probability that the overall rate of return will equal −5 percent?

(d) What is the probability that the overall rate of return will equal +5 percent?

(e) What is the probability that the overall rate of return will equal zero?

(f) What is the probability distribution of the overall rate of return?

Multiple-Choice Questions

1. The random variable X has the following probability distribution:

Value of X	Probability
0	.1
1	.2
2	.4
3	.2
4	.1

Its expected value is

(a) 1.6.
(b) 1.8.
(c) 2.0.
(d) 2.2.
(e) 2.4.

2. J. East, Inc., a roofing firm, tests a batch of shingles it purchases to determine whether the batch contains defective shingles. The shingle manufacturer states

that 1/10 of 1 percent of such batches contain defective shingles. If the batch received by East was picked at random from those produced by the manufacturer, whether or not the batch contains defective shingles is

(a) not a random variable since it is not in numerical form.
(b) a random variable with three possible values.
(c) known with certainty prior to testing.
(d) a random variable with an asymmetrical probability distribution, if the manufacturer's statement is correct.
(e) none of the above.

3. In the situation in question 2, suppose that East must decide whether or not to use the batch before it can test whether it contains defective shingles. If the firm uses this batch, and if it contains defective shingles, East will lose $2,000. If East uses this batch and it does not contain defective shingles, East will gain $1,000. If East does not use the batch, it will gain (and lose) nothing. The expected monetary gain if the company uses the batch (and if the manufacturer's statement is correct) is

(a) $2.
(b) $1,000.
(c) $997.
(d) –$2,000.
(e) zero.

4. In the situation in question 3, East's monetary gain, if it does not use the batch, is

(a) $2.
(b) $1,000.
(c) $997.
(d) –$2,000.
(e) zero.

5. In question 3, the decision that maximizes East's expected gain is

(a) to use the shingles.
(b) the same as the decision that maximizes maximum gain.
(c) the same as the decision that minimizes maximum loss.
(d) only (a) and (b).
(e) all of the above.

6. A coal mine's records indicate that the average age of its miners is 35 and that the standard deviation of their ages is 10 years. The proportion of the miners who are over 65 must therefore be

(a) greater than 1/9.
(b) 1/9.
(c) less than 1/9.
(d) completely unknown.
(e) greater than the proportion of miners under 25 years of age.

Problems and Problem Sets

1. Grace Andrews, a stockbroker, recommends two stocks (Hewlett Packard and Citibank) to her customers. Suppose that the probability that each stock's price will go up next year is .6, and that each stock's price behavior is independent of the price behavior of the other stock.

    (a) What is the probability that *neither* stock will go up next year? What is the probability that *both* stocks will go up next year? What is the probability that *one* of these stocks will go up next year?

    (b) What is the expected number of these stocks that will go up next year?

2. J. East, the local roofing firm, feels that there is a 50-50 chance of landing a big industrial job which will keep one of its crews busy for all of July. East also feels that there is a 30 percent chance that it will get the contract to do the roofing of the new courthouse, which will occupy one crew for the first two weeks of July.

    (a) The chance of getting one job is not affected by whether East gets the other job. If these are the only two jobs that East has any chance of getting during July, is the number of crews that the firm can keep busy during the first week of July a random variable? If so, what is its probability distribution?

(b) Is the number of crews that East can keep busy during the last week of July a random variable? If so, plot its probability distribution in the graph below.

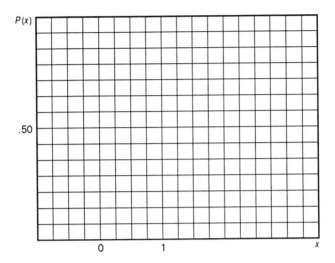

(c) Plot the probability distribution of the number of crews that East can keep busy during the first week of July in the graph below.

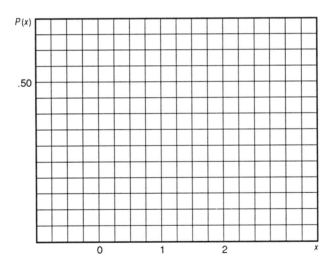

(d) What is the expected number of crews that East can keep busy during the first week of July? During the second week of July? During the third week of July? During the last week of July?

(e) Suppose that East must hire crews by the week and that it must decide (before knowing whether it will get the industrial job, or the courthouse job, or both) how many crews to hire for the first week in July. Given the number of crews it hires and the number of jobs it gets, its profits are as follows:

Number of crews hired	Number of crews East can keep busy		
	0	1	2
	(thousands of dollars)		
0	−1	−1	−1
1	−2	2	2
2	−3	1	5

What is the probability distribution of the firm's profits if it hires no crews? If it hires one crew? If it hires two crews?

(f) What is the firm's expected profit if it hires no crews? If it hires one crew? If it hires two crews?

(g) How many crews should East hire if it wants to maximize expected profit?

3. Based on past experience, a tire manufacturer knows that the mean number of defective tires that its inspectors fail to identify and that are sold to a particular customer is 100 per year. The standard deviation of this number is known to be 10. The contract with this customer states that the tire manufacturer must pay the customer $10,000 if the number of defective tires shipped to this customer exceeds 150 per year. The president of the tire-manufacturing firm states that the expected value of the cost to the firm of this provision per year is less than $500. Is this correct? Why, or why not?

4. Suppose that the city of Hanover, in an effort to solve its fiscal difficulties, introduces a lottery. Suppose that 1,000,000 people buy tickets at $1 apiece, and that two tickets are drawn at random by the city. The holder of the first ticket receives $600,000, and the holder of the second ticket receives $300,000. No other prizes are awarded.

   (a) What is the expected value of the gamble to any purchaser of a ticket?

   (b) Would someone who maximizes expected profit buy such a ticket?

5. John Malone has 10 plots of land. He knows that plot A contains valuable minerals, whereas the other plots do not. He feels that the fair market value of plot A is $200,000, and that of the other plots is $20,000 each. He asks you to consider the following gamble: He will pick a number from 1 to 10 at random. Then he will let you pick a number from 1 to 10 at random. If the number you pick equals the number he picked, you get plot A; otherwise you get one of the other plots. For this to be a fair bet, how much must he charge you to engage in this gamble?

*6. The Atlas Corporation is uncertain concerning its output rate in 1997. Its total cost during the year equals its fixed costs ($200,000) plus $3 times the number of units of output it produces during 1997.

(a) If the expected number of units of output it will produce in 1997 is 10,000, what is the firm's expected total cost in 1997?

(b) The Atlas Corporation has already decided to charge $25 for each unit of its output. What is the firm's expected total profit in 1997?

Answers

The Overall Rate of Return: A Case Study

(a) Since the amount invested in each stock is the same, the overall rate of return is the mean of the rates of return from the two stocks. If the overall rate of return equals −10 percent, the rate of return from each stock must equal −10 percent (since each stock's rate of return can equal only −10, 0, or +10 percent). The probability that this will occur is $(1/3)(1/3) = 1/9$.

(b) If the overall rate of return equals +10 percent, the rate of return from each stock must equal +10 percent. The probability that this will occur is $(1/3)(1/3) = 1/9$.

(c) If the overall rate of return equals −5 percent, the rate of return from the first stock must equal −10 percent and the rate of return from the second stock must equal zero, or the rate of return from the first stock must equal zero and the rate of return from the second stock must equal −10 percent. The probability that each will occur is $(1/3)(1/3) = 1/9$. Thus, the probability that the overall rate of return equals −5 percent is $1/9 + 1/9 = 2/9$.

(d) If the overall rate of return equals +5 percent, the rate of return from the first stock must equal +10 percent and the rate of return from the second stock must equal zero, or the rate of return from the first stock must equal zero and the rate of return from the second stock must equal +10 percent. The probability that each will occur is $(1/3)(1/3) = 1/9$. Thus, the probability that the overall rate of return equals +5 percent is $1/9 + 1/9 = 2/9$.

* Material pertaining to the chapter appendix.

(e) Since the overall rate of return can assume only five values (which are mutually exclusive), the probability that the overall rate of return equals zero must equal 1 minus the sum of the probabilities that the overall rate of return equals −10, +10, −5, or +5 percent. Thus, it must equal $1 - (1/9 + 1/9 + 2/9 + 2/9) = 3/9$.

(f) The probability distribution is as follows:

Overall rate of return (percent)	Probability
−10	1/9
−5	2/9
0	3/9
+5	2/9
+10	1/9

Multiple-Choice Questions
1. (c) 2. (a) 3. (c) 4. (e) 5. (d) 6. (c)

Problems and Problem Sets
1. (a) $(.4)(.4) = .16$.
   $(.6)(.6) = .36$.
   $1 - .16 - .36 = .48$.
   (b) $.16(0) + .48(1) + .36(2) = 1.2$.
2. (a) Yes. If $P(x)$ is the probability of x crews being kept busy,
   $$P(0) = (.50)(.70) = .35,$$
   $$P(1) = (.50)(.70) + (.50)(.30) = .50,$$
   and $$P(2) = (.50)(.30) = .15.$$
   (b) Yes. $P(0) = 1/2$ and $P(1) = 1/2$.

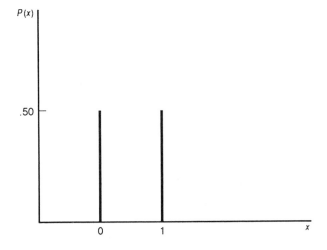

(c)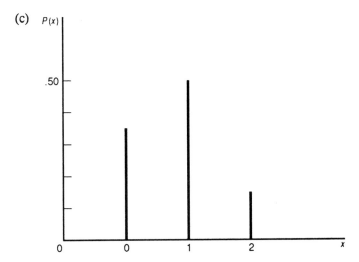

(d) $(.35)(0) + (.50)(1) + (.15)(2) = .80, .80, (.50)(0) + (.50)(1) = .50, .50.$

(e) If it hires no crews, the probability distribution is $P(-1) = 1$. That is, the probability that profits (in thousands of dollars) equal -1 is 1. If it hires one crew, the probability distribution is

$$P(-2) = .35$$

and $\qquad P(2) = .65.$

That is, the probability that profits equal -2 is .35, and the probability that profits equal 2 is .65. If it hires two crews, the probability distribution is

$$P(-3) = .35,$$
$$P(1) = .50,$$

and $\qquad P(5) = .15.$

(f) If it hires no crews, the expected profit is $1(-1) = -1$, or $-\$1,000$. If it hires one crew, the expected profit is

$$.35(-2) + .65(2) = -.70 + 1.30 = .60, \text{ or } \$600.$$

If it hires two crews, the expected profit is

$$.35(-3) + .50(1) + .15(5) = -1.05 + .50 + .75 = .20, \text{ or } \$200.$$

(g) It should hire one crew.

3. Using Chebyshev's inequality, the probability is less than 1/25 that the number of defective tires shipped to this customer exceeds 150 per year. Thus, the expected value of this cost is less than $1/25(\$10,000) = \$400$. Thus, the president is right.

4. (a) The expected profit is

$$\frac{1}{1,000,000}(\$600,000) + \frac{1}{1,000,000}(\$300,000) - \$1 = \$0.90 - \$1 = -\$0.10.$$

(b) No.

5. The expected value of the gamble is

$$(1/10)(\$200,000) + (9/10)(\$20,000) = \$38,000.$$

Thus, he should charge you $38,000.

6. (a) If C equals total cost, $C = 200,000 + 3X$, where X is the number of units of output produced. Based on Appendix 4.1, it follows that

$$E(C) = 200,000 + 3E(X).$$

Since $E(X) = 10,000$, $E(C)$ must equal $230,000.

(b) If Y is the firm's total profit, $Y = 25X - 200,000 - 3X = -200,000 + 22X$. Thus,

$$E(Y) = -200,000 + 22E(X).$$

Since $E(X) = 10,000$, $E(Y)$ must equal $20,000.

CHAPTER 5

The Binomial and Poisson Distributions

Chapter Profile

A *binomial* distribution represents the number of successes in n Bernoulli trials. That is, if each trial can result in success or failure, and if the probability of a success equals Π on each trial (and if the outcomes of the trials are independent), the number of successes that occur in n trials has a binomial distribution. The probability that the number of successes equals x is

$$P(x) = \frac{n!}{(n-x)!x!}\Pi^x (1-\Pi)^{n-x}.$$

The number of successes has a mean of $n\Pi$, and its standard deviation is

$$\sqrt{n\Pi(1-\Pi)}.$$

The *Poisson distribution* can be used to approximate the binomial distribution if n is very large and Π is very small. Under these circumstances,

$$P(x) = \frac{\mu^x e^{-\mu}}{x!}.$$

This is the probability distribution of a Poisson random variable. The mean is μ, and the standard deviation is $\sqrt{\mu}$. Besides being useful as an approximation to the binomial distribution, the Poisson distribution represents the number of events that occur in a time interval under the following circumstances: (1) The probability that an event occurs in a very short time interval is proportional to the length of the time interval and does not depend on when the interval occurs or on how many events occurred before the beginning of the interval. (2) The probability that more than one event will occur in a very short time interval is negligible.

Behavioral Objectives

A. You should be able to define the following key concepts in this chapter:

Bernoulli process	binomial distribution
Bernoulli trials	Poisson distribution

B. Be sure that you can do each of the following:
   1. Calculate the probability that a binomial variable will equal a certain value (or values), given n and Π.
   2. Calculate the mean and standard deviation of a binomial variable, given n and Π.
   3. State the conditions under which the Poisson distribution arises.
   4. Calculate the probability that a Poisson variable will equal a certain value or values, given μ (or $\lambda\Delta$).

5. Use the Poisson distribution to approximate the binomial distribution.
6. Compute the mean and standard deviation of a Poisson variable, given μ (or $\lambda\Delta$).

Power Utilization in a Factory: A Case Study[1]

In a particular factory, a motor generates power to be used intermittently by five workers. At any given time each worker has the same probability of requiring a unit of power. The workers perform independently, with the result that the probability that one worker will require power at a certain moment is the same, whether or not any other worker requires power then. According to a study carried out by the factory's engineers, each worker uses power for an average of 12 minutes per hour.

(a) At a given point in time, what is the probability that a given worker will require power?
(b) What is the probability distribution for the number of workers requiring power at any given point in time?
(c) In the following graph draw the probability distribution of the number of workers requiring power at any given point in time.

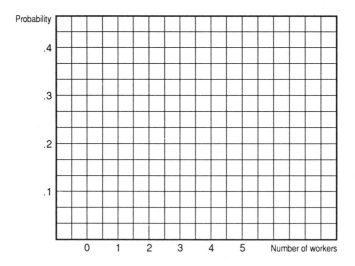

(d) If more than two workers require power at the same time, the motor will not function properly. What is the probability of such a malfunction at any given moment?
(e) What is the expected number of workers requiring power at any given point in time?
(f) What is the standard deviation of the number of workers requiring power at any given point in time?

---

1. This case is based on a section of W. Feller, *Probability Theory and Its Applications.*

Multiple-Choice Questions

1. An automobile manufacturer has 10 plants, and it feels there is a 5 percent chance of a wildcat strike at each plant. According to the firm's managers, whether or not a wildcat strike occurs at one plant is independent of whether one occurs at another plant. The probability that no plants will have a wildcat strike equals

   (a) $10(.05)(.95^9)$.
   (b) $10(.05)$.
   (c) $(.95)^5$.
   (d) $.05^{10}$.
   (e) none of the above.

2. In question 1, the expected number of the auto manufacturer's plants that will have wildcat strikes is

   (a) $10(.05)(.95^9)$.
   (b) $10(.05)$.
   (c) $\sqrt{.475}$.
   (d) $.05^{10}$.
   (e) none of the above.

3. In question 1, the standard deviation of the number of plants that will have wildcat strikes is

   (a) $10(.05)(.95^9)$.
   (b) $10(.05)$.
   (c) $\sqrt{.475}$.
   (d) $.05^{10}$.
   (e) none of the above.

4. The probability that the automobile manufacturer in question 1 will have a wildcat strike in one of its plants is

   (a) $10(.05)(.95^9)$.
   (b) $10(.05)$.
   (c) $\sqrt{.475}$.
   (d) $.05^{10}$.
   (e) none of the above.

5. A shipping company finds that the probability distribution of the number of its ships running aground in a particular period of time conforms to the Poisson distribution. The mean number of its ships running aground per year is 0.5. The probability that two of its ships will run aground next year equals

   (a) $.5e^{-.5}$.
   (b) $.5^2e^{-.5}$.
   (c) $.5^2e^{-.5} \div 2$.
   (d) $\sqrt{.5}$.
   (e) none of the above.

6. The same shipping company enters into an agreement with the firm insuring its ships whereby the shipping company will pay the insurance company $1,000 next year if any of its ships run aground, and the insurance company will reduce the shipping company's premium by $50 next year if none of its ships run aground. To the shipping company, the expected profit next year from this agreement is

(a) $e^{-.5}(\$50) - (1 - e^{-.5})(\$1,000)$.
(b) $(1 - e^{-.5})(\$50) - e^{-.5}(\$1,000)$.
(c) $(1 - e^{-.5})(\$1,000) - e^{-.5}(\$50)$.
(d) $e^{-.5}(\$1,000) - (1 - e^{-.5})(\$50)$.
(e) none of the above.

Problems and Problem Sets

1. The expected value of a binomial random variable is equal to double its variance. If its expected value is 3, what is the probability that the random variable equals zero?

2. If X is a random variable with a binomial distribution and its mean equals 1 and its variance equals 0.9, what is the value of Π for this random variable? What is the value of n for this random variable?

3. A motion picture theater finds that the probability that a science-fiction movie will prove profitable, if such a film is shown for a week, is .6. The theater shows six such films, each for a period of one week. Whether or not one film is successful is independent of the outcome of the others. What is the probability distribution of the number of weeks during this six-week period that the theater made money?

4. The motion picture theater (in problem 3) does not know the probability that a sports film will be profitable, but a consultant says that it is .5 if the film is run for a week. The theater shows three such films, each for a period of one week. The outcome of one movie is independent of the outcome of the others. All are profitable. The consultant says that this does not mean that the probability is not .5. Further, the consultant says that such an occurrence can be expected about 10 percent of the time. Is this correct? Why, or why not?

5. An automobile manufacturer buys radios from a supplier. When each shipment of radios arrives, the automobile manufacturer takes a random sample of 10 radios from the shipment of 10,000. If any radio in the sample is defective, the automobile manufacturer rejects the shipment.

   (a) If 2 percent of the radios in a shipment are defective, what is the probability that the shipment will be rejected?

   (b) If 5 percent of the radios in a shipment are defective, what is the probability that the shipment will be accepted?

6. The Bainbridge Company is uncertain concerning the number of its salespeople who will be out sick on a particular day. Its sales force consists of three individuals, and the manager believes that the chance that each one will be out sick is .01. If whether or not one person is out sick is independent of whether or not another is out sick, show that the probability distribution of x, the number of persons out sick, is

$$P(x) = \frac{3!}{x!(3-x)!}(.01)^x(.99)^{3-x}.$$

7. Use Minitab (or some other computer package) to calculate the binomial distribution for $n = 25$ and $\Pi = .4$.

8. The following is a binomial distribution. What is its value of n? What is its value of Π?

x	$P(x)$
0	.49
1	.42
2	.09

9. The annual number of oil spills in the Atlantic off the New England coast is found to be a Poisson random variable. If the probability of one oil spill annually is the same as the probability of two oil spills annually, what is the value of each of these probabilities?

10. An insurance company finds that .003 percent of the population dies of a certain disease each year. The company has insured 100,000 people against death from this disease.

   (a) What is the probability that the firm must pay off in three or more cases next year? (Use the Poisson distribution)

   (b) What is the expected number of persons insured by this company who will die of the disease next year? What is the *most likely* number of persons who will die of the disease next year?

11. An airplane manufacturer operates a large machine tool. The number of times that this tool breaks down per month can be represented as a Poisson variable. The probability that this tool will not break down at all during a month is .3679. If the tool breaks down two or more times in a month, the aircraft manufacturer must shift some of the work to another location. What is the probability that such a shift will occur next month?

Answers

Power Utilization in a Factory: A Case Study

(a) The probability that a given worker will require power at a given point in time is approximately 1/5, since each worker uses power for, on the average, 12 minutes per hour.

(b) The probability that x workers will require power is

$$P(x) = \frac{5!}{(5-x)!x!}\left(\frac{1}{5}\right)^x\left(\frac{4}{5}\right)^{5-x}.$$

(c) Based on Appendix Table 1, the graph is:

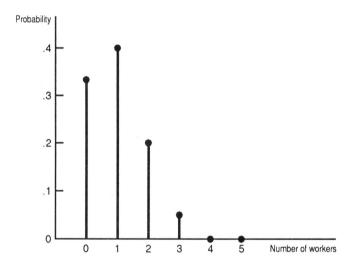

(d) Based on Appendix Table 1, this probability equals .0512 + .0064 + .0003 = .0579.

(e) (5)(1/5) = 1 worker.

(f) $\sqrt{5(1/5)(4/5)} = \sqrt{20/25} = .89$ worker.

Multiple-Choice Questions

1. (e)   2. (b)   3. (c)   4. (a)   5. (c)   6. (a)

Problems and Problem Sets

1. Since $n\Pi = 2[n\Pi(1 - \Pi)]$, $\Pi = 1/2$. And since $n\Pi = 3$, $n = 6$. Thus, based on Appendix Table 1, this probability equals .0156.

2. Since $n\Pi = 1$, and $n\Pi(1 - \Pi) = 0.9$, $(1 - \Pi)$ must equal 0.9. Thus, Π must equal 0.1. Since $\Pi = 0.1$, n must equal 10.

3. If x is the number of weeks that the theater made money,

$$P(x) = \frac{6!}{x!(6-x)!}(.6)^x(.4)^{6-x}, \quad \text{for } x = 0, 1, \ldots, 6.$$

4. If the probability that a sports film is successful equals .50, the probability that all three will be successful is $(.50)^3 = .125$. This is not too different from the consultant's figure of 10 percent.

5. (a) If $\Pi = .02$, the probability of no defectives in 10 trials equals $(.98)^{10}$. Thus, the probability of rejection equals $1 - (.98)^{10}$. Since $(.98)^{10} = .82$, the probability of rejection equals .18.

   (b) If $\Pi = .05$, the probability of no defectives in 10 trials equals $(.95)^{10}$. Appendix Table 1 shows that this probability equals .60.

6. The number of persons out sick is a binomial random variable with $n = 3$ and $\Pi = .01$, so it follows that this is the correct probability distribution.

7. MTB> PDF;
   SUBC> BINOMIAL N = 25, P = .4.

   BINOMIAL WITH N = 25 P = 0.400000

K	P(X = K)
1	0.0000
2	0.0004
3	0.0019
4	0.0071
5	0.0199
6	0.0442
7	0.0800
8	0.1200
9	0.1511
10	0.1612
11	0.1465
12	0.1140
13	0.0760
14	0.0434
15	0.0212
16	0.0088
17	0.0031
18	0.0009
19	0.0002
20	0.0000

   For $K = 21$ to 25, $P(X = K)$ is very close to zero.

8. $n = 2$, $\Pi = .3$.

9. $\mu e^{-\mu} = \mu^2 e^{-\mu}/2$. Thus,

$$\mu = \frac{\mu^2}{2}.$$

   This implies that $\mu = 2$. So, from Appendix Table 3, we see that both probabilities equal .2707.

10. (a) The expected number of cases per year is $(.00003)(100,000) = 3$. Since $\mu = 3$, the probability that $x = 3$ or more equals 1 minus the probability that a

Poisson variable (with $\mu = 3$) equals 0, 1, or 2. From Appendix Table 3 we see that this equals

$$1 - (.0498 + .1494 + .2240) = 1 - .4232 = .5768.$$

(b) Since $\mu = 3$, the expected number is 3. The most likely numbers are 2 or 3, based on Appendix Table 3; they are equally likely.

11. The probability of no breakdown equals $\mu^0 e^{-\mu}/0! = e^{-\mu}$. Thus, $e^{-\mu} = .3679$. Appendix Table 4 shows that μ must equal 1. Given that $\mu = 1$, the probability of 0 or 1 breakdown per month is $.3679 + .3679 = .7358$, according to Appendix Table 3. Thus, the probability of 2 or more breakdowns equals

$$1 - .7358 = .2642.$$

CHAPTER 6

The Normal Distribution

Chapter Profile

The probability density function of a *normal random variable* is

$$f(x) = \frac{1}{\sqrt{2\pi}\sigma} e^{-1/2[(x-\mu)/\sigma]^2}$$

where μ is the mean and σ is the standard deviation. It is continuous, symmetrical, and bell-shaped. When n is large and Π is not too close to zero or 1, the normal curve is a good approximation to the binomial distribution. The probability that a *standard normal variable* (a normal variable with zero mean and standard deviation equal to 1) falls between any two numbers has been tabled. This table can be used to calculate the probability that any normal variable will fall between some particular pair of numbers.

Behavioral Objectives

A. You should be able to define the following key concepts in this chapter:

probability density function	standard normal distribution
standard units	normal distribution
Z value	continuity correction
*exponential distribution	*waiting lines

B. Make sure that you can do each of the following:
1. Describe how the probability distribution of a continuous random variable can be characterized graphically.
2. Express observations in standard units, that is, as Z values.
3. Use the table of the standard normal distribution to find the probability that a normal variable will fall in a specified range, given the mean and standard deviation of the normal variable.
4. Use the normal distribution to approximate the binomial distribution.

Lengths of Metal Parts: A Case Study

A manufacturing firm has produced a particular metal part for many years. The firm is sure that the length of the part is normally distributed. That is, due to machine wear, machine variability, and other factors, the length of one metal part will differ from that of another metal part produced on the same day, and if one plots the frequency distribution of lengths of the metal parts produced on a given day, the

* Concept described in chapter appendix.

result will conform to a normal distribution. If the length of a part is less than 0.78 inch or more than 0.82 inch, the part is defective and must be discarded or reworked.

(a) If the standard deviation of the lengths of metal parts produced on a certain day is 0.01 inch, what proportion of the day's output of metal parts is defective if the mean length is 0.80 inch?

(b) If the standard deviation remains at 0.01 inch, but the mean length increases to 0.81 inch, what proportion will be defective?

(c) If the standard deviation increases to 0.02 inch, at what level should the firm attempt to set the mean length if it wants to minimize the proportion defective?

(d) If the mean length is set at 0.79 inch, what value of the standard deviation would minimize the proportion defective? Why?

Suppose that the cost of making a part too long is less than the cost of making it too short (parts that are too long can be reworked, whereas parts that are too short must be thrown away). Specifically, the cost of a part that is too long is $0.01 and the cost of one that is too short is $0.02.

(e) What is the expected cost (due to defective length) per part if the standard deviation is 0.01 inches and the mean length is 0.80 inch?

(f) What is the expected cost (due to defective length) per part if the standard deviation is 0.01 inches and the mean length is 0.81 inch?

Multiple-Choice Questions

1. The scores on a particular psychological test are normally distributed with a mean equal to 100 and standard deviation equal to 20. The probability that a score will exceed 130 equals

   (a) .4332.
   (b) .0668.
   (c) .3413.
   (d) .1587.
   (e) none of the above.

2. A manufacturer of pipe knows that the pipe lengths it produces vary in diameter and that the diameters are normally distributed. The mean diameter is 1 inch, and the probability that a length of pipe will have a diameter exceeding 1.1 inches is .1587. The standard deviation of the diameters must therefore be

   (a) 1 inch.
   (b) 0.1 inch.
   (c) 2 inches.
   (d) 0.2 inch.
   (e) none of the above.

3. The pipe manufacturer in the previous questions wants to know what the probability is that a diameter will exceed 1.2 inches. You are hired as a consultant. Your answer should be

    (a) .05.
    (b) .10.
    (c) .0228.
    (d) .0793.
    (e) none of the above.

4. The probability that the value of a standard normal variable is less than 1.0 equals

    (a) .0228.
    (b) .0287.
    (c) .6915.
    (d) .8413.
    (e) .0919.

5. The probability that the value of a standard normal variable exceeds 1.9 equals

    (a) .0228.
    (b) .0287.
    (c) .6915.
    (d) .8413.
    (e) .0919.

6. If X is normally distributed with a mean of 2 and a standard deviation of 2, the probability that X is less than 3 equals

    (a) .0228.
    (b) .0287.
    (c) .6915.
    (d) .8413.
    (e) .0919.

7. In the previous question, the probability that X lies between 4 and 5 equals

    (a) .0228.
    (b) .0287.
    (c) .6915.
    (d) .8413.
    (e) .0919.

8. In question 6, the probability that X exceeds 6 equals

    (a) .0228.
    (b) .0287.
    (c) .6915.
    (d) .8413.
    (e) .0919.

Problems and Problem Sets

1. According to Robert Klitgaard,[1] the distribution of population density per
    square kilometer for 71 countries is as follows:

Middle of interval	Number of countries
25	49
75	6
125	4
175	5
225	1
275	1
325	2
375	1
1,250	1
2,750	1

    Does population per square kilometer seem to be normally distributed? Why or
    why not?

2. A statistician employed by the housing industry constructs a frequency
    distribution of single-family houses by the number of bedrooms they contain.
    Will the result be a normal distribution? Why or why not?

1. Robert Klitgaard, *Data Analysis for Development* (Oxford: Oxford University Press, 1985), p. 9.

3. The length of a rod produced by the Cascade Manufacturing Company is normally distributed with mean equal to 3 inches and standard deviation equal to 0.001 inch.

(a) What point on the standard normal distribution corresponds to a rod length of 2.9984 inches?

(b) What is the probability that a rod's length will be less than 2.9984 inches?

(c) What point on the standard normal distribution corresponds to a rod length of 2.9979 inches?

(d) What is the probability that a rod's length will be greater than 2.9979 inches?

4. A gasoline station knows that the number of gallons of gasoline it sells each day is normally distributed. The probability that it sells more than 139.2 gallons per day equals .025. The probability that it sells less than 60.8 gallons per day equals .025.

   (a) What is the expected number of gallons sold per day?

   (b) What is the standard deviation of the number of gallons sold per day?

5. The diameters of the tires produced by a tire manufacturer vary from tire to tire, and are normally distributed. The probability that a tire will have a diameter exceeding 25.128 inches is .10. The probability that a tire will have a diameter exceeding 25.164 inches is .05.

   (a) What is the median diameter of the tires produced by the firm?

(b) What is the variance of the diameters of the tires produced by the firm?

(c) What is the probability that a tire will have a diameter of less than 24.90 inches?

(d) What is the probability that a tire will have a diameter of less than 24.85 inches?

6. John Black is a roofer. He telephones homes at random in the area where he works and asks whether the roof is at least 20 years old. If so, he asks if he can reroof the house. In 10 percent of such cases, Black gets the job. There are 20,000 houses with telephones in the area where he works. The ages of the roofs in this area are normally distributed, with mean equal to 10 years and standard deviation equal to 5 years.

(a) If Black telephones 50 houses in a particular week, what is the expected number of jobs he will get?

(b) Suppose that John Black telephones 10 houses. What is the probability that none has a roof at least 20 years old? What is the probability that all have a roof at least 20 years old?

7. The Ajax Manufacturing Company owns and operates two air conditioners. If the temperature on a particular day exceeds 90°, it uses both air conditioners. If the temperature is between 80 and 90°F, it uses one air conditioner. If the temperature is below 80°F, it uses neither air conditioner. The cost of operating each air conditioner for one day is $5. If the temperature tomorrow is a normally distributed random variable with a mean of 75°F and a standard deviation of 10°F, what is the expected value of the firm's cost of operating its air conditioners tomorrow?

8. To reduce its costs, the Ajax Manufacturing Company revises the operating rules given in the previous problem. It now uses one rather than two air conditioners if the temperature exceeds 90°F. What is the expected value of the saving per day?

*9. If X is a normally distributed random variable with a mean of 100 and a standard deviation of 10, and if $Y = 2X - 4$, what is the probability that Y is greater than 200?

10. A manufacturer of shingles finds that 60 percent of the roofs covered with its shingles last for more than 20 years. In a particular community 500 roofs have been covered with this firm's shingles. What is the probability that more than 300 but less than 321 of these roofs will last for more than 20 years?

*This problem assumes that Appendix 4.1 has been read.

Answers

Lengths of Metal Parts: A Case Study

(a) The probability that the length of a part exceeds 0.82 inch or is less than 0.78 inch equals the probability that the standard normal variable exceeds 2.00 or is less than –2.00. According to Appendix Table 2 this probability equals .0228 + .0228 = .0456. Thus, 4.56 percent will be defective.

(b) The desired probability equals the probability that the standard normal variable exceeds 1.00 or is less than –3.00. According to Appendix Table 2 this probability equals .1587 + .0013 = .1600. Thus, 16 percent will be defective.

(c) The firm should set the mean at 0.80 inch because this will minimize the proportion defective.

(d) Zero, because none of the parts would be defective.

(e) Under these circumstances, the probability that a part is too long is .0228, and the probability that it is too short is .0228. See (a) above. Thus, the expected cost equals

$$(.0228)(\$.01) + (.0228)(\$.02) = \$.000684.$$

That is, the expected cost per part equals about 7/100 of a cent.

(f) The probability that a part is too long is .1587, and the probability that it is too short is .0013. See (b) above. Thus, the expected cost equals

$$(.1587)(\$.01) + (.0013)(\$.02) = \$.001613.$$

That is, the expected cost per part equals about 16/100 of a cent.

Multiple-Choice Questions

    1. (b)   2. (b)   3. (c)   4. (d)   5. (b)   6. (c)   7. (e)   8. (a)

Problems and Problem Sets

1. No. The distribution seems skewed to the right, not bell-shaped.

2. No. The result will not be a continuous distribution. Also, skewness is likely to be present.

3. (a) –1.6.
   (b) .0548.
   (c) –2.1.
   (d) .9821.

4. (a) $(139.2 + 60.8)/2 = 100$.
   (b) $139.2 - 100 = 1.96\sigma$
           $39.2 = 1.96\sigma$
             $\sigma = 20$.

5. (a) $\mu + 1.28\sigma = 25.128$.
       $\mu + 1.64\sigma = 25.164$.
       Thus,
       $1.64\sigma - 1.28\sigma = 25.164 - 25.128$,
       or $.36\sigma = .036$,
       so $\sigma = .10$.
       Thus, $\mu = 25.128 - (1.28)(.10) = 25$.
       Since the median and mean are equal, the median equals 25 inches.
   (b) The variance equals $(.10)^2$, or 0.01 inches ^{2}.

  (c) $Z = (24.90 - 25)/.10 = -1$.

      Thus, the probability equals .1587.

  (d) $Z = (24.85 - 25)/.10 = -1.5$.

      Thus, the probability equals .0668.

6. (a) The probability that a roof's age is at least 20 years equals the probability that the standard normal variable is at least 2, which is .0228.

      Given that a roof is this old, the probability that Black will get the job is .1, so the expected number is $(.0228)(.1)(50) = .114$ jobs per week.

  (b) The first probability equals $(.9772)^{10}$. The second equals $(.0228)^{10}$.

7. The probability that the temperature exceeds 90°F equals the probability that the standard normal variable exceeds 1.5, and thus is .0668.

The probability that the temperature is between 80 and 90°F equals the probability that the standard normal variable is between 0.5 and 1.5, and thus is .4332 − .1915 = .2417.

The probability that the temperature is below 80°F equals the probability that the standard normal variable is below 0.5, and thus is .6915.

The expected value of the cost is

$$(.6915)(0) + (.2417)(\$5) + (.0668)(\$10) = \$1.21 + \$0.67 = \$1.88.$$

8. The expected value of the cost is

$$(.2417 + .0668)(\$5) = (.3085)(\$5) = \$1.54.$$

Thus, the expected savings is 34 cents per day.

9. Based on Appendix 4.1, we know that

$$E(Y) = 2E(X) - 4$$

and
$$\sigma(Y) = 2\sigma(X).$$

Thus, the expected value of Y equals $2(100) - 4 = 196$, and the standard deviation of Y equals $2(10) = 20$. Thus, the probability that Y is greater than 200 equals the probability that the standard normal variable exceeds $(200 - 196) \div 20 = 0.2$. Appendix Table 2 indicates that this probability equals .4207.

10. Let X be the number of roofs lasting more than 20 years. Its probability distribution is

$$P(x) = \frac{500!}{(500 - x)!x!}(.6)^x(.4)^{500 - x}.$$

To estimate the probability that $300 < X < 321$, we use the normal approximation to the binomial distribution. The mean of the binomial distribution is $(500)(.6) = 300$, and its standard deviation is

$\sqrt{500(.6)(.4)} = \sqrt{120} = 0.95$. The probability that a normal variable with a mean of 300 and a standard deviation of 10.95 will lie between 300.5 and 320.5 equals the probability that the standard normal variable will lie between

$$\frac{300.5 - 300}{10.95} = .05 \quad \text{and} \quad \frac{320.5 - 300}{10.95} = 1.87.$$

Based on Appendix Table 2, this probability equals .4693 − .0199 = .4494.

CHAPTER 7

Sample Designs and Sampling Distributions

Chapter Profile

Sample designs can be divided into two broad classes: *probability samples* and *judgment samples*. A *probability sample* is one where the probability that each member of the population will be chosen in the sample is known. A *judgment sample* is chosen on the basis of personal judgment. One of the most important disadvantages of a judgment sample is that one cannot calculate the sampling distributions of the sample statistics, and so there is no way to tell "how far off" the sample results are likely to be.

One of the most important ways that expert judgment can be used to design a probability sample is in the construction of *strata,* or subdivisions of the population. A more precise estimate often can be obtained from a sample of given size if the population is stratified first, and if a random sample is chosen from each stratum. This is called *stratified random sampling.* The basic idea in formulating strata is to subdivide the population so that the strata differ greatly with regard to the characteristic that is measured, and so that there is as little variation as possible within each stratum with regard to this characteristic. To maximize the precision of the sample results, the sample size in each stratum should be proportional to the product of the number of items in the stratum and the standard deviation of the characteristic being measured in the stratum.

In *cluster sampling,* the population is divided into a number of clusters, and a sample of these clusters is chosen, after which a random sample of the items in each of the chosen clusters is taken. The major advantage of cluster sampling is that it is relatively cheap to sample items that are physically or geographically close to one another.

A *population* is composed of the entire set of observations in which one is interested, whereas a *sample* is composed of a part of the population. Populations may be *finite* or *infinite*. In a finite population composed of N items, a random sample of n items is a sample chosen so that each of the $N! \div [(N-n)! \times n!]$ different samples that could be chosen has an equal chance of being picked. To choose a random sample, a *table of random numbers* can be used.

Three very useful statements can be made about the probability distribution of the sample mean:

(1) The mean of this probability distribution is equal to the population mean.

(2) The standard deviation of this probability distribution is equal to $\sigma/\sqrt{n}$, where σ is the population standard deviation and n is the sample size. (This is for an infinite population. For a finite population, the standard deviation of this probability distribution equals $\sigma/\sqrt{n}$ multiplied by $\sqrt{(N-n)/(N-1)}$, where N is the number of items in the population.)

(3) If the sample size is large, this probability distribution can be approximated by the normal distribution.

These propositions concerning the probability distribution of the sample mean are of great practical importance, since they allow us to calculate how reliable a sample mean or sample proportion is likely to be.

Behavioral Objectives

A. You should be able to define the following key concepts in this chapter:

population
finite population
infinite population
parameter
cluster sample
systematic sample
statistic
random sample
table of random numbers
sampling distribution
finite population correction factor

mean of the probability distribution
    of the sample mean
optimum allocation
stratified random sample
standard deviation of the probability
    distribution of the sample mean
central limit theorem
probability sample
judgment sample
proportional allocation

B. Make sure that you can do each of the following:
   1. Distinguish between a finite population and an infinite population and between a population and a sample.
   2. Use a table of random numbers to pick a random sample.
   3. Calculate the standard deviation of a sample mean, given the population standard deviation.
   4. Describe the mean, standard deviation, and shape (for large samples) of the probability distribution of the sample mean.
   5. Compute the probability that a sample mean (from a large sample) will depart from the population mean by at least a given amount.
   6. Describe the nature of simple random sampling.
   7. Describe the nature of systematic sampling.
   8. Describe the nature and advantages of stratified random sampling.
   9. Distinguish between probability samples and judgment samples.
   10. Describe the nature and advantages of cluster sampling.

The Chesapeake and Ohio Railroad: A Case Study[1]

The Chesapeake and Ohio Railroad Company made a study some years ago to determine the revenue due them on interline, less-than-carload, freight shipments during a particular six-month period. It wanted to determine whether it could sample its waybills to determine how much it was owed for such shipments. (A waybill is a document describing the goods to be shipped, the route, and the charges for a particular shipment of freight. Each shipment is issued a waybill.) Such a sampling

---

1. This case is adapted from John Neter, "How Accountants Save Money by Sampling," *Statistics: A Guide to the Unknown*, J. Tanur et al. (San Francisco: Holden-Day, 1972).

procedure would be cheaper than going through all of the waybills to get this information.

The firm divided all the waybills issued during this six-month period into five groups: (1) those where the freight charges were $5.00 or less, (2) those where they were $5.01 to $10.00, (3) those where they were $10.01 to $20.00, (4) those where they were $20.01 to $40.00, and (5) those where they were over $40.00. For each waybill one can compute the amount due to the firm on interline, less-than-carload shipments. This amount varies, of course, from waybill to waybill in each of the above groups. The firm believed that the standard deviation of this amount was 10 percent as large in group 1 as in group 2, that it was one-half as large in group 2 as in group 3, that it was 40 percent as large in group 3 as in group 4, and that it was one-half as large in group 4 as in group 5.

(a) If the firm decided to sample 1 percent of the waybills in group 1, what percentage should it sample in group 2 if it wanted to achieve optimum allocation?
(b) If the firm decided to sample 10 percent in group 3, what percentage should it sample in group 4 in order to achieve optimum allocation?
(c) Waybills are numbered serially, and there is no reason to expect that a waybill's serial number is related in any systematic way to the amount it contains that is due the firm on interline, less-than-carload shipments. If this is the case, suggest a relatively simple way of drawing what amounts to a 1 percent random sample of waybills in group 1.
(d) Suppose that the firm decides to take a 20 percent sample of the waybills in group 3. Suggest a relatively simple way of drawing what amounts to a 20 percent random sample from this population.
(e) In fact, the Chesapeake and Ohio found that its sample (which contained less than 10 percent of all waybills) provided an estimate which was in error by $83. On the basis of this evidence, does it appear that sampling is worthwhile? What information would you need to provide a better answer to this question?

Multiple-Choice Questions

1. A firm has 70 employees. The firm's president wants to estimate the mean number of years they have worked for the firm. The president chooses a random sample of 36 employees and finds that the sample mean is 7 years. If the standard deviation of the number of years worked for the firm is 4 years for the 70 employees, the standard error of the sample mean equals

   (a) .693.
   (b) .674.
   (c) .667.
   (d) .513.
   (e) .468.

2. The mean of the probability distribution of the sample mean is

   (a) a statistic.
   (b) a random variable.
   (c) a parameter.
   (d) always equal to the sample mean.
   (e) none of the above.

3. The sample mean is

   (a) a parameter.
   (b) always equal to the population mean.
   (c) a statistic.
   (d) never equal to the population mean.
   (e) none of the above.

4. When N is large, the finite population correction factor is approximately equal to

   (a) $\sqrt{1 - N/n}$.
   (b) $\sqrt{1 + N/n}$.
   (c) $\sqrt{1 - n/N}$.
   (d) $\sqrt{1 + n/N}$.
   (e) none of the above.

5. A random sample of 16 observations is taken from an infinite population with a standard deviation equal to 10. The standard deviation of the probability distribution of the sample mean equals

   (a) 10.
   (b) 4.
   (c) 2.5.
   (d) 10/16.
   (e) none of the above.

6. A random sample of four observations is taken from an infinite population with a standard deviation equal to 10. The probability that the sample mean will differ from the population mean by more than 20 is

   (a) 2/16.
   (b) between 1/16 and 2/16.
   (c) less than 1/16.
   (d) completely unknown.
   (e) none of the above.

7. If the sample size is multiplied by 10, the standard deviation of the sample mean is

   (a) multiplied by 10.
   (b) divided by 10.
   (c) unaffected.
   (d) divided by $\sqrt{10}$.
   (e) none of the above.

8. A random sample of 100 observations is taken from an infinite population with a standard deviation equal to 10. The probability that the sample mean will differ from the population mean by more than 2 is

   (a) .0456.
   (b) .0228.
   (c) .4772.
   (d) .0114.
   (e) none of the above.

9. If the sample size in question 8 is increased from 100 to 400, the probability is .95 that the sample mean will differ from the population mean by less than

   (a) .82.
   (b) .50.
   (c) .98.
   (d) 1.00.
   (e) none of the above.

10. Ten percent of the male adults in a large city are unemployed. A random sample of 25 male adults is chosen from this city's adult male population. The standard deviation of the number of unemployed in the sample is

   (a) .06.
   (b) 1.5.
   (c) $\sqrt{7.5}$.
   (d) 2.25.
   (e) none of the above.

Problems and Problem Sets

1. According to the *Statistical Abstract of the United States,* there are 434 municipal governments in Alabama. How would you pick a random sample of 10 of them?

2. If the variance of an infinite population is 64, what is the probability of drawing a simple random sample of size 49 with a mean of 50 or more from a population with a mean of 51?

3. Suppose that a company has six plants, which are designated as plant 1, plant 2, . . . , plant 6.

   (a) If sampling occurs without replacement, how many samples of size 3 can be chosen from these plants?

   (b) List all the possible samples of size 3.

4. A company has eight plants: plant 1, plant 2, . . . , plant 8. It chooses a random sample of two of these plants (*with replacement*).

   (a) What is the probability that plant 2 is the first chosen?

(b) What is the probability that plant 2 is chosen both times?

5. A company has eight plants: plant 1, plant 2, . . . , plant 8. It chooses a random sample of two of these plants (*without replacement*).

(a) What is the probability that each possible sample of size 2 will be drawn?

(b) What is the probability that plant 2 is included in the sample?

(c) What is the probability that both plant 2 and plant 3 are included in the sample?

6. Obtain a list of the names of the students in your statistics class. Use a table of random numbers to obtain a random sample of four students in your class

    (a) without replacement;

    (b) with replacement.

7. A random sample of size n is drawn (without replacement) from a population with N members.

    (a) How many different samples of size n can be drawn?

(b) How many different samples of size n can be drawn if we stipulate that the ith member of the population must be included in the sample?

(c) What is the probability that the ith member of the population will be included in a random sample of size n?

8. The Beta Corporation has five machines, and their costs (in thousands of dollars) are 7, 8, 9, 2, and 4.

(a) Calculate the mean and standard deviation of the costs of the machines. (Note that these five machines are the population.)

(b) List all possible samples (without replacement) of size 2 from this population of the costs of the five machines.

(c) Given that the probabilities of choosing each of the samples in (b) are equal, derive the sampling distribution of the sample mean from random samples of size 2 from this finite population.

(d) Compute the mean and standard deviation of the sampling distribution, and compare them with the results predicted by the propositions in the text.

9. In the previous problem, suppose that the sampling was with replacement.

(a) List all possible samples of size 2 from this population of the costs of the five machines. (In this case, consider different permutations as different samples.)

(b) Given that the probabilities of choosing each of the samples in (a) are equal, derive the sampling distribution of the sample mean from random samples of size 2 from this infinite population.

(c) Compute the mean and standard deviation of the sampling distribution, and compare these with the results predicted by the propositions in the text.

10. A supermarket receives a shipment of 20,000 cans of beans. The supermarket picks a random sample of 16 cans and finds that their weights (in ounces) are as follows:

21.1	21.0	21.2	20.7
21.3	20.9	21.3	21.0
21.2	20.8	21.0	20.9
21.6	21.0	20.9	21.1

If the standard deviation of the weights of the cans in the shipment is known to equal 0.2 oz. and if the weights of the cans in the shipment are normally distributed, find an interval within which the mean weight of all cans in the shipment will lie with probability equal to .90.

11. A random sample of 49 cans of peas is selected from a large shipment, and each can is weighed. The mean of the sample is used to estimate the mean weight of the cans in the shipment. The weights of the cans in the shipment are known to have a standard deviation equal to 0.1 oz. What is the probability that the sample mean will depart from the population mean by more than 0.005 oz.?

12. Based on data concerning the performance of 1,000 machine tools owned by the Zorro Company, it is known that the length of time a machine can go without repair is distributed approximately as a normal distribution with a mean of 250 hours and a standard deviation of 50 hours. What is the probability that the mean number of hours between repairs of a random sample of 25 of these machines is

   (a) less than 240 hours?

   (b) greater than 270 hours?

   (c) between 240 and 250 hours?

13. Suppose that the Alpha Corporation has six typewriters (A, B, . . . , F) and that typewriters A, B, D, and E do not need repairs, whereas the other two typewriters do.

    (a) Letting a 0 stand for a typewriter that does not need repairs and a 1 stand for a typewriter that does, list all possible samples (without replacement) of size 2 from this population.

    (b) Derive the sampling distribution of the sample proportion of typewriters needing repairs from samples of size 2 from this finite population. Compute the mean and standard deviation of this sampling distribution, and compare these with the results predicted by the propositions in the text. (Note: The standard deviation of a random variable that assumes the value of 1 with probability Π and the value of zero with probability $(1 - \Pi)$ equals $\sqrt{\Pi(1 - \Pi)}$.)

14. The Alliance Company buys four trucks from a truck dealer. These four trucks can be regarded as a random sample from this dealer's entire stock. The dealer knows that for the entire stock of trucks, the mean mileage before a major repair is 25,000 miles, the standard deviation is 5,000 miles, and the distribution is approximately normal. The Alliance Company asks the truck dealer to enter into an agreement whereby it would pay Alliance $1,000 if the mean mileage before a major repair for these four trucks is less than 20,000 miles.

   (a) What is the expected value of the cost of this agreement to the dealer?

   (b) Suppose that the dealer responds to Alliance's request by saying that it will enter into the agreement described in the previous problem providing Alliance agrees to pay the dealer $1,000 if the mean mileage before a major repair for these four trucks is greater than 29,000 miles. What is the expected value of the cost of the combination of these two agreements to the dealer? To Alliance?

15. A pollster is asked to construct a random sample of the population of New York City. The pollster obtains the telephone directories of Manhattan and the Bronx and uses a table of random numbers to select people at random from these directories. Is the result a random sample? Why, or why not?

16. A buyer receives a large shipment of tires, draws a random sample of the tires, and measures the diameter of each tire. From past experience it is known that the standard deviation of the diameters in such a shipment equals 0.1 inch. The buyer wants to take a large enough sample so as to have a probability of only .10 that the mean of the diameters in the sample will differ from the mean of the diameters in the entire shipment by more than 0.2 inch. How big a sample should be taken?

17. In estimating unemployment in the United States, Labor Department interviewers asked people somewhat different questions, depending on their sex. Adult women were asked: "What were you doing last week, keeping house or something else?" In 1993, this question was changed because it was felt that it biased the female unemployment rate downward. Why?

18. If a pipe's diameter exceeds 24 inches, it is useless to a buyer. A buyer receives a shipment of 10,000 pieces of pipe, and knows from past experience that the standard deviation of the diameters of the pieces of pipe in such a shipment equals 0.2 inch and that the diameters are normally distributed. The buyer draws a random sample of 100 pieces of pipe from the shipment. If the proportion of useless pieces of pipe in the entire shipment equals 10 percent, what is the probability that the mean diameter in the sample is greater than 23.9 inches?

19. Use Minitab to generate 25 randomly chosen observations from a normal population with mean of 20 and standard deviation of 10.

Answers

The Chesapeake and Ohio Railroad: A Case Study

(a) To achieve optimum allocation, the proportion of the waybills sampled in a group should be proportional to the standard deviation in the group. Since the standard deviation in group 2 is 10 times that in group 1, and 1 percent of the waybills are to be sampled in group 1, 10 percent of the waybills should be sampled in group 2.

(b) Since the standard deviation in group 4 is 2.5 times as big as that in group 3, 25 percent of the waybills in group 4 should be sampled.

(c) Pick a number between 1 and 100 at random. Let this number be x. Then include the waybills with serial number x, $100 + x$, $200 + x$, and so on, in the sample.

(d) Pick a number between 1 and 5 at random. Let this number be x. Include in the sample the waybills with serial numbers x, $5 + x$, $10 + x$, $15 + x$, $20 + x$, and so forth.

(e) It depends on the cost of sampling. If the sample costs essentially as much as the complete count, there is little point in sampling. It also depends on whether $83 is regarded as a substantial error. In fact, however, the Chesapeake and Ohio did regard the sampling procedure as advantageous, since the savings were worthwhile and the error was of little consequence.

Multiple-Choice Questions

1. (e) 2. (c) 3. (c) 4. (c) 5. (c) 6. (c) 7. (d) 8. (a) 9. (c)
10. (b)

Problems and Problem Sets

1. Number them from 1 to 434, and use a table of random numbers to pick 10 of them, as indicated in the text.

2. The sample mean is distributed normally with mean equal to 51 and standard deviation equal to $8 \div \sqrt{49} = 8/7$. Thus, the probability that the sample mean exceeds 50 is equal to the probability that a standard normal variable exceeds $(50 - 51) \div 8/7 = -.875$. According to Appendix Table 2, this probability is approximately equal to $.31 + .50 = .81$.

3. (a) $\dfrac{6!}{3!3!} = \dfrac{(6)(5)(4)}{(3)(2)(1)} = 20$.

   (b)
123	134	146	236	345
124	135	156	245	346
125	136	234	246	356
126	145	235	256	456

4. (a) There are eight possibilities, each of which is equally likely. Thus, the probability equals 1/8.

   (b) The probability that plant 2 is the first drawn is 1/8. The probability that it is the second drawn is 1/8. The probability that it is drawn in both cases is $(1/8)(1/8) = 1/64$.

5. (a) There are $8!/6!2! = 28$ possible samples that can be drawn. Thus the answer is 1/28.

   (b) The probability is 1/8 that plant 2 is the first drawn. It is $(7/8)(1/7)$ that it is the second drawn. Since sampling is without replacement, the probability is zero that plant 2 is both the first and second drawn. Thus, the probability that plant 2 is included in the sample equals $1/8 + 1/8 = 1/4$.

   (c) Of the 28 possible samples, only one contains both plant 2 and plant 3. Thus, the probability equals 1/28.

7. (a) $N!/(N - n)!n!$

   (b) $(N - 1)!/(N - n)!(n - 1)!$

   (c) n/N.

8. (a) $\mu = 6$, $\sigma = \sqrt{6.8} = 2.61$.

   (b)
7,8	8,2
7,9	8,4
7,2	9,2
7,4	9,4
8,9	2,4

(c) The sample means are 7.5; 8.0; 4.5; 5.5; 8.5; 5.0; 6.0; 5.5; 6.5; and 3.0. Each has a probability of 1/10. Thus, the sampling distribution is

x	P(x)
3.0	1/10
4.5	1/10
5.0	1/10
5.5	2/10
6.0	1/10
6.5	1/10
7.5	1/10
8.0	1/10
8.5	1/10

(d) The mean is $(1/10)(3.0 + 4.5 + 5.0 + 11.0 + 6.0 + 6.5 + 7.5 + 8.0 + 8.5)$, which equals 6. This is the same as μ, which is in accord with the propositions in the text.
The standard deviation is

$$\sqrt{(1/10)(3^2 + 1.5^2 + 1^2 + 2(.5)^2 + .5^2 + 1.5^2 + 2^2 + 2.5^2}$$

$$= \sqrt{(1/10)(25.50)} = 1.60.$$

This equals

$$\frac{\sigma}{\sqrt{n}}\sqrt{\frac{N-n}{N-1}} = \frac{2.61}{\sqrt{2}}\sqrt{\frac{3}{4}} = 2.61\sqrt{.375} = 1.60.$$

This, too, is in accord with the predictions in the text.

9. (a) If different orders are regarded as different samples, we have

7,7	8,7	9,7	2,7	4,7
7,8	8,8	9,8	2,8	4,8
7,9	8,9	9,9	2,9	4,9
7,2	8,2	9,2	2,2	4,2
7,4	8,4	9,4	2,4	4,4

(b) The means of the 25 samples are 7.0; 7.5; 8.0; 4.5; 5.5; 7.5; 8.0; 8.5; 5.0; 6.0; 8.0; 8.5; 9.0; 5.5; 6.5; 4.5; 5.0; 5.5; 2.0; 3.0; 5.5; 6.0; 6.5; 3.0; and 4.0. Each has a probability of 1/25. Thus, the sampling distribution is

x	P(x)
2.0	1/25
3.0	2/25
4.0	1/25
4.5	2/25
5.0	2/25
5.5	4/25
6.0	2/25
6.5	2/25
7.0	1/25
7.5	2/25
8.0	3/25
8.5	2/25
9.0	1/25

(c) The mean is $(1/25)(2 + 6 + 4 + 9 + 10 + 22 + 12 + 13 + 7 + 15 + 24 + 17 + 9) = 6$, which is the same as μ. This is in accord with the propositions in the text.

The standard deviation is

$$\left\{ \frac{1}{25}(4^2 + 2(3)^2 + 2^2 + 2(1.5)^2 + 2(1)^2 + 4(.5)^2 + 2(.5)^2 + 1^2 \right.$$
$$\left. + 2(1.5)^2 + 3(2)^2 + 2(2.5)^2 + 3^2) \right\}^{1/2}$$

$$= \sqrt{\frac{1}{25}(16 + 18 + 4 + 4.5 + 2 + 1 + .5 + 1 + 4.5 + 12 + 12.5 + 9)}$$

$$= \sqrt{\frac{85}{25}} = 1.84 .$$

Except for rounding errors, this equals $2.61 \div \sqrt{2}$, in accord with the propositions in the text.

10. $\sigma_{\bar{x}} = 0.2 \div \sqrt{16} = 0.05$ oz.
$\bar{x} = 21.0625$.

The interval is $\bar{x} \pm 1.64\sigma_{\bar{x}} = 21.0625 \pm (1.64)(.05)$. That is, it is $21.0625 \pm .0820$, or 20.9805 to 21.1445 oz.

11. $\sigma_{\bar{x}} = 0.1 / \sqrt{49} = .01428$ oz. Since $\bar{x}$ is distributed normally with a mean of μ and a standard deviation of .01428 oz., the probability that it will depart from μ by more than .005 oz. equals the probability that the standard normal variable will exceed $.005 \div .01428$ or will fall short of $-.005 \div .01428$. Since $.005 \div .01428 = .35$, this probability is $2(.3632) = .7264$.

12. (a) The sample mean is normally distributed, with a mean of 250 hours and a standard deviation of 10 hours. Thus, the desired probability equals the probability that the standard normal variable assumes a value below -1.00, which is .1587.

(b) The desired probability equals the probability that the value of the standard normal variable exceeds 2.00, which is .0228.

(c) The desired probability equals the probability that the value of the standard normal variable lies between -1.00 and zero, which is .3413.

13. (a) AB, which is 00; AC, which is 01; AD, which is 00; AE, which is 00; AF, which is 01; BC, which is 01; BD, which is 00; BE, which is 00; BF, which is 01; CD, which is 10; CE, which is 10; CF, which is 11; DE, which is 00; DF, which is 01; and EF, which is 01.

(b) The sample proportions in the 15 samples in part (a) are: 0; 1/2; 0; 0; 1/2; 1/2; 0; 0; 1/2; 1/2; 1/2; 1; 0; 1/2; and 1/2. Thus, the sampling distribution of the sample proportion (x/n) is

x/n	$P(x/n)$
0	6/15
1/2	8/15
1	1/15

The mean of this distribution equals $(8/15)(1/2) + (1/15)(1) = 1/3$. The standard deviation of this distribution equals

$$\sqrt{\frac{6}{15}\left(\frac{1}{3}\right)^2 + \frac{8}{15}\left(\frac{1}{6}\right)^2 + \frac{1}{15}\left(\frac{2}{3}\right)^2} = \sqrt{\frac{6}{135} + \frac{8}{540} + \frac{4}{135}} = \sqrt{\frac{12}{135}}$$

$$= \sqrt{.08889} = .30.$$

Note that the sample proportion is a sample mean where the observations are 0 or 1. Thus, according to the propositions in the text, its standard deviation should equal

$$\frac{\sqrt{\Pi(1-\Pi)}}{\sqrt{n}}\sqrt{\frac{N-n}{N-1}},$$

since $\sqrt{\Pi(1-\Pi)}$ is the standard deviation of a random variable that assumes the value of 1 with probability Π and the value of zero with probability $1 - \Pi$. This is true, since

$$\sqrt{\frac{\Pi(1-\Pi)}{n}}\sqrt{\frac{N-n}{N-1}} = \sqrt{\frac{(1/3)(2/3)}{2}}\sqrt{\frac{4}{5}} = \sqrt{\frac{8}{90}}$$

$$= \sqrt{.08889} = .30.$$

14. (a) The probability that $\overline{X} < 20{,}000$ miles equals the probability that the value of the standard normal variable is less than -2.00, since $\mu = 25{,}000$ miles and $\sigma_{\overline{x}} = 2{,}500$ miles. This probability is .0228. Thus, the expected cost equals

$$.0228(\$1{,}000) = \$22.80.$$

(b) The probability that $\overline{X} > 29{,}000$ miles equals the probability that the value of the standard normal variable exceeds $4{,}000 \div 2{,}500$, or 1.60. This probability is .0548. Thus, the expected cost to the dealer is

$$22.80 - .0548(\$1{,}000) = 22.80 - 54.80 = -\$32.00.$$

The expected cost to Alliance is $+\$32.00$.

15. No, for at least two reasons. Not all New Yorkers have telephones, and most do not live in Manhattan or the Bronx.

16. The buyer wants .10 to equal the probability that $|\overline{X} - \mu| > .02$. If this is true and if $\overline{X}$ is normally distributed, 0.02 must equal 1.64 $\sigma_{\overline{x}}$. If the shipment is very large, $\sigma_{\overline{x}} = \sigma / \sqrt{n} = 0.1 / \sqrt{n}$, since $\sigma = 0.1$. Thus,

$$0.02 = \frac{(1.64)(0.1)}{\sqrt{n}},$$

so

$$n = \left[\frac{(1.64)(0.1)}{0.02} \right]^2 = 8.2^2 = 67.$$

Consequently, the buyer should take a sample of 67 tires.

17. Interviewers often assumed that women who were keeping house were out of the labor force. Thus, they did not ask them whether they were laid off or seeking employment.[2]

18. If the proportion that exceeds 24 inches is .10, and $\sigma = 0.2$ inches, it follows that $\mu = 24 - 1.28(0.2)$, since 24 inches must be 1.28 standard deviations above the mean. (See Appendix Table 2.) Thus, $\mu = 23.744$ inches. If $\mu = 23.744$ and $\sigma = 0.2$, what is the probability that $\overline{X} > 23.9$ inches? Since $n = 100$, $\overline{X}$ is distributed normally with a mean of 23.744 inches and a standard deviation of .02 inch. Thus, this probability equals the probability that the standard normal variable exceeds $(23.900 - 23.744) \div .02$, or 7.8. Based on Appendix Table 2, this probability is essentially zero.

19. MTB> RANDOM 25 OBSERVATIONS INTO C2;
    SUBC> NORMAL MU = 20   SIGMA = 10.
    MTB> PRINT C2
    C2

43.3396	10.4134	15.7107	19.9674	24.1440	16.5887	18.5687
18.5306	27.2196	20.3743	17.0122	8.7985	15.1986	20.3279
27.0790	26.6757	15.6880	4.1174	2.7882	15.6498	17.9853
23.3297	−3.0515	3.2741	31.2580			

---

2. *New York Times*, November 17, 1993, p. A1.

CASE TWO

Estimates of Unmeasured Television Viewing*

Network Television Association

NEW YORK, March 12, 1993. According to a new study of total television viewing conducted by Nielsen Media Research, each week more than 28 million adults in the United States watch television in out-of-home locations. This number includes viewing to ABC, CBS, NBC, basic and pay cable, syndication, FOX, and independent stations that is not currently reflected in television ratings used by the advertising industry.

Furthermore, 23 percent of the total viewing done by these 28 million adults (representing an average of 5 hours and 49 minutes each week) is in currently unmeasured locations, such as the workplace, college facilities, hotels, motels, restaurants/bars, and second homes. This is incremental to television viewing as currently reported by Nielsen ratings, which include persons watching TV in their own homes and viewing done by visitors.

"Lifestyle changes in the 90s have led to a rise in the number of working women, college students, and business travelers. This study indicates it is increasingly important for the industry to quantify all television viewing, regardless of viewing location, and to track the viewing behavior of these important demographic groups," said Steve Singer, senior vice president/director of research for the NTA.

A special ratings pocketpiece, *Total Television Viewing Report: ABC, CBS, NBC,* is being mailed today to all subscribers of Nielsen's national TV ratings services. For the first time, total television average audience viewing information by program is being reported for all ABC, CBS, and NBC programs, except for specials and children's programming. Data are reported for 14 gender and age demographics based on averages for the October–November 1992 survey period.

A series of special analyses are being conducted on this database. Preliminary examination of these analyses indicates that young and active demographic groups traditionally thought to be light television viewers do a significant proportion of their viewing in unmeasured locations.

Highlights from *Total TV Viewing Report: ABC, CBS, NBC* and from a special analysis of out-of-home viewing by location for the three broadcast networks include:

- Two-thirds of out-of-home viewers, 19 million adults 18 years or older, view the three broadcast networks in out-of-home viewing locations each week.

*Reprinted with permission of the Network Television Association.

- Viewing in unmeasured out-of-home locations delivers an average of 4 percent more adult audience to ABC, CBS, and NBC than is currently reported in NTI average audience viewership.
- Almost three-quarters of all out-of-home viewing is done in the workplace, college facilities, and hotels/motels.

Distribution of OOH Viewing to ABC, CBS, NBC by Location: Mon–Sun, 24 hours/adults 18+	
Workplace	27.6
College	27.6
Hotels/motels	17.3
Restaurants/bars	10.6
Second homes	2.7
Other*	14.2

*Viewing to network programs at all other locations including hospitals, airports, recreational vehicles, boats, cars, etc.

- The study sheds new light on the perception that visitor viewing (which is measured and included in Nielsen ratings) is greater than unmeasured viewing done in all other out-of-home locations: Viewing in unmeasured out-of-home locations contributed the same percentage of viewers to a network's A18–49 total viewing average audience as viewing done when visiting someone else's home (i.e., 4.5 percent).
- Out-of-home viewing levels and viewing distribution by location varies significantly by demography, daypart, program type, and individual programs. (See the analysis below of out-of-home viewing by daypart.)

The report is based on a nationally, projectable sample of 3,494 respondents, 12 years of age and older, who completed a personal, paper diary for one week within the survey period. In addition to ratings and audience projections, an index which summarizes the total audience to in-home audience relationship was developed for each program. The index was then applied to NTI people-meter-based in-home ratings to produce total audience estimates.

Network TV Out-of-Home Analysis by Daypart

1. *Primetime:* There are 4 percent more adults 18–34 watching primetime network television than reported by Nielsen based on in-home viewing measures.

A18–34:	*Law and Order*	+9%
	CBS Sunday Movie	+9%
	Family Matters	+7%

- 75% of out-of-home viewing by adults 18–34 years old in primetime is done in college facilities (48%), hotels/motels (14%), and the workplace (13%).

---

2. *Early Morning News:* Men 25–54 total TV audiences for weekday morning programming are 7 percent higher than in-home-based levels.

M25–54:	*CBS This Morning*	+8%
	Good Morning America	+6%
	The Today Show	+6%

- 89% of out-of-home viewing by Men 25–54 in this daypart is done either in the workplace (47%) or in hotels/motels (42%).

---

3. *Daytime Dramas:* Women 18–49 Total TV audiences are 7 percent greater than its reported in-home-based measurement.

W18–49:	*Another World*	+12%
	All My Children	+10%
	As the World Turns	+8%

- 78% of this daypart's out-of-home viewing by women 18–49 is done in the workplace (40%) and college facilities (38%).

_____

4. Evening News: Men 18–49 total TV audiences are 5 percent higher than in-home viewing levels.

M18–49: *CBS Evening News* +9%
ABC World News
Tonight +5%
NBC Nightly News +3%

- 78% of the out-of-home viewing for these three news programs is done by men 18–49 in the workplace (52%) and college facilities (26%).

_____

5. Late Night: Out-of-home viewing during this daypart is driven by two demographic groups, women 18–34 and men 25–54. Women 18–34 total TV audience is 8 percent higher than the in-home measurement. Men 25–54 total TV audience is 4 percent higher than in-home-based measures.

W18–34: *Late Night with
David Letterman* +27%
The Tonight Show
with Jay Leno +10%
M25–54: *CBS Late Night
I & II* +5%

- Among women 18+ viewing all late-night programming, 80% of out-of-home viewing is done in college facilities (54%) and hotels/motels (26%).
- For men 18+, 93% of out-of-home viewing during late night is done in the workplace (48%), college facilities (24%), and hotels/motels (21%).

_____

6. Sports: The M18–34-year-old audience for weekend sports on the

networks is 14 percent higher than reported in-home levels.

M18–34: *ABC College
Football* +16%
CBS NFL Football +12%
NBC Football +11%

- 68% of the out-of-home viewing for all weekend sports by men 18–34 is done in college facilities (42%) and the workplace (26%). Furthermore, contrary to the perceptions of some in the industry, viewing done in restaurants/bars accounts for only 22% of men 18–34 of out-of-home viewing for weekend sports.

_____

Questions

1. According to the *New York Times,* "Nielsen counts viewers at home using what is known as the people meter. Members of Nielsen homes are supposed to press a button on the meter whenever they start and stop watching television. Visitors to Nielsen homes are also supposed to log in on the meter, although the networks contend that many fail to do so."[1] Why didn't Nielsen use people meters to measure television watching in out-of-home locations?

2. In fact, Nielsen used diaries that respondents filled out by hand to measure television watching in out-of-home locations. The total cost of the survey was over $500,000. The study was financed by the Network Television Association, a trade group representing ABC, CBS, and NBC. Why would these three networks be interested in such a survey?

3. The networks have been steadily losing their share of the tele-vision audience to cable. Would this

_____

1. New York Times, March 15, 1993.

help to explain their interest in such a survey?

4. According to the *New York Times,* "Were [the out-of-home] audience incorporated into Nielsen's ratings reports, as many network executives would like, it could have a significant effect on the rates advertisers are charged."[2] Why?

5. Advertising executives do not feel such an increase in rates would be justified. For example, Steven Auerbach of Dewitt Media is quoted as saying: "We all understand that there's out-of-home viewing. It's a bonus. Fifteen years ago, the networks might have been able to get us to pay for it. But they have no leverage to make us pay for it now."[3] What arguments would the advertising executives make to support their position?

2. *Ibid.*

3. *Ibid.*

PART III

Estimation and Hypothesis Testing

CHAPTER 8

Statistical Estimation

Chapter Profile

One form of estimate is a *point estimate*, which is a single number. Another form of estimate is a *confidence interval*, which is constructed in such a way that there is a specified probability (called the *confidence coefficient*) that this interval will include the parameter we are trying to estimate. One disadvantage of a point estimate relative to a confidence interval is that it contains no information concerning the extent to which the single number may be in error.

The point estimate generally used to estimate the *population mean* is the sample mean. If the population standard deviation σ is known, the confidence interval for the population mean is

$$\bar{x} \pm z_{\alpha/2} \sigma / \sqrt{n}.$$

If σ is unknown and the sample size (n) is greater than 30, the confidence interval is

$$\bar{x} \pm z_{\alpha/2} s / \sqrt{n},$$

where $z_{\alpha/2}$ is the value of the standard normal variable that is exceeded with probability equal to $\alpha/2$. If σ is unknown and the sample size (n) is less than or equal to 30, the confidence interval is

$$\bar{x} \pm t_{\alpha/2} s / \sqrt{n},$$

where $t_{\alpha/2}$ is defined by the *t distribution*. Specifically, $t_{\alpha/2}$ is the number which will be exceeded with probability equal to $\alpha/2$ by a random variable with a *t* distribution. The *t* distribution is symmetrical, bell-shaped, and its mean equals zero. Its shape depends on the number of degrees of freedom, which is ($n - 1$) in confidence intervals of this sort.

The point estimate generally used to estimate the *population proportion* is the sample proportion. Special graphs are available for constructing confidence intervals for the population proportion. If the sample size is large, this confidence interval equals

$$p \pm z_{\alpha/2} \sqrt{p(1 - p) \div n},$$

where p is the sample proportion.

If it is desired that the probability be ($1 - \alpha$) that the sample mean differs from the population mean by no more than some number, δ, the sample size must equal

$$n = \left(\frac{z_{\alpha/2} \sigma}{\delta} \right)^2.$$

This assumes that the normal approximation can be used and that the population is large relative to the sample.

An estimator is *unbiased* if the mean of its sampling distribution equals the parameter that is being estimated. One unbiased estimator is more *efficient* than another unbiased estimator if the standard deviation of its sampling distribution is less than that of the other estimator.

If independent samples of sizes n_1 and n_2 are chosen from two populations, we can calculate a confidence interval for the difference between the population means, $\mu_1 - \mu_2$. The following formula is applicable if both n_1 and n_2 are large:

$$\bar{x}_1 - \bar{x}_2 - z_{\alpha/2} \sqrt{\frac{s_1^2}{n_1} + \frac{s_2^2}{n_2}} < \mu_1 - \mu_2 < \bar{x}_1 - \bar{x}_2 + z_{\alpha/2} \sqrt{\frac{s_1^2}{n_1} + \frac{s_2^2}{n_2}},$$

where the confidence coefficient equals $(1 - \alpha)$. A confidence interval can also be constructed for the difference between two population proportions.

Behavioral Objectives

A. You should be able to define the following key concepts in this chapter:

point estimate	degrees of freedom
confidence interval	unbiasedness
confidence coefficient	efficiency
consistency	*t* distribution

B. Make sure that you can do each of the following:

1. Calculate a confidence interval for the population mean (a) if σ is known; (b) if σ is unknown.
2. Calculate an estimate of the population standard deviation.
3. Use tables of the *t* distribution to find the value of $t_{\alpha/2}$ corresponding to a particular value of α and a certain number of degrees of freedom.
4. Determine how large the sample must be so that there is a given probability that the sample mean differs from the population mean by no more than a certain amount.
5. Use graphs to calculate a confidence interval for the population proportion.
6. For large samples use the normal distribution to calculate a confidence interval for the population proportion.
7. Determine how large the sample must be so that there is a given probability that the sample proportion differs from the population proportion by no more than a certain amount.
8. Describe some of the major properties of a good estimator.
9. Calculate (for large samples) a confidence interval for the difference between two population means.
10. Compute (for large samples) a confidence interval for the difference between two population proportions.

Unpaid Department Store Bills: A Case Study[1]

A large department store has more than 100,000 customers who owe money for goods purchased. The store wants to determine the proportion of these customers having bills that have not been paid for more than 10 months. The store carries out a random sample of 40 of its customers with unpaid bills, and finds that 7 have bills unpaid for over 10 months.

(a) What is your best estimate of the proportion of the store's customers with unpaid bills who have bills unpaid for over 10 months?
(b) Calculate a 95 percent confidence interval for this proportion.

Based on the information obtained from this sample, the store decides that it wants to take a larger sample to obtain a more accurate estimate of this proportion. Specifically, it wants the probability to be only 5 percent that the sample proportion will differ from the true proportion by more than 1 percentage point.

(c) How large a sample do you think that the store must take to accomplish this objective?
(d) Suppose that the store takes a random sample of 900 customers with unpaid bills and finds that 99 have bills unpaid for over 10 months. Does this sample provide the desired degree of accuracy? Why, or why not?

Multiple-Choice Questions

1. The probability that the value of a random variable with the t distribution with 10 degrees of freedom will lie above _____ is equal to .05.

   (a) 1.645
   (b) 1.960
   (c) 1.282
   (d) 1.812
   (e) 2.228

2. If the standard deviation of the population is known, the confidence interval for the population mean is based on

   (a) the t distribution.
   (b) the normal distribution.
   (c) the binomial distribution.
   (d) the Poisson distribution.
   (e) none of the above.

1. For an actual case involving the aging of accounts receivable in a department store, see R. Trueblood and R. Cyert, *Sampling Techniques in Accounting* (Englewood Cliffs, N.J.: Prentice-Hall, 1957).

3. If the standard deviation of the population is unknown, and the sample size is less than 10, the confidence interval for the population mean is based on

    (a) the t distribution.
    (b) the normal distribution.
    (c) the binomial distribution.
    (d) the Poisson distribution.
    (e) none of the above.

4. If σ doubles, the width of the confidence interval for the population mean (that is, the upper limit of the confidence interval minus the lower limit) will

    (a) be multiplied by $\sqrt{2}$.
    (b) double.
    (c) quadruple.
    (d) decrease.
    (e) do none of the above.

5. If a sample consists of three observations, 1, 2, 3, an estimate of the population standard deviation equals

    (a) $\sqrt{2/3}$.
    (b) $\sqrt{1/2}$.
    (c) 1.
    (d) $\sqrt{3/2}$.
    (e) none of the above.

6. If $\alpha = .20$, and $n = 20$, $t_{\alpha/2}$ equals

    (a) 1.325.
    (b) 1.282.
    (c) 1.328.
    (d) 1.729.
    (e) none of the above.

7. A statistician wants to estimate the mean of a population. From past experience, it is known that the standard deviation of the population is 10. If the statistician wants the probability to be .90 that the sample mean will differ from the population mean by no more than 2, the size of the sample must be

    (a) 8.
    (b) 34.
    (c) 67.
    (d) 16.
    (e) none of the above.

8. A statistician wants to estimate a population proportion, which is known to be about 0.2. To be sure that the normal approximation is a valid basis for

constructing a confidence interval for the population proportion, the sample size (according to William Cochran) must be at least

(a) 30.
(b) 50.
(c) 80.
(d) 200.
(e) 600.

9. A sample is to be taken to estimate a population proportion. Statistician A suggests that the sample be constructed so that the probability is .9 that the sample proportion differs by no more than 2 percentage points from the population proportion. Statistician B would like to see the sample constructed so that the probability is .9 that the sample proportion differs by no more than 4 percentage points from the population proportion. If statistician A's advice is taken, the sample size must be

(a) double what it would be if statistician B's advice were taken.
(b) quadruple what it would be if statistician B's advice were taken.
(c) triple what it would be if statistician B's advice were taken.
(d) bigger than if statistician B's advice were taken, but how much bigger depends on the population proportion.
(e) none of the above.

10. The following statistics are unbiased estimators:

(a) The sample mean
(b) The sample proportion
(c) The sample variance
(d) The sample standard deviation.
(e) All the above
(f) All the above except (d)

11. If one unbiased estimator has a smaller standard deviation than another unbiased estimator, it follows that

(a) the expected value of this estimator equals that of the other estimator.
(b) its mean square error is less than that of the other estimator.
(c) it is more efficient than the other estimator.
(d) all the above are true.
(e) all the above except (a) are true.

Problems and Problem Sets

1. Using the technique described in the text (where σ is known), a statistician calculates a 95 percent confidence interval for the mean income of the

depositors at Bank A, which is located in a poverty-stricken area. The confidence interval is $18,201 to $21,799.

(a) What is the mean income in the sample?

(b) If $\sigma = \$8,000$, what was the sample size, n?

2. A supermarket wants to estimate the mean error made by clerk A in adding up customers' bills. From past experience, the supermarket knows that the standard deviation of the errors made by clerk A equals 60 cents. The supermarket draws a random sample of nine customers' bills added up by clerk A, and finds that the errors in them are as follows:

$0.52	−$0.10	−$0.70
−$0.58	$0.20	−$0.40
$0.96	$1.40	$0.50

(a) If the errors made by clerk A are normally distributed, calculate a 90 percent confidence interval for the mean of the population of errors made by clerk A.

(b) Suppose that the supermarket had no idea what the standard deviation of the errors made by clerk A might be. Under these circumstances, what is a 90 percent confidence interval for the mean of the population of errors made by clerk A?

3. A tire manufacturer wants to estimate the mean weight of the tires produced by one of its plants. It takes a random sample of 100 of the tires produced at this plant and finds that the sample mean is 48.1 lbs. and the sample standard deviation is 0.12 lb. Calculate a 95 percent confidence interval for the population mean.

4. Using the tables of the standard normal distribution and the t distribution, show that as the number of degrees of freedom grows larger and larger, the t distribution gets closer and closer to the standard normal distribution.

5. A firm that prepares income tax returns for clients wants to determine the proportion of returns prepared by one of its employees, John Adams, that contains major errors.

   (a) If Adams makes major errors on 25 percent of the returns he fills out, and if the firm wants the probability to be .90 that the sample proportion will not differ from the population proportion by more than 5 percentage points, how large a sample of Adams's returns must the firm take?

   (b) If the firm draws a random sample of 100 returns prepared by another of its employees, Grace Black, and if 22 percent turn out to contain major errors, construct a 95 percent confidence interval for the population proportion of returns prepared by Black containing major errors.

6. A tire manufacturer draws a random sample of 160 tires produced by a new process and finds that 40 percent wear better than required by specifications.

(a) Construct a 95 percent confidence interval for the population proportion of the tires produced by the new process that will wear better than required by specifications.

(b) The tire manufacturer finds that the sample standard deviation of the number of miles the tires can be used without a major repair is 1,200 miles. Calculate a 90 percent confidence interval for the population standard deviation. (Hint: See Exercise 8.17 in the text.)

7. A firm wants to estimate the mean lifetime of a particular kind of tool. From previous experience, it knows that the lifetimes are normally distributed. It draws a random sample of four of these tools and finds that their lifetimes are 7.9; 9.3; 10.8; and 11.4 years. Calculate a 90 percent confidence interval for the mean lifetime of this kind of tool.

8. Ten pieces of a new type of material have breaking strengths (in hundreds of pounds per square inch) of 8; 7; 6; 9; 10; 8; 7; 6; 11; and 8. Calculate a 99 percent confidence interval for the proportion of such pieces of material having breaking strengths of 7 or less.

9. An advertising agency wants to estimate the mean income of families located in a particular 50-block area of a low-income section of Chicago. There are 10,000 families in this area, and the agency chooses a random sample of 100. The mean income of these families is $18,000 per year.

   (a) Compute a 95 percent confidence interval for the population mean, if the population standard deviation is known to be $5,000.

   (b) If there were 20,000 families (rather than 10,000 families) in this area, would your answer to part (a) be altered?

10. Two independent samples of the diameters of tires are drawn, one from a batch of tires produced at plant A, and another from a batch of tires produced at plant B. The samples are independent. The results are as follows:

Sample	Sample size	Sample mean (inches)	Sample standard deviation (inches)
Plant A	100	50.3	0.2
Plant B	100	50.7	0.3

Calculate a 95 percent confidence interval for the difference between the mean diameter of the entire batch produced at plant B and the mean diameter of the entire batch produced at plant A.

11. A bank conducts a random sample of 40 of its employees and finds that 20 percent have more than 20 years of experience in banking. Construct a 99 percent confidence interval for the proportion of all the bank's employees who have more than 20 years of experience in banking.

12. A personnel agency wants to determine the proportion of individuals it has helped get jobs who are currently earning more than $40,000 per year. It selects a random sample of 50 such persons and finds that 70 percent earn above $40,000 per year.

  (a) Construct a 95 percent confidence interval for the population proportion.

(b) The personnel agency decides that the sample of 50 is too small to result in the desired degree of accuracy. It would like the probability to be .90 that the sample proportion will differ by no more than 2 percentage points from the population proportion. Approximately how large a sample should the agency take?

13. A bank administers an aptitude test to 16 job applicants, and the scores are as follows:

80	92	94	78
70	78	86	74
72	83	82	70
76	75	68	66

The bank has not administered such tests to any of its job applicants in the past. If these 16 people can be regarded as a random sample of all the bank's job applicants, and if the scores are normally distributed, calculate a 90 percent confidence interval for the population mean score.

14. A firm has factories in New York and Florida. It picks a random sample of 100 of its workers from each factory. In New York, 32 percent say that they buy the firm's product; in Florida, 27 percent say this.

    (a) Construct a 95 percent confidence interval for the difference between the New York and Florida factories in the proportion of workers who say they buy the firm's product.

    (b) Calculate a 95 percent confidence interval for the proportion of workers at the New York factory who say they buy the firm's product.

    (c) Calculate a 95 percent confidence interval for the proportion of workers at the Florida factory who say they buy the firm's product.

15. Minitab is used to calculate a 95 percent confidence interval for a mean. The sample is 22, 14, 16, 30, 11, and 42. Interpret the computer output, which is as follows:

```
MTB>   SET INTO C3
DATA>   22   14   16   30   11   42
DATA>   END
MTB>   TINTERVAL 95 PERCENT FOR DATA IN C3
```

	N	MEAN	STDEV	SE MEAN	95.0 PERCENT C.I.
C3	6	22.50	11.69	4.77	(10.23. 34.77)

16. A sample consists of the following eight observations: 8, 9, 7, 6, 9, 10, 7, and 9. Use Minitab (or some other computer package) to calculate a 99 percent confidence interval for the mean. If no computer package is available, do it by hand.

Answers

Unpaid Department Store Bills: A Case Study

(a) $7/40 = 0.175$.

(b) Based on Appendix Table 7(a), the confidence interval is .08 to .33.

(c) $n = (1.96/.01)^2(.175)(.825) = (38,416)(.144375) = 5,546$.

(d) No. The 95 percent confidence interval is

$$.11 - 1.96\sqrt{\frac{(.11)(.89)}{900}} < \Pi < .11 + 1.96\sqrt{\frac{(.11)(.89)}{900}},$$

or $\quad .11 - \dfrac{1.96}{30}\sqrt{.0979} < \Pi < .11 + \dfrac{1.96}{30}\sqrt{.0979}$,

or $\quad .11 - \dfrac{1.96(.3129)}{30} < \Pi < .11 + \dfrac{1.96(.3129)}{30}$,

or $\quad .11 - \dfrac{.6133}{30} < \Pi < .11 + \dfrac{.6133}{30}$,

or $\quad .09 < \Pi < .13$.

Multiple-Choice Questions

1. (d) 2. (b) 3. (a) 4. (b) 5. (c) 6. (c) 7. (c) 8. (d) 9. (b)
10. (f) 11. (d)

Problems and Problem Sets

1. (a) $20,000.

   (b) $\sqrt{n} = 1.96(\$8,000)/\$1,799$. Thus, $n = 76$.

2. (a) The confidence interval is

$$\bar{x} - z_{\alpha/2}\sigma/\sqrt{n} < \mu < \bar{x} + z_{\alpha/2}\sigma/\sqrt{n},$$

   or $\quad\quad 20 - 1.64(60/3) < \mu < 20 + 1.64(60/3)$,

   or $\quad\quad -12.8$ cents $< \mu < 52.8$ cents.

   (b) The confidence interval is

$$\bar{x} - t_{\alpha/2}\frac{s}{\sqrt{n}} < \mu < \bar{x} + t_{\alpha/2}\frac{s}{\sqrt{n}}.$$

The deviation (in cents) of each observation from the sample mean is:

32	30	90
78	0	60
76	120	30

Thus, $\displaystyle\sum_{i=1}^{9}(x_i - \bar{x})^2 = 1{,}024 + 6{,}084 + 5{,}776 + 900 + 0 + 14{,}400 + 8{,}100$

$+ 3{,}600 + 900 = 40{,}784$,

and $s = \sqrt{40,784/8} = \sqrt{5,098} = 71.4$ cents.

Thus, the confidence interval is

$$20 - (1.86)\left(\frac{71.4}{3}\right) < \mu < 20 + (1.86)\left(\frac{71.4}{3}\right),$$

or $\qquad\qquad 20 - 44.3 < \mu < 20 + 44.3,$

or $\qquad\qquad -24.3$ cents $< \mu < 64.3$ cents.

3. The confidence interval is

$$\bar{x} - 1.96\frac{s}{\sqrt{n}} < \mu < \bar{x} + 1.96\frac{s}{\sqrt{n}},$$

or $\qquad\quad 48.1 - 1.96\left(\frac{.12}{10}\right) < \mu < 48.1 + 1.96\left(\frac{.12}{10}\right),$

or $\qquad\qquad 48.1 - .0235 < \mu < 48.1 + .0235,$

or $\qquad\qquad 48.0765$ lbs. $< \mu < 48.1235$ lbs.

4. A comparison of Appendix Tables 2 and 6 demonstrates that this is true.

5. (a) $\quad n = \left(\dfrac{z_{\alpha/2}}{\delta}\right)^2 \hat{\Pi}(1 - \hat{\Pi})$

$$= \left(\frac{1.64}{.05}\right)^2\left(\frac{1}{4}\right)\left(\frac{3}{4}\right)$$

$$= (32.8)^2\left(\frac{3}{16}\right)\left(\frac{3,228}{16}\right) = 202.$$

(b) $.14 < \Pi < .31$, based on Appendix Table 7a.

6. (a) The confidence interval is

$$p - z_{\alpha/2}\sqrt{\frac{p(1-p)}{n}} < \Pi < p + z_{\alpha/2}\sqrt{\frac{p(1-p)}{n}},$$

or $\qquad .40 - 1.96\sqrt{\dfrac{(.40)(.60)}{160}} < \Pi < .40 + 1.96\sqrt{\dfrac{(.40)(.60)}{160}},$

or $\qquad\qquad .40 - 1.96(.0387) < \Pi < .40 + 1.96(.0387),$

or $\qquad\qquad .324 < \Pi < .476.$

(b) The confidence interval is

$$\frac{s}{1 + z_{\alpha/2}/\sqrt{320}} < \sigma < \frac{s}{1 - z_{\alpha/2}/\sqrt{320}},$$

or $\qquad\qquad \dfrac{1200}{1 + 1.64/\sqrt{320}} < \sigma < \dfrac{1200}{1 - 1.64/\sqrt{320}},$

or $$\frac{1200}{1.0917} < \sigma < \frac{1200}{.9083},$$

or $$1{,}099 \text{ miles} < \sigma < 1{,}321 \text{ miles.}$$

7. The confidence interval is

$$\bar{x} - t_{\alpha/2}\frac{s}{\sqrt{n}} < \mu < \bar{x} + t_{\alpha/2}\frac{s}{\sqrt{n}},$$

$$\bar{x} = 9.85 \text{ years.}$$

The deviations of the observations from $\bar{x}$ are 1.95; .55; .95; and 1.55. Thus,

$$s = \sqrt{\frac{3.8025 + .3025 + .9025 + 2.4025}{3}} = \sqrt{\frac{7.41}{3}} = \sqrt{2.47} = 1.57.$$

So, the confidence interval is

$$9.85 - (2.353)\left(\frac{1.57}{2}\right) < \mu < 9.85 + (2.353)\left(\frac{1.57}{2}\right),$$

or $$9.85 - 1.85 < \mu < 9.85 + 1.85,$$

or $$8.0 \text{ years} < \mu < 11.7 \text{ years.}$$

8. Four of the 10 pieces have breaking strengths of 7 or less. Thus, $p = .40$. Using Appendix Table 7b, the confidence interval is 8 percent to 81 percent.

9. (a) The confidence interval is

$$\bar{x} - 1.96\frac{\sigma}{\sqrt{n}} < \mu < \bar{x} + 1.96\frac{\sigma}{\sqrt{n}},$$

or $$18{,}000 - 1.96\left(\frac{5{,}000}{10}\right) < \mu < 18{,}000 + 1.96\left(\frac{5{,}000}{10}\right),$$

or $$\$17{,}020 < \mu < \$18{,}980.$$

(b) No.

10. The confidence interval is

$$\bar{x}_1 - \bar{x}_2 - z_{\alpha/2}\sqrt{\frac{s_1^2}{n_1} + \frac{s_2^2}{n_2}} < \mu_1 - \mu_2 < \bar{x}_1 - \bar{x}_2 + z_{\alpha/2}\sqrt{\frac{s_1^2}{n_1} + \frac{s_2^2}{n_2}},$$

or $$50.7 - 50.3 - 1.96\sqrt{(.09/100) + (.04/100)} < \mu_1 - \mu_2$$
$$< 50.7 - 50.3 + 1.96\sqrt{(.09/100) + (.04/100)}$$

or $$0.4 - \frac{1.96}{10}\sqrt{.13} < \mu_1 - \mu_2 < .04 + \frac{1.96}{10}\sqrt{.13},$$

or $$0.4 - .071 < \mu_1 - \mu_2 < 0.4 + .071,$$

or $$0.329 \text{ inch} < \mu_1 - \mu_2 < 0.471 \text{ inch.}$$

11. From Appendix Table 7b, the confidence interval is 7 percent to 41 percent.

12. (a) From Appendix Table 7a, the confidence interval is about 55 percent to 82 percent.

(b) $n = (z_{.05}/\delta)^2 \hat{\Pi}(1-\hat{\Pi})$.

Since $\delta = .02$, $z_{.05} = 1.64$, and a reasonable estimate of Π (based on the previous sample) is 0.7,

$$n = \left(\frac{1.64}{.02}\right)^2 (.7)(.3) = (82)^2(.21) = (6,724)(.21)$$

$$= 1,412 \text{ people}.$$

13. $\bar{x} = 77.75$.

$s = 8.153$.

The confidence interval is

$$\bar{x} - t_{\alpha/2}\frac{s}{\sqrt{n}} < \mu < \bar{x} + t_{\alpha/2}\frac{s}{\sqrt{n}}.$$

Since there are 15 degrees of freedom, $t_{.05} = 1.753$. Thus,

$$77.75 - 1.753\left(\frac{8.153}{4}\right) < \mu < 77.75 + 1.753\left(\frac{8.153}{4}\right),$$

or
$$77.75 - 3.57 < \mu < 77.75 + 3.57,$$

or
$$74.18 < \mu < 81.32.$$

14. (a) The confidence interval is

$$p_1 - p_2 - 1.96\sqrt{\frac{p_1(1-p_1)}{n_1} + \frac{p_2(1-p_2)}{n_2}} < \Pi_1 - \Pi_2 < p_1 - p_2$$

$$+ 1.96\sqrt{\frac{p_1(1-p_1)}{n_1} + \frac{p_2(1-p_2)}{n_2}},$$

or $.32 - .27 - 1.96\sqrt{\frac{(.32)(.68)}{100} + \frac{(.27)(.73)}{100}} < \Pi_1 - \Pi_2 < .32 - .27$

$$+ 1.96\sqrt{\frac{(.32)(.68)}{100} + \frac{(.27)(.73)}{100}},$$

or $.05 - 1.96\sqrt{\frac{.2176 + .1971}{100}} < \Pi_1 - \Pi_2 < .05$

$$+ 1.96\sqrt{\frac{.2176 + .1971}{100}},$$

or $.05 - 1.96(.0644) < \Pi_1 - \Pi_2 < .05 + 1.96(.0644)$,

or $.05 - .126 < \Pi_1 - \Pi_2 < .05 + .126$,

or $-.076 < \Pi_1 - \Pi_2 < .176$.

(b) According to Appendix Table 7a, the confidence interval is 23 percent to 42 percent.

(c) According to Appendix Table 7a, the confidence interval is 18 percent to 37 percent.

15. The confidence interval is 10.23 to 34.77.

16. MTB>   SET INTO C4
DATA> 8 9 7 6 9 10 7 9
DATA> END
MTB> TINTERVAL 99 PERCENT FOR DATA IN C4

	N	MEAN	STDEV	SE MEAN	99.0 PERCENT C.I.
C4	8	8.125	1.356	0.479	(6.447. 9.803)

CHAPTER 9

Hypothesis Testing

Chapter Profile

The first step in establishing a test procedure is to formulate the hypothesis that is being tested (the *null hypothesis*) and the *alternative hypothesis*. The alternative hypothesis may be *one-sided* (if one wants to detect only positive differences or only negative differences from the null hypothesis) or *two-sided* (if one wants to detect differences, positive or negative, from the null hypothesis). In choosing between the null hypothesis and the alternative hypothesis, the decision maker can make two types of error. First, he or she can reject the null hypothesis when it is true. This is a *Type I error*. Second, he or she can fail to reject the null hypothesis when it is false. This is a *Type II error*. Any test procedure results in a certain value of α, the probability of Type I error, and β, the probability of Type II error. The test's *operating characteristic curve* shows β as a function of the specific alternative hypothesis.

To test whether a population mean equals a specified value μ_0 the test procedures are as follows: If σ is known, and the alternative hypothesis is two-sided, one computes

$$(\bar{x} - \mu_0) \div \sigma / \sqrt{n},$$

and rejects the null hypothesis if it exceeds $z_{\alpha/2}$ or is less than $-z_{\alpha/2}$. If the alternative hypothesis is $\mu > \mu_0$, the null hypothesis should be rejected if this statistic exceeds z_α. If the alternative hypothesis is $\mu < \mu_0$, the null hypothesis should be rejected if this statistic is less than $-z_\alpha$.

If σ is unknown and $n > 30$, the sample standard deviation can be used in place of σ in this statistic. If σ is unknown and $n < 30$, the t distribution should be used in place of the standard normal distribution.

To test whether the mean of one population equals the mean of another population, the test procedure (for a two-sided alternative) is to compute

$(\bar{x}_1 - \bar{x}_2) \div \sqrt{s_1^2 / n_1 + s_2^2 / n_2}$, and reject the null hypothesis if it exceeds $z_{\alpha/2}$ or is less than $-z_{\alpha/2}$. This assumes that one does not know the standard deviation of the two populations, and that both the size of the sample taken from the first population (n_1) and the size of that taken from the second population (n_2) exceed 30. If n_1 or n_2 is less than 30, a test based on the t distribution, not the standard normal distribution, can be used.

To test whether a population proportion equals a specified value, Π_0, the test procedure (for a two-sided alternative) is to compute $(p - \Pi_0) \div \sqrt{\Pi_0(1 - \Pi_0)/n}$ and reject the null hypothesis if it exceeds $z_{\alpha/2}$ or falls below $-z_{\alpha/2}$. This assumes that the sample is large.

Behavioral Objectives

A. You should be able to define the following key concepts in this chapter:

null hypothesis	operating characteristic curve
alternative hypothesis	test statistic
Type I error	one-sided alternative
Type II error	two-sided alternative
α	significance level
β	

B. Make sure that you can do each of the following:

1. Explain the nature of a Type I and a Type II error and the way in which the operating characteristic curve characterizes a test.
2. Explain the considerations leading up to the choice of what is the null hypothesis and what is the alternative hypothesis in a particular situation.
3. Test whether the population mean equals a particular value, given that the population standard deviation is known.
4. Test whether the population mean equals a particular value, given that the population standard deviation is unknown and that the sample size is at least 30.
5. Test whether the population mean equals a particular value, given that the population standard deviation is unknown and that the sample size is less than 30.
6. Test whether the means of two populations are equal, given that the standard deviations of both populations are known.
7. Test whether the means of two populations are equal, given that the standard deviation of both populations is unknown and that the sample size in each population is at least 30.
8. Test whether the means of two populations are equal, given that the standard deviation of both populations is unknown and that the sample size in each population is less than 30.
9. Test whether a population proportion equals a certain value.

The Amount of Fat in Meat: A Case Study

Two analytical methods—the AOAC method and the Babcock method—have been used to determine the amount of fat in meat. W. J. Youden, in an article in *Analytical Chemistry,* provided results comparing the findings of these two methods. Twenty pieces of meat were chosen at random. Each piece was subjected to both methods, and the percentage of fat estimated for it by each method was recorded. The estimates for each piece of meat, as well as the difference between the estimates for each piece of meat, are shown below:[1]

---

1. The data are from W. J. Youden, *Analytical Chemistry XIX.*

Piece of meat	AOAC method	Babcock method	Difference
	(estimated percent of fat)		
1	22.0	22.3	0.3
2	22.1	21.8	−0.3
3	22.1	22.4	0.3
4	22.2	22.5	0.3
5	24.6	24.9	0.3
6	25.3	25.6	0.3
7	25.3	25.8	0.5
8	25.6	26.2	0.6
9	25.6	26.1	0.5
10	25.9	26.7	0.8
11	26.0	26.3	0.3
12	26.2	24.9	−1.3
13	27.0	26.9	−0.1
14	27.3	28.4	1.1
15	27.7	27.1	−0.6
16	41.5	41.4	−0.1
17	41.6	41.4	−0.2
18	45.5	45.5	0.0
19	48.5	48.2	−0.3
20	49.1	47.5	−1.6

(a) Can we use the standard test for equality of two means (described in the text section Two-Sample Test of Means: Small Samples) to test whether on the average the results of the two methods are the same? Why, or why not?

(b) Can you see how this problem can be transformed into a problem of testing whether a single mean equals zero? How?

(c) Carry out the test alluded to in (b) to determine whether on the average the two methods yield the same results.

Multiple-Choice Questions

1. Morton Smart is testing whether $\mu = 300$ on the basis of a random sample of 100 observations from a very large population. He knows that $\sigma = 10$, and the test is two-tailed. If $\overline{X} = 298$, he should reject the null hypothesis if

    (a) $\alpha = .05$.
    (b) $\alpha = .03$.
    (c) $\alpha = .02$.
    (d) $\alpha = .01$.
    (e) $\alpha = .001$.

2. An advertising agency wants to test the hypothesis that the proportion of adults in San Francisco who read a particular magazine is 20 percent. The null hypothesis is that the proportion reading the magazine

    (a) is different from 20 percent.
    (b) is less than 20 percent.
    (c) is greater than 20 percent.
    (d) equals 20 percent.
    (e) is none of the above.

3. In the previous question the advertising agency, in carrying out this test, wants to detect whether the proportion is less than 20 percent. If this is the case, the agency wants to reject the hypothesis that it equals 20 percent. The agency does not care if the proportion is above 20 percent. In this situation, the alternative hypothesis is

    (a) that the proportion is greater than 20 percent.
    (b) that the proportion equals 20 percent.
    (c) that the proportion is less than 20 percent.
    (d) undefined.
    (e) none of the above.

4. In the previous question the alternative hypothesis is

    (a) no-sided.
    (b) one-sided.
    (c) two-sided.
    (d) three-sided.
    (e) none of the above.

5. Suppose that the null hypothesis is true and that it is rejected. This is

    (a) a Type I error, and its probability is β.
    (b) a Type II error, and its probability is β.
    (c) a Type I error, and its probability is α.
    (d) a Type II error, and its probability is α.
    (e) none of the above.

6. If the alternative hypothesis is two-sided, the operating characteristic curve of a test that $\mu = \mu_0$ is

    (a) always downward sloping.
    (b) always upward-sloping.
    (c) U-shaped.
    (d) shaped like ⌢⌣.
    (e) none of the above.

7. If the null hypothesis is that the mean of a particular population is μ_0, and the alternative hypothesis is that the mean exceeds μ_0, the operating characteristics of the tests recommended in the text are shaped like

    (a) ∫ .
    (b) a horizontal line.
    (c) ╲ .
    (d) U-shaped.
    (e) none of the above.

8. If the null hypothesis is that the mean of a particular population is μ_0, and the alternative hypothesis is that the mean is less than μ_0, the operating characteristics of the tests recommended in the text are shaped like

    (a) ╱ .
    (b) a horizontal line.
    (c) ╲ .
    (d) U-shaped.
    (e) none of the above.

9. If the mean of a particular population is μ_0, $(\bar{x} - \mu_0) \div \sigma / \sqrt{n}$ is distributed

    (a) as a standard normal variable, if the population is normal.
    (b) as a standard normal variable, if the sample is large.
    (c) as the t distribution with $(n - 1)$ degrees of freedom.
    (d) as both (a) and (b) state.
    (e) as none of the above.

10. If the mean of one population is μ_1 and the mean of a second population is μ_2, $[(\bar{x}_1 - \bar{x}_2) - (\mu_1 - \mu_2)] \div \sqrt{\sigma_1^2 / n_1 + \sigma_2^2 / n_2}$ is distributed

    (a) as a standard normal variable, if both populations are normal and if the samples are independent.
    (b) as a standard normal variable, if both samples are large and if the samples are independent.
    (c) as the t distribution with $n_1 + n_2 - 2$ degrees of freedom.
    (d) as both (a) and (b) state.
    (e) as none of the above.

11. If the population proportion equals Π_0, then $(p - \Pi_0) \div \sqrt{\Pi_0(1-\Pi_0)/n}$ is distributed

   (a) as a Poisson variable.
   (b) as a standard normal variable, if the sample is very large.
   (c) as the t distribution with $(n - 1)$ degrees of freedom.
   (d) as both (a) and (b) state.
   (e) as none of the above.

Problems and Problem Sets

1. A university hospital wants to make sure that the probability is .8 (no more, no less) that a person arriving at the hospital will have been seen by a physician within 15 minutes of his or her arrival. A random sample of 200 persons is chosen, and it is determined that 150 of them are seen by a physician within 15 minutes of their arrival. If α is set at .05, is the difference between the sample proportion and .8 statistically significant?

2. An automobile producer receives a large shipment of steel parts. It draws a random sample of 60 of the parts in the shipment and rejects the shipment if one or more are defective. Give an equation for the operating characteristic curve of this test.

3. (a)   A retailer of electronic equipment receives a very large batch of receivers from the manufacturer. It tests 100 of them and rejects the batch if two or more are defective. What is the probability that it will reject the batch if 5 percent of the batch is defective? If 2 percent of the batch is defective?

(b) The statistician working for the retailer of electronic equipment says that the null hypothesis is that 1 percent of the batch is defective. What is the value of α for the test specified above?

(c) Suppose that the retailer increases the sample size from 100 to 200 and that it continues to reject the batch if two or more are defective. What is the probability of Type I error for this test, and how does it compare with the probability of Type I error for the test specified above?

(d) Suppose that the alternative hypothesis in both (a) and (c) is that the proportion of defective receivers in the batch is 2 percent. What is the probability of Type II error for the test in (c), and how does it compare with the probability of Type II error for the test in (a)?

(e) Based on your answers to (c) and (d), write a brief report to the retailer describing the pros and cons of substituting the test in (c) for that in (a).

4. A tire producer wants to test whether the mean diameter of the tires produced on a given day equals 36 inches. Whether the mean diameter is less than 36 inches is of little or no importance, but it is important for the firm to determine whether or not the mean diameter is more than 36 inches. The firm chooses a random sample of 36 tires, and finds that their mean diameter is 36.4 inches.

   (a) If the firm knows that the standard deviation of the diameters is 0.8 inch, should the firm reject the hypothesis that the mean diameter is 36 inches? (It wants the probability of rejecting the hypothesis that the mean diameter is 36 inches, when it is true, to equal .05.)

   (b) In (a), what is the null hypothesis? What is the alternative hypothesis? What is the test statistic? What value of α are you using? Is there a unique value of β?

5. A supermarket wants to test whether the mean weight of the cans of peas sold by a particular maker equals 24 oz. It chooses a random sample of 16 cans and finds that the sample mean is 23.3 oz. and the sample standard deviation is 0.4 oz.

   (a) If the supermarket wants α to be .05, should it reject the hypothesis that the mean equals 24 oz. on the basis of this evidence? (Assume a two-sided alternative hypothesis.)

   (b) Suppose that this supermarket is interested only in determining whether or not the mean weight is less than 24 oz. Indicate why the supermarket might feel this way, and see whether it should reject the hypothesis that the mean equals 24 oz. on the basis of the evidence in (a).

6. A maker of refrigerators buys bolts from two suppliers, and it is very important that the mean widths of the bolts received from both suppliers are equal since they must be used interchangeably. The refrigerator maker receives a large shipment of bolts from each supplier and draws a random sample of 49 bolts from each shipment. It wants to test whether the mean width is the same in both shipments.

(a) What is the null hypothesis? What is the alternative hypothesis? Is the alternative hypothesis one-sided or two-sided?

(b) Suppose that the refrigerator manufacturer finds that the mean width of the bolts taken from the one shipment is 1.14 inches, and that the mean width of the bolts taken from the other shipment is 1.09 inches. From past experience it is known that the standard deviation of the widths of the bolts in each shipment is 0.1 inch. Based on this evidence, would the manufacturer reject the hypothesis that the mean widths are equal, if it sets α equal to .05? If it sets α equal to .01? Why, or why not?

(c) Suppose that the refrigerator manufacturer does not know the population standard deviations. The firm knows only that the sample standard deviation of the widths of the bolts taken from the one shipment is 0.09 inch, and the sample standard deviation of the widths of the bolts taken from the other shipment is 0.11 inch. Should the manufacturer reject the hypothesis that the mean widths are equal, if it sets α equal to .05? If it sets α equal to .01? Why, or why not? (Use the test in the text section Two-Sample Test of Means: Small Samples. If its assumptions hold, this test is valid even though the sample size in each population exceeds 30.)

7. An advertising agency wants to test whether the proportion of subscribers to a particular magazine who remember an ad paid for by one of its clients is .5 (the figure that the magazine claims). The agency doesn't much care whether the figure is greater than .5, but it wants to determine whether it falls short of .5. It conducts a random sample of 100 subscribers and determines how many remembered the ad in question.

(a) In this case, what is the null hypothesis? What is the alternative hypothesis? Is the alternative hypothesis one-sided or two-sided? What factors govern the value of α that should be set?

(b) Suppose that this advertising agency finds that 43 percent of the subscribers in its sample remembered the ad. If α is set equal to .05, should the advertising agency conclude that the population proportion is less than .5?

8. A beer company wants to determine whether 60 percent of the viewers of a sports program it sponsors prefer a new TV commercial over the old one it has been using, as its advertising agency claims. The company draws a random sample of 16 viewers of its program and asks them to indicate whether they prefer the new commercial over the old one. It is interested in detecting both positive and negative deviations from 60 percent.

(a) What is the null hypothesis? What is the alternative hypothesis? Is it one-sided or two-sided? What factors influence the choice of α?

(b) The beer company finds that none of the viewers in the sample prefer the new commercial over the old one. Should it conclude that the proportion preferring the new commercial over the old one does not equal .6 if $\alpha = .05$? If $\alpha = .10$? Why, or why not?

9. Minitab is used to test the hypothesis that the population mean is 20. The sample is 22, 14, 16, 30, 11, 42. Interpret the computer output, which is as follows:

MTB> TTEST MU = 20 ON DATA IN C3

TEST OF MU = 20.00 VS MU N.E. 20.00

	N	MEAN	STDEV	SE MEAN	T	P VALUE
C3	6	22.50	11.69	4.77	0.52	0.62

10. A sample consists of the following eight observations: 8, 9, 7, 6, 9, 10, 7, 9. Use Minitab (or some other computer package) to test the hypothesis that the population mean equals 7. If no computer package is available, do it by hand.

Answers

The Amount of Fat in Meat: A Case Study
(a) No, because the observations are paired, not independent.
(b) We can test whether the mean of the differences equals zero.
(c) The mean of the differences, $\bar{x}$, equals .04. The standard deviation of the differences, s, equals .65.

$$t = (\bar{x} - \mu_0) \div s/\sqrt{n} = (.04 - 0) \div .65/\sqrt{20}$$
$$= \frac{(.04)(4.47)}{.65} = \frac{.1788}{.65}$$
$$= .275.$$

If $\alpha = .05$, we should not reject the null hypothesis that the mean of the differences equals zero, since the observed value of t is not greater than $t_{.025}$ or less than $-t_{.025}$. (With 19 degrees of freedom, $t_{.025} = 2.093$.)

Multiple-Choice Questions
1. (a) 2. (d) 3. (c) 4. (b) 5. (c) 6. (d) 7. (c) 8. (a) 9. (d) 10. (d) 11. (b)

Problems and Problem Sets
1. $z_{\alpha/2}\sqrt{\Pi_0(1-\Pi_0)/n} = 1.96\sqrt{.8(.2)/200}$
$$= .055.$$

Since $p(= 150/200 = 0.75)$ exceeds $.8 - .055(= .745)$ and is less than $.8 + .055(= .855)$, the difference is not statistically significant.[2]

---

2. Note that this is an alternative way of carrying out the test described in the text section One-Sample Test of a Proportion: Large Samples.

2. Given that Π is the proportion of parts in the shipment that are defective, the probability of accepting the shipment (that is, of not rejecting the null hypothesis) is

$$(1 - \Pi)^{60}.$$

3. (a) The probability of accepting the batch if 5 percent are defective is the probability of 0 or 1 defective in the sample. Thus, the probability of rejecting the batch equals

$$1 - [(.95)^{100} + 100(.95)^{99}(.05)] \doteq .96.$$

If 2 percent are defective, it equals

$$1 - [(.98)^{100} + 100(.98)^{99}(.02)] \doteq .59.$$

(b) The probability of rejecting the null hypothesis, given that it is true, equals

$$1 - [(.99)^{100} + 100(.99)^{99}(.01)] \doteq .26.$$

(c) The probability of rejecting the null hypothesis, given that it is true, equals

$$1 - [(.99)^{200} + 200(.99)^{199}(.01)] \doteq .59.$$

And α is higher than in the test specified in (a).

(d) The probability of Type II error in (c) is

$$(.98)^{200} + 200(.98)^{199}(.02) \doteq .09.$$

In (a) it is

$$(.98)^{100} + 100(.98)^{99}(.02) \doteq .41.$$

(e) The test in (c) has a higher probability of Type I error than the test in (a). Specifically, α equals .59 for the test in (c), and .26 for the test in (a). On the other hand, the test in (c) has a lower probability of Type II error than the test in (a). Specifically, β equals .09 for the test in (c), and .41 for the test in (a). The test in (c) is more expensive than the one in (a) because an additional 100 receivers must be tested. Also, it is possible that other tests using the same sample size might be better from the point of view of the retailer.

4. (a) If we let $\alpha = .05$, $\mu_0 + z_\alpha \dfrac{\sigma}{\sqrt{n}} = 36 + 1.64 \dfrac{(0.8)}{\sqrt{36}}$

$$= 36.22.$$

Since $\bar{x} = 36.4$, the firm should reject the hypothesis that the mean equals 36 inches.[3]

(b) The null hypothesis is that $\mu = 36$ inches. The alternative hypothesis is that $\mu > 36$ inches. The test statistic is $\bar{x}$. The value of α we used is .05. The value of β depends on the true value of μ.

---

3. Note that this is an alternative way of carrying out the test described in the text section One-Sample Test of a Mean: Large Samples.

5. (a) $\mu_0 - t_{.025}\dfrac{s}{\sqrt{n}} = 24 - (2.131)\dfrac{(0.4)}{\sqrt{16}} = 23.79$.

$\mu_0 + t_{.025}\dfrac{s}{\sqrt{n}} = 24 + (2.131)\dfrac{(0.4)}{\sqrt{16}} = 24.21$.

Since 23.2 (the observed value of $\bar{x}$) is less than 23.79, the supermarket should reject the hypothesis that $\mu = 24$.[4]

(b) It might not care whether the weight was greater than 24 oz., since the consumer would not be shortchanged. If $\alpha = .05$,

$$\mu_0 - t_{.05}\dfrac{s}{\sqrt{n}} = 24 - 1.753\dfrac{(0.4)}{\sqrt{16}} = 23.82.$$

Since the observed value of $\bar{x}$ is less than 23.82, the hypothesis that $\mu = 24$ should be rejected.

6. (a) The null hypothesis is that the two population means are equal. The alternative hypothesis is that they are not equal. The alternative hypothesis is two-sided.

(b) $z = (1.14 - 1.09) \div \sqrt{\dfrac{(.1)^2}{49} + \dfrac{(.1)^2}{49}} = .05 \div \dfrac{\sqrt{.02}}{7} = \dfrac{.35}{.1414}$

$= 2.48$.

Since $z > z_{.025} = 1.96$, the refrigerator manufacturer should reject the hypothesis that the mean widths are equal, if $\alpha = .05$. If $\alpha = .01$, the refrigerator manufacturer should not reject this hypothesis, since $z_{.005} = 2.58$.

(c) $s^2 = \dfrac{(48)(.09)^2 + (48)(.11)^2}{49 + 49 - 2} = \dfrac{48}{96}(.0081 + .0121) = \dfrac{.0202}{2}$

$= .0101$.

$t = (1.14 - 1.09) \div \sqrt{.0101\left(\dfrac{2}{49}\right)} = \dfrac{(.05)(7)}{\sqrt{.0202}} = \dfrac{.35}{.1421}$

$= 2.463$.

Since $t_{.025} = 1.99$ and $t_{.005} = 2.64$, the refrigerator manufacturer should reject the hypothesis that the mean widths are equal if $\alpha = .05$, but not if $\alpha = .01$.

7. (a) The null hypothesis is that $\Pi = 0.5$. The alternative hypothesis is that $\Pi < 0.5$. The alternative hypothesis is one-sided. The relative costs of Type I and Type II errors govern the value of α that should be set.

(b) $\Pi_0 - z_{.05}\sqrt{\dfrac{\Pi_0(1 - \Pi_0)}{n}} = .5 - 1.64\sqrt{\dfrac{.5^2}{100}} = .5 - 1.64(.05)$

$= .418$.

---

4. Note that this is an alternative way of carrying out the test described in the text section One-Sample Test of a Mean: Small Samples.

Since the observed value of p is not less than .418, the advertising agency should not reject the hypothesis that $\Pi = .5$.[5]

8. (a) The null hypothesis is that the proportion preferring the new commercial equals .6. The alternative hypothesis is that this proportion does not equal .6. The alternative hypothesis is two-sided. The choice of α is affected by the relative cost of Type I and Type II errors.

(b) The probability of this occurring, given that $\Pi = 0.6$, equals $(.40)^{16}$, which is less than .0001, according to Appendix Table 1. Thus, if we use the sample proportion as the test statistic, it appears that the beer company should conclude that the proportion does not equal .6.

9. There is no reason to reject the null hypothesis that the mean is 20. The p-value is .62. Thus, so long as one uses a significance level less than .62, this null hypothesis will not be rejected.

10. MTB>   TTEST MU = 7 ON DATA IN C4

TEST OF MU = 7.000 VS MU N.E. 7.000

	N	MEAN	STDEV	SE MEAN	T	P VALUE
C4	8	8.125	1.356	0.479	2.35	0.051

Whether one should reject the null hypothesis that the population mean equals 7 depends on the significance level that is chosen. If α exceeds .051, this hypothesis should be rejected; if α is less than .051, it should not be rejected.

5. Note that this is an alternative way of carrying out the test described in the text section One-Sample Test of a Proportion: Large Samples.

The Louisiana State Museum*

Caroline M. Fisher and Claire J. Anderson

Claire Brown, Director of Marketing and Public Relations for the Louisiana State Museum, pondered the results of three recent surveys prior to developing her 1990 marketing plan for the museum's holdings in New Orleans. The museum relied heavily on state financing, philanthropy, and, to a lesser degree, membership fees. Dramatic decreases in state support over the past five years made attracting more contributors and more members imperative.

Background

The Louisiana State Museum, one of the largest historical museum complexes in the United States, was founded in 1906. By 1989, the museum operated ten historic properties in the state, of which eight were in the historic New Orleans French Quarter. Five of the ten properties across the state were open to the public, three of them in New Orleans: the Cabildo, the Presbytere, and the Old U.S. Mint. The first two flanked the St. Louis Cathedral on Jackson Square, a prime tourist location. (See Exhibit 1 for a listing of all the Louisiana State Museum properties.)

An estimated half million visitors frequented the five public museum properties annually. New Orleans, by far, had the largest number of adult public visitors, likely a result of the number of attractions and their proximity to hotel and convention accommodations.

The purpose and responsibility of the museum, as written by the museum board and professional staff, was:

> "to preserve, augment and present historical buildings and collections as cultural, educational and economic benefits for the state of Louisiana. The Museum makes certain that Louisiana has a memory and that its people and institutions have access to historical documents, artifacts, photographs and other materials that are necessary to understand the past and present and plan for the future. The Museum also serves as one of Louisiana's major tourist attractions."

The collections included important and irreplaceable fine, decorative, folk, fabric and inventive arts, and historical manuscripts, prints, maps, and photographs. At the New Orleans sites, exhibitions focused on Louisiana history, New

*This case was prepared for classroom discussion and was not intended to illustrate either effective or ineffective handling of administrative situations. Appreciation is expressed to the Louisiana State Museum for its support in developing this case. Distributed by the North American Case Research Association. © 1991. All rights reserved to the authors and the North American Case Research Association. Permission to publish has been obtained from the authors and the North American Case Research Association.

Orleans jazz, Mardi Gras, costumes, and other aspects of Louisiana's cultural heritage. The collections were made accessible to the public, students, and scholars through a number of programs including exhibitions, education programs, symposia, and lecture series. (Exhibit 2 contains a list of the exhibitions and nonexhibit programs for the 1989 season.) The museum also published materials and produced video documentaries related to history and preservation.

Louisiana and the City of New Orleans

Louisiana was, in 1989, still staggering under the blow of the precipitous drop in oil prices (one of the primary state industries) and suffering high unemployment and a decreasing population as people moved to find work. One consequence of the weak economic conditions was severe limitations on state revenues. The governor tried to balance the state's budget by passing new revenues, but fought strong opposition from citizens and the legislature. Many government and cultural activities suffered increasing cutbacks during the 1980s.

The City of New Orleans fared a bit better than the rest of the state. The Port of New Orleans, which suffered from the recession during the early 1980s, made a substantial comeback during the latter part of the decade. Tourism remained strong throughout the decade and became an increasingly substantial portion of the city's revenue generators. A new convention center on the site of the 1984 Louisiana World's Fair and hotel availability made the city attractive to conventions and tourists.

Other Local Attractions

Visitors to New Orleans had easy access to a wide variety of entertainment. A riverside development on the Mississippi River adjacent to the Convention Center formed a natural extension to the historic French Quarter with its many attractions. For the footsore, a riverfront streetcar provided transportation from the French Quarter to the end of Canal Street, where most of the major hotels were located. In addition to the traditional attractions of the French Quarter, visitors could enjoy a riverboat ride, visit the widely acclaimed Audubon Zoo, or frequent antique shops on Royal Street.

New Orleans was famous for its multitude of festivals which were almost continuous throughout the year. Mardi Gras was the most noted of the festivals, but the Jazz Fest grew each year and attracted increasing numbers of tourists. New Orleans (the Big Easy) was noted for being a 24-hour party town.

The home of five universities, New Orleans supported many cultural activities. The Symphony, the Opera, two ballet companies, and numerous theatre and musical groups offered series of performances each year. The New Orleans Museum of Art, the Contemporary Arts Center, and many private galleries presented collections for public viewing.

The New Orleans Museum of Art, a fine-arts museum, was located several miles away from the French Quarter. The New Orleans Museum of Art was a separate entity from the Louisiana State Museum, funded partially by the City of New Orleans and partly by philanthropy, membership, and admissions. It had a high profile with local residents, but attracted fewer tourists because of its location and transportation difficulties.

Popular Museum Attractions

The Louisiana State Museum was not all dusty documents and antiquities. In 1985 the Presbytere featured a new exhibit called "Intimately Revealing" which featured women's underclothes during various historical periods. In 1986, the Cabildo highlighted popular exhibits such as Napoleon's death mask and bottles stuffed with border agreements which at one time were buried in mounds a mile apart along the disputed Texas-Louisiana border. At the Old Mint, two new permanent displays focused on the best-known traditions of the city of New Orleans, jazz and Mardi Gras.

The Old Mint, built in the 1830s, had a colorful history. It was turning out more than $10 million in coins by 1851. Early in the nineteenth century, the Old Mint was used as a federal prison, chiefly for bootleggers. The federal government gave the building to the state in 1966 on the condition that it be used as a museum. In 1982, the Old Mint was restored to serve as a treasure source for serious researchers and a meeting place for nonprofit groups.

In Fall 1983, a Jazz and Mardi Gras museum opened at the Old Mint. The exhibit was expected to draw swarms of tourists and local residents. Exhibits chronicled the history of jazz. Early great names in jazz were represented by their instruments, including Louis Armstrong's battered bugle and Kid Ory's trombone. The Mardi Gras Museum displayed the artifacts of the large, high-society Mardi Gras

krewes[1] including glittering costumes, royal crowns and scepters, and gilt-edged ball invitations. In addition the exhibits chronicled street masking, neighborhood floats, and marching clubs, all significant parts of the Mardi Gras celebration.

The Sun King Exhibition

In the early 1980s, the museum attracted national attention with the announcement of the upcoming exhibit of "The Sun King: Louis XIV and the New World" to take place concurrently with the 1984 Louisiana World's Fair. Three years of delicate negotiations with museum directors across France cleared the way for an exhibit of artifacts of the days of Louis XIV. The exhibition was insured by the U.S. government for $100 million. The artifacts, to be housed in the Cabildo, consisted of a collection of over 200 objects, paintings, and tapestries woven together to present the story of the king who sent explorers to the New World and claimed the territory later named after him—Louisiana. The show would not have been possible without the World's Fair. According to Robert McDonald, assistant department secretary for the Office of the State Museum, "The proximity of the Sun King exhibition in the Cabildo to the World's Fair was a major factor in our obtaining the

---

1. A krewe is a social group which bands together to construct and man the many Mardi Gras floats. Traditionally the krewe members came from upper social classes and sponsored glittering balls and receptions during the Mardi Gras season. By the late 1980s, upper-class domination was fading with many new well-recognized krewes emerging, including those sponsored by blacks, women, and the art community.

support we needed to host this event."[2]

The excitement over the Sun King exhibit spread to the state government. The governor placed an additional $50,000 in the museum's 1982–83 budget to initiate the project. The effort was not totally financed by the state; a large band of volunteers joined in the effort. The arrival of the exhibition in 1984 was met in typical New Orleans fashion with a three-day *divertissement*[3] reminiscent of the grand days of Louis XIV, ranging from a black tie dinner New Orleans style ($500 to $1500 per ticket) to a performance by the New Orleans Philharmonic Symphony and Chorus of seventeenth century French music, presented in the historic St. Louis Cathedral adjacent to the Cabildo. Before the exhibit closed, the State spent $1.1 million from general and capital outlay money to fund the visit.

After a seven-month run of the Sun King exhibition, the Louisiana Museum took in far less than expected. Blame was placed on the low attendance at the 1984 Louisiana World's Fair. The World's Fair was a failure ending in a declaration of bankruptcy. Rather than 4 percent of the projected 11 million visitors, the exhibit drew slightly less than 4 percent of the actual 7 million who came to the fair. The financial outcome was a shortfall of $300,000 for the Museum.

The Fire at the Cabildo

The financial failure of the Sun King exhibition was a setback for the

high hopes of the museum. However, in 1988, an even greater blow came with a fire in the Cabildo.

The Cabildo was the center of attention for the museum. Dating back to 1795, the Cabildo was Louisiana's first seat of government. On May 11, 1988, a fire broke out in the tinder-dry building. The building lost its roof and sustained severe damage to its third floor and many exhibits. Restoration work was estimated to cost $4 million, of which the state had to pay the first $1 million. A $2 million fund-raising campaign was launched almost immediately after the fire to help cover the deductible; $1.2 million for improvements to the building's heating, air-conditioning, safety, and drainage systems and new exhibits. Firms such as Entergy, a local utility company, contributed large sums to the rebuilding fund. Yet in mid-1989, the fund was still over $1 million short of its goal. The Cabildo remained closed to the public throughout 1989; the anticipated reopening was set for late in 1991.[4]

Internal Operations

Board of Directors

The museum's board of directors consisted of 21 members, of which 10 were appointed by the governor. By law, the Friends of the Cabildo, a membership support group, had two representatives on the board, who might be included in those named by the governor. The board oversaw the operation of the 10 historic buildings of the Louisiana State Museum, voting on such diverse issues as

2. Allan Katz, "The Sun King will shine on fair art lovers," *Times Picayune*, New Orleans, March 5, 1983, p. A 13.

3. A *divertissement* is a series of diversions or entertainments popular during the time of Louis XIV.

4. Bruce Eggler, "Cabildo gets boost from LP&L, NOPSI," *Times Picayune*, New Orleans, July 1, 1989, p. B 8.

hours, admission fees, budgets, and promotions.

The Museum Director

Robert R. MacDonald, who served as museum director from 1974 to 1985, coincidentally resigned just before the financial roof fell in for the state. In August 1985, he left to become the director of the Museum of the City of New York.

George Rollie Adams, previously executive director of the Buffalo and Erie County Historical Society in Buffalo, New York, took over as museum Director in 1986. His tenure started out on an upbeat note, "to dust cobwebs from the museum and make it a fun place to come."[5] He set out to create a long-range plan for the museum saying, "There has never been a thorough modern computerized inventory of our collections which include about 3 million items." His tenure, however, was marked by cutbacks brought on by state budget crunches; the Museum's budget shrank from $2.8 million in 1985–86 to $1.9 million in 1986–87. When Adams moved to the Margaret Wood-bury Strong Museum in Rochester, New York, in 1987, his new salary was 30 percent higher than that he received at the Louisiana State Museum.

Adams was followed by James F. Sefcik, who previously was the assistant director of the State Historical Society of Wisconsin in Madison. Sefcik's first impression of the Cabildo and the Presbytere was that the two buildings were "dark and dank [and] not welcoming."[6] Yet, he was impressed with "the size and scope and quality of the exhibits here." He went on to say, "I think this museum is an underrated jewel in the museum world."[7] By 1989 he was totally frustrated with the continuing lack of adequate funding from the State.

Staff

The losses incurred during the Sun King exhibition, combined with the economic woes emanating from the crisis in the oil industry, resulted in a number of cuts in staffing. In 1985–86, the museum had 127 employees. This number shrank to 64 in 1986–87 and was only 66 in 1989–90.

The regular staff was augmented by volunteer workers from the Friends of the Cabildo. Volunteers developed educational programs, organized galas and benefits to raise money for projects and programs, provided volunteers to supplement the museum's professional staff, operated the museum store, gave daily walking tours of the French Quarter for tourists and special groups, and participated in outreach programs.

Financing

Financing came from a number of sources with state government appropriations providing the bulk of the operational support. Other sources of funds included grants, philanthropy, facility rentals, and membership admission fees. The admission fees went directly to the state and did not provide the museum with additional operating funds. Most of the staff of the museum was paid through state funds; a notable

5. Marjorie Roehl, "New director to try to dust cobwebs from state museum," *Times Picayune,* New Orleans, April 7, 1986, pp. A 13–14.

6. "After the fire: A chance for change," *Times Picayune*, New Orleans, May 19, 1988, p. A 31.

7. Roehl, "New director to try to dust cobwebs from state museum." *Picayune.*

exception was Claire Brown, the director of marketing and public relations.

In virtually all cases, the monies from philanthropy and grants were earmarked for specific purposes (part of the Louisiana Museum Foundation) and could not be used to meet operating costs. For example, a 1983 Kellogg Foundation project underwrote a community education program to "take the museum to the community."[8]

In the late 1980s the state was experiencing severe shortfalls in revenue and the museum was faced with drastic budget cuts. In 1985–86, the museum had a budget of $2.8 million ($2.6 million from the State), but it dropped to $1.9 million ($1.8 million from the state) in 1986–87. By 1989–90 the budget returned to $2.1 million ($2.0 million from the state), with cuts threatened if state revenues ran short.[9] (Exhibit 3 presents the budgets for 1985–86 to 1989–90. Further breakdowns of the data were unavailable.) Self-generated funds came from admission fees and rental of the Old Mint and Presbytere for parties and receptions.

Support Groups

The Friends of the Cabildo was a museum membership group organized in 1956 to provide support for the museum, its projects, and its property. Various membership categories existed, ranging from $20 for an individual membership to $100 for a family member plus 10 guest passes per year. In addition to free admission to all public museum buildings, members received invitations to exhibition previews, special showings, cultural programs, and special events; the Friends of the Cabildo quarterly publication; discounts at the museum store; and volunteer opportunities.

By 1989, the membership was approximately 3,000. The membership turnover rate ranged from five to six hundred members annually. According to Claire Brown, members tended to be over 65 years old and have relatively high incomes; members were frequent visitors to the museum.

The funds raised from membership sales were kept separate from the museum budget. Membership revenues of approximately $200,000 per year covered the expenses of special events and financed all marketing and public relations, including the salary of the director of marketing and public relations, as mentioned above.

Groups similar to the Friends of the Cabildo functioned outside the New Orleans area. These support groups were quite small and provided limited revenues which were used only for the buildings in Baton Rouge and Shreveport, Louisiana.

The Louisiana Museum Foundation provided financial support restricted to exhibits. Funds from foundations and grants were part of this foundation, kept separate from the museum's operating budget.

Admission Fees

Admission was free at the Baton Rouge and Shreveport locations. A price increase from $1 to $2 was adopted in July 1983 for the New Orleans locations. By 1989, admission fees were $3.00 per adult, $1.50 for students and senior citizens, and free for children under the age of

8. "Louisiana State Museum admission will be $2 as of July 1," *Times Picayune,* New Orleans, April 11, 1983, p. A 23.

9. Bruce Eggler, "U.S. Mint museum stays in the money, will remain open," *Times Picayune,* New Orleans, August 1, 1989, p. B 2.

12 or organized educational groups. Claire Brown did not consider an increase in admission fees to be a viable option, because of the mission of the museum. In addition, as stated above, the admission fees went directly to the state and did not provide additional operating funds for the museum.

In 1989, volunteer guides from the Friends of the Cabildo conducted walking tours of the French Quarter. The tour price of $7 for adults and $3.50 for students and seniors included admission to two museum buildings. The Friends also offered a guided tour of the historic 1850 House. The tour price of $5 for adults and $3 for children also included admission. All tour revenues went directly to the museum.

Hours of Operation

The New Orleans buildings were open Wednesday through Sunday from 10 a.m. to 5 p.m. The buildings were closed on Mondays, Tuesdays, and evenings except for special functions.

Location

The two main buildings, the Cabildo and Presbytere, had prime locations flanking St. Louis Cathedral on historic Jackson Square, the heart of the French Quarter. One drawback was the fact that the buildings themselves were old; the facades of the buildings seemed to fade into the background, given the colorful nature of the French Quarter. All the properties bore U.S. historical landmark signs, but the signs were inconspicuous. Without having read of the Louisiana State Museum, the casual passerby would find little to lure him [or her] in. The Vieux Carre Commission, a preservationist group

with authority over businesses in the French Quarter, opposed the idea of large outdoor signs. While public agencies like the museum do not need commission approval for signs or changes in buildings, they normally seek it. And the possibility of alienating their neighbors had to be considered in any decision that the museum made.

The Louisiana State Museum's location made access unattractive for local visitors because of heavy traffic, concerns over crime, and crowded parking facilities in the French Quarter. On the other hand, the buildings were in close proximity to popular tourist sites. The French Quarter with its shops and street entertainers offered a number of events for both locals and tourists, such as the French Quarter Festival and Christmas caroling in Jackson Square.

Marketing

The museum's directors were conservative in their approach to marketing the museum. George Rollie Adams, who took charge of the museum in 1986, used a marketing approach to managing a museum. He noted that museums may take one of three approaches in creating an exhibit, "You can decide what artifacts you have available and build an exhibit around them, or you can decide what you think people should know and what you want to tell them, and then get the necessary materials for that kind of exhibit. Or you can use the third approach, plan something they want and will enjoy—and that's the way we're going."[10]

---

10. Roehl, "New director to try to dust cobwebs from state museum."

While the museum was responsible for preserving collections and creating exhibits, Adams set out to make the collections and Louisiana history entertaining in addition to being educational. He envisioned sending people out to roam Jackson Square portraying General Andrew Jackson, pirate Jean Lafitte, and other historical figures to lure visitors into the Cabildo and Presbytere. Another dream of Adams was a multimedia show that would enhance the Mardi Gras exhibit by involving visitors in the Carnival atmosphere.[11]

In 1987 James F. Sefcik replaced Adams as director. Sefcik also believed that, like any business, museums should be "consumer and not producer oriented. I think we need to ask ourselves, "Who comes to the museum? Is it mainly tourists and conventioneers?' Of course we are delighted to have them but we should reach as much as possible, too, to the community—our own citizens in New Orleans and Louisiana."[12] His first concern was to "determine who comes to the museum—and who doesn't. We're looking into some figures that show a 50-50 mix of tourists and local people."[13]

While attendance was thought to be down in 1988–89, specific figures were not available.

Promotion

According to Claire Brown, advertising was not considered appropriate or possible given the budgetary constraints. Promotion,

11. Millie Ball, "Caught in crunch, director dreams, plans the possible," *Times Picayune,* September 14, 1986, pp. E 1–2.

12. Marjorie Roehl, "New director: Museum is 'underrated jewel,'" *Times Picayune,* New Orleans, December 3, 1987, p. B 10.

13. Marjorie Roehl, "Museum director takes reins," *Times Picayune,* February 29, 1988, pp. B 5–6.

used in lieu of advertising, was limited to direct mail to museum members, tourist brochures, public relations and publicity, and links with the U.S. Park Service, which maintained an office near the Cabildo. The Park Service offered free walking tours of the French Quarter in competition with the Friends of the Cabildo.

The promotions budget was provided by the Friends of the Cabildo and included the salary of the director of marketing and public relations, Claire Brown. The budget of $25,000 in 1985–86 had doubled by 1989–90 to $50,000 and included a second professional staff position, community relations coordinator. Further breakdown of the promotions budget was not available.

Research Results

Who Visits the Museum?

In recent years, arts organizations have attempted to identify their customers and potential customers. While several national surveys have been conducted to determine the characteristics of the arts patron, little is known about the specific segment that visits historic museums. Few historic museums enjoy any national reputation with the exception of Washington, D.C.'s prestigious Smithsonian Museum. A 1987 Louis Harris survey provided some idea of the typical arts patron. The only data on museums addressed fine arts; as might be expected, the typical museum goer was an upper-income college graduate. (See Exhibit 4.)

The New Orleans staff of the museum attempted to identify the characteristics of their visitors. In Fall 1988 and Spring 1989, museum employees undertook two surveys. The first was a tourist intercept interview in the arcade outside the Presbytere. (See Exhibit 5.) The second survey was accomplished by asking visitors to the Old Mint, the 1850 House, and the Presbytere to fill in questionnaires. (See Exhibit 6.)

The surveys gave a clear message: visitors during the October 1988 to May 1989 period were overwhelmingly non-museum members (99%) and were not local residents. Nineteen percent of the respondents were residents of Louisiana and only 9% were local residents. A large proportion (89%) were first time visitors to the museum's attractions.

The Telephone Survey

The earlier surveys pointed to the question of how to tap the local market, which was not only under-represented among visitors, but also posed the potential for repeat visits and memberships in the Friends of the Cabildo. In Fall 1989, a telephone survey questioned local residents concerning their museum attendance and support. (See Exhibit 7.) One thing clearly indicated by the survey results was that people were more likely to respond positively to specific exhibits or locations, such as jazz or the Cabildo, rather than the Louisiana State Museum name.

The Dilemma

Claire Brown had reviewed the survey results and now had to get to the serious work of developing her strategy for increasing self-generated funds. She faced severe constraints in the available budget, which would restrict her options in the short run. Yet she wanted to increase memberships, contributions, and the number of visitors to the museum.

One option that Claire was considering was to go back to the Vieux Carre Commission to again request permission for outdoor signs. The research results might give her enough additional ammunition to convince the commission. Alternatively the museum board could go ahead with the signs without approaching the commission.

Another option was to focus on the most appealing exhibits and concentrate her efforts on gaining publicity for these exhibits. This had been her approach for the past several years, and she was good at getting the desired publicity. But would this approach create the type of funding that the museum needed for operations?

Claire was also interested in how she could convince local residents that visiting the museum was not inconvenient, if that was a serious impediment to attendance. She did not think that she could get adequate funding to run an advertising campaign that would change any existing negative attitudes, however.

Exhibit 1
Properties of the Louisiana State Museum

The Cabildo, A National Historic Landmark, New Orleans (1795).*
The Presbytere, A National Historic Landmark, New Orleans (1791).
Madame John's Legacy, A National Historic Landmark, New Orleans (1726, 1788).*
The Old U.S. Mint, A National Historic Landmark, New Orleans (1835).
The 1850 House of the Lower Pontalba Building, A National Historic Landmark, New Orleans (1850).
The Arsenal, New Orleans (1839).*
The Creole House, New Orleans (1842).*
The Jackson House, New Orleans (1842).*
The Old State Capitol, A National Historic Landmark, Baton Rouge (1847–49).
The State Exhibit Museum, Shreveport (1838).

*Building under restoration or used for administrative or support activities.
SOURCE: Louisiana State Museum.

Exhibit 2
Louisiana State Museum
Summer/Fall 1989 Exhibition Schedule

Location	Exhibit
Presbytere	Zachary Taylor: The Louisiana President
	Uptown New Orleans: Historic Jefferson City
	On Louisiana Waters
	The Musical Interlude
	Crafts of the Newcomb Style
	Louisiana Portrait Gallery
Old U.S. Mint	The New Orleans Branch of the U.S. Mint
	Carnival in New Orleans
	New Orleans Jazz
	My Dear Mother: Letters from a Confederate Soldier
Historic 1850 House	Antebellum New Orleans
Old State Capitol (Baton Rouge)	Old State Capitol Building
State Exhibit Museum (Shreveport)	Dioramas of Industry and Agriculture
	Louisiana's First Families

SOURCE: Louisiana State Museum.

Exhibit 3
Operations Budget
Louisiana State Museum
(July 1 to June 30 fiscal year, thousands of dollars)

Revenues	1989–90	1988–89	1987–88	1986–87	1985–86
State general					
fund*	$1,968	$1,908	$2,194	$1,758	$2,639
Self-generated†	120	120	150	150	187
Total revenues	$2,088	$2,028	$2,344	$1,908	$2,826
Expenses					
Personnel	$1,299	$1,323	$1,635	$1,205	$2,038
Operating					
expenses	610	580	700	701	785
Acquisitions &					
repairs	36	1	6	0	2
Interagency					
transfers	144	123	2	1	1
Total expenses	$2,088	$2,028	$2,344	$1,908	$2,826
Positions	66	73	79	64	127

*These figures reflect appropriate levels at the beginnings of the fiscal years and do not account for numerous budget reductions made by State government during each year.
†Facility rentals, grants and gifts, and admission fees.
SOURCE: Louisiana State Museum.

Exhibit 4
Attendance at Art Museums
*Results of a 1987 National Survey**

	Attend	Do not Attend
Total public	55%	45%
Education		
High school or less	43%	57%
Some college	63	37
College graduate	70	30
Post graduate	76	24
Income		
$15,000 or less	39%	61%
$15,001–$25,000	57	43
$25,001–$35,000	59	41
$35,001–$50,000	61	39
Over $50,000	73	27

*Americans and the Arts, Nationwide Survey of Public Opinion, Louis Harris & Associates, 1988.

Exhibit 5
Visitor Survey
Interviews of 33 Tourists Outside the Presbytere, Spring 1989

Prior knowledge of LSM	52%

Sources of information about LSM*

Participation in this survey	6%
Newspaper or magazine	11
Radio or television	2
Brochure or tourist guide	33
Saw building while passing by	42
Recommendation of family/friend	15
Other	21

Exhibition preferences*

History of New Orleans	72%
Historical maps and documents	57
History of New Orleans music	49
Politics	4
Costumes/clothes	38
Mississippi River	24
History of Louisiana	65
History of Mardi Gras	47
New Orleans food	31
Civil War	46
Louisiana ethnic diversity	22

Household income

$10,000–$19,999	21%
$20–$29,999	6
$30–$49,999	30
$50,000 & over	15
No response	27

Residence

New Orleans	14%
Other Louisiana	25
Other U.S.	46
Foreign countries	9
No response	6

Age

18–25	15%
26–35	33
36–50	30
51–64	12
Over 65	3
No response	6

Education

High school	9%
College	55
Graduate school	27
No response	9

*Percentages add to more than 100 due to multiple responses.
SOURCE: Louisiana State Museum.

Exhibit 6
1988–1989 Survey of Louisiana State Museum Visitors
New Orleans Locations
(response rate = 19%, N = 840)

Museum membership   1%

Visited Louisiana State Museum before   12%

Exhibit preference *		*Sources of information about LSM* *	
History of New Orleans	74%	Newspaper or magazine	7%
New Orleans food	29	Radio or television	9
Mississippi River	39	Local hotels, restaurants	8
Costumes and clothing	39	Tourist publications	36
Mardi Gras	35	Saw building	28
History of Louisiana	40	Recommendation of family/	
Civil War	35	friend	8
Historical documents		Riverfront streetcar	6
and maps	31	Other	6
Local architecture	40		
Politics	13		
New Orleans music	24		
Louisiana's melting pot	36		
Other	9		

Motivation for visit *		*Gender of visitor*	
Add to knowledge	63%	Male	35%
Do something with others	18	Female	48
Experience something		No response	17
different	27		
See valuable objects	20		
Be entertained	17		
Other	8		

Residence		*Income*	
New Orleans	9%	$10,000–$19,999	10%
Louisiana	11	$20,000–$29,999	14
Other states	64	$30,000–$49,999	21
Foreign	16	$50,000 & over	24
No response	0	No response	31

Age		*Education*	
18–25	9%	High school or less	13%
26–35	19	College	36
36–50	26	Graduate school	26
51–64	17	No response	25
65 and older	10		
No response	19		

*Percentages add to more than 100 due to multiple responses.
SOURCE: Louisiana State Museum.

Exhibit 7
1989 Telephone Survey of New Orleans Area Residents
(response rate = 35%, N = 760)

Visited a museum in the past year	32%

Museums visited in past year*

New Orleans Museum of Art	16%
Louisiana State Museum	10
Other	24

Heard of the Louisiana State Museum or one of its buildings	81%
Ever visited the Louisiana State Museum	46%

Reason for not visiting the Louisiana State Museum

Not enough time	32%
Hadn't heard of it	27
Not interested in museums	20
Don't know where it is	4
Fear for safety	3
Parking problems	2
Other	12

Visited the French Quarter or riverfront in the past year	83%

Reason for going to the French Quarter or riverfront*

Entertainment	49%
Guests	14
Shopping	14
Eating	11
Work	6
Other	11

Exhibit preference	Degree of interest in exhibit types		
	Very	*A little*	*Not at all*
New Orleans history	66	23	11
New Orleans food	62	25	13
New Orleans music	62	25	13
Louisiana history	56	30	13
Mardi Gras and parades	44	32	24
Mississippi River	44	39	17
Costumes and clothing	38	35	28
Historical documents and maps	36	35	29
Civil War history	35	38	27
Local architecture	33	40	27
Louisiana ethnic diversity	30	35	35

Exhibit 7 (continued)
1989 Telephone Survey of New Orleans Area Residents
(N = 760)

Percent of demographic categories who had visited the LSM

Occupation

Student	24%	Professional	56%
White collar		Blue collar	38
(management)	58	Homemaker	38
Clerical	49	Unemployed	34
Retired	60		

Education

Less than 12th grade	20%	High school degree	44%
College degree	58	Graduate degree	72

Age

15 to 24	28%	25 to 39	42%
40 to 64	57	Over 65	58

Demographic characteristics of sample

Gender

Male	37%	Female	63%

Occupation

Student	12%	Professional	23%
White collar		Blue collar	13
(management)	12	Homemaker	14
Clerical	7	Unemployed	5
Retired	13		

Education

Less than 12th grade	14%	High school degree	54%
College degree	24	Graduate degree	8

Age

15 to 24	18%	25 to 39	35%
40 to 64	32	Over 65	15

*Percentages add to more than 100 due to multiple responses.
SOURCE: Louisiana State Museum.

Questions

1. If the respondents in Exhibit 7 can be regarded as a random sample, construct a 95 percent confidence interval for:

(a) the proportion of New Orleans area residents (with telephones) who visited the Louisiana State Museum in the previous year.

(b) the proportion of New Orleans area residents (with telephones) who had ever visited the Louisiana State Museum.

2. Based on the results of Exhibit 6, does it appear that Mr. Sefcik was right in saying that about 50 percent of the visitors to the museum were local people? Can you test this hypothesis?

3. Summarize the results of the surveys in Exhibits 4, 5, 6, and 7.

4. What possible biases might be present in these results?

5. Of what use are the survey results to Claire Brown? Can they help her devise a better strategy? If so, how?

PART IV

Chi-Square Tests, Nonparametric Techniques, and the Analysis of Variance

CHAPTER 10

Chi-Square Tests and Nonparametric Techniques

Chapter Profile

A χ^2 *distribution* (with v degrees of freedom) is the probability distribution of the sum of squares of v independent standard normal variables, v being the number of degrees of freedom. To test the null hypothesis that a number of proportions are equal, we compute $\Sigma(f-e)^2/e$ where f is the actual frequency, e is the expected frequency (if all proportions are equal), and the summation is over all frequencies. The null hypothesis is rejected if this statistic exceeds χ_α^2, where α is the desired significance level of the test.

A *contingency table* contains a number of rows and columns, and the decision maker wants to know whether the probability distribution across rows varies from column to column. To test the hypothesis that the distribution across rows is independent of which column is chosen, one computes $\Sigma(f-e)^2/e$ and rejects this hypothesis if it exceeds χ_α^2.

Given a certain theoretical frequency distribution, a χ^2 test can be applied to determine whether discrepancies between this theoretical distribution and an actual distribution are due to chance. If the theoretical distribution is correct, $\Sigma(f-e)^2/e$ has a χ^2 distribution. Thus, one should reject the hypothesis that the theoretical distribution is correct if $\Sigma(f-e)^2/e$ exceeds χ_α^2.

The *sign test* is used to test the null hypothesis that the population median equals a certain amount. A plus sign is put next to sample observations exceeding this amount; a minus sign is put next to those that fall below it. The number of plus signs, x, has a binomial distribution (where $\Pi = 1/2$) if the null hypothesis is true. For large samples the null hypothesis should be rejected if $x < n/2 - z_{\alpha/2}\sqrt{n/4}$ or if $x > n/2 + z_{\alpha/2}\sqrt{n/4}$, assuming that a two-tailed test is appropriate.

The Mann-Whitney test is used to test the null hypothesis that two samples come from the same population. The first step is to rank all observations in both samples combined and then compute R_1, the sum of the ranks for the first sample. Then one computes

$$\frac{n_1 n_2 + n_1(n_1+1)/2 - R_1 - n_1 n_2/2}{\sqrt{n_1 n_2(n_1 + n_2 + 1)/12}}$$

where n_1 is the number of observations in the first sample and n_2 is the number of observations in the second sample. If this test statistic is greater than $z_{\alpha/2}$ or less than $-z_{\alpha/2}$, the null hypothesis should be rejected (if n_1 and n_2 are at least 10).

The runs test is designed to test the null hypothesis that a sequence of numbers (or symbols or objects) is in random order. Like the sign test and the Mann-Whitney test, the runs test is a nonparametric test. Nonparametric tests do not assume that the relevant population is normal, and they often are easier to compute than the tests described in Chapter 9. However, they are less powerful than the latter tests if the assumptions underlying these latter tests are approximately true.

Behavioral Objectives

A. You should be able to define the following key concepts in this chapter:

χ^2 distribution	degrees of freedom
contingency tables	runs test
expected frequency	nonparametric techniques
actual frequency	sign test
goodness-of-fit tests	Mann-Whitney test

B. Make sure that you can do each of the following:
1. Describe the conditions under which the χ^2 distribution arises, the meaning of its degrees of freedom, and its expected value and standard deviation.
2. Use the tables of the χ^2 distribution to test whether a number of proportions are equal.
3. Use the χ^2 distribution to test whether the frequency distribution in one row of a contingency table differs from that in the other rows.
4. Use the χ^2 distribution to test whether an observed frequency distribution corresponds to a theoretical distribution.
5. Use the χ^2 distribution to test whether the variance of a normal population equals a specified amount.
6. Use the χ^2 distribution to calculate a confidence interval for the variance of a normal population.
7. Describe the nature of nonparametric techniques.
8. Use the sign test to test whether a population median equals a certain value.
9. Use the Mann-Whitney test to find out whether two samples come from the same population.
10. Use the runs test to find out whether a sequence of numbers or symbols is in random order.

Reasons for Component Failure: A Case Study[1]

In the development of a particular new device, an industrial laboratory was interested in the reasons why an electronic component of this device failed. There were four possible reasons why this component might fail. (Let's call these reasons A, B, C, and D.) The engineers at the laboratory were considering placing the electronic component in two possible positions in the new device. (Let's call them positions I and II.) They tested the new device a large number of times, and each time the electronic component failed, they noted the particular reason. The number

---

1. This case is based on an actual case described in a statistical journal article, but the figures are disguised.

of times when the reason was A, B, C, or D is shown below. Note that the times when the electronic component was in position I are distinguished from those when it was in position II.

Position of electronic component	Reason for failure			
	A	B	C	D
I	20	32	44	10
II	10	48	21	15

(a) Based on these data, would you conclude that the relative frequency of various causes of failure is the same, regardless of the position of the electronic component? Why, or why not? (Let $\alpha = .05$)

(b) If you conclude that the relative frequency of various causes of failure is not the same, describe the differences in this respect that seem to exist, depending on the position of the electronic component.

(c) Of what practical usefulness might information of this sort be to an industrial laboratory? What decisions might it influence?

Multiple-Choice Questions

1. X is a random variable with the χ^2 distribution. The probability that it exceeds 29.1413 equals .01. Its number of degrees of freedom is

    (a) 12.
    (b) 14.
    (c) 16.
    (d) 18.
    (e) 20.

2. A random variable has a χ^2 distribution with 18 degrees of freedom. Its mean is

    (a) 18.
    (b) 3 times its standard deviation.
    (c) unknown.
    (d) both (a) and (b).
    (e) none of the above.

3. If a random variable has a χ^2 distribution with 6 degrees of freedom, $\chi^2_{.05}$ equals

    (a) 14.4494.
    (b) 16.8119.
    (c) 12.5916.
    (d) less than 12.
    (e) none of the above.

4. In testing independence in a 2×2 contingency table, χ^2 has _____ degrees of freedom.

   (a) 1
   (b) 2
   (c) 3
   (d) 4
   (e) none of the above.

5. If the variance of a normal population equals 10, then $\left(\dfrac{n-1}{10}\right)s^2$ has the following distribution:

   (a) normal.
   (b) binomial.
   (c) χ^2 with n degrees of freedom.
   (d) χ^2 with $(n-1)$ degrees of freedom.
   (e) none of the above.

6. If a sequence is in random order, and if there are n_1 objects of one kind and n_2 objects of another kind, the expected number of runs is

   (a) $2n_1n_2/(n_1 + n_2) + 1$.
   (b) $n_1 \div (n_1 + n_2)$.
   (c) $(n_1 + n_2) \div n_1$.
   (d) $\sqrt{2n_1n_2 \div (n_1 + n_2)}$.
   (e) none of the above.

7. The sign test

   (a) specifies that each observation be given a plus or minus sign.
   (b) uses the binomial distribution.
   (c) assumes normality.
   (d) does both (a) and (b).
   (e) does none of the above.

8. The Mann-Whitney test

   (a) is also known as the Wilcoxon test.
   (b) is also known as the U test.
   (c) ranks the observations in both samples combined.
   (d) does all of the above.
   (e) does none of the above.

9. To test whether IQ scores in a certain high school are normally distributed, one should use

   (a) a runs test.
   (b) acceptance sampling.
   (c) a contingency table.
   (d) the Mann-Whitney test.
   (e) none of the above.

Problems and Problem Sets

1. An automobile manufacturer receives steel parts in 1994 from eight suppliers. It receives a large shipment of these parts from each of the suppliers and draws a random sample of 100 parts from each shipment. The percentage defective of each sample respectively is 7; 8; 9; 6; 10; 11; 9; 6. Test the hypothesis that the proportion defective is the same in all suppliers' shipments. (Set $\alpha = .05$.)

2. To test the null hypothesis of independence in a 2×2 contingency table, a statistician calculates $\sum \left(\frac{f - e}{e} \right)^2$. Is this correct? If not, why not?

3. A testing organization examines the contents of cans of three brands of peaches to determine whether they are in strict accord with what is on the label. The organization examines a random sample of 64 cans of each brand and finds that the number of cans in each sample that are not in accord with the label is as follows:

Brand	Number of cans not in accord with label
A	7
B	5
C	10

Test the hypothesis that the proportion of cans not in accord with the label is the same for one brand as for another. (Set $\alpha = .01$.)

4. The U.S. Air Force wants to devise a test to predict whether a particular candidate for officer's rank will be able to succeed in its program leading to a second lieutenancy. A team of psychologists develops a test, which is administered to 500 officer candidates. The results are as follows:

	Succeeded in program	Failed in program	Total
Passed test	103	102	205
Failed test	37	258	295
Total	140	360	500

Test whether the test itself is effective as a predictor. (Let $\alpha = .05$.)

5. The following are data concerning the number of nylon bars classed as brittle or tough, depending on the length of the heating process. These data are meant to shed light on whether the length of the heating process has any effect on the probability that a nylon bar will be classed as brittle rather than tough. Based on these data, what would you conclude on this score? (Let $\alpha = .01$.)

Length of heating cycle (seconds)	Number of bars classed as brittle	Number of bars classed as tough	Total
30	106	294	400
90	148	252	400
Total	254	546	800

6. A study was made some years ago to determine whether front tires get more wear than rear tires and whether left tires get more wear than right tires. After a certain amount of mileage, the tires that had to be scrapped were distributed in the following way:

	Front	Rear
Right	115	65
Left	125	95

Is there any evidence that the probability that a left (rather than a right) tire must be scrapped depends on whether the tire is a front or a rear tire? (Set $\alpha = .05$.)

7. An electronics firm has six plants, and the firm's top management feels that the probability is .10 that each plant manager will have to travel to corporate headquarters during a time interval of one month, that each plant's experience in this regard is independent of the others', and that each month's experience in this regard is independent of the others. During the past 100 months, the number of plant managers traveling to corporate headquarters was as follows:

Number of managers traveling to corporate headquarters per month	Number of months
0	45
1	30
2	15
3	4
4	2
5	2
6	2

Test whether the firm's hypotheses are correct. (Let $\alpha = .01$.)

8. A company reports the following data for 1994 concerning the percent of its 1,000 workers who were absent for 0, 1, 2, 3, or 4-or-more periods of time (of one day or longer) due to illness:

Number of absences	Percent of workers
0	49
1	27
2	13
3	7
4 or more	4

Test whether the number of absences conforms to a Poisson distribution with mean equal to 1. (Let $\alpha = .01$.)

9. A rifle manufacturer claims that the standard deviation of the diameters of the rifle barrels it makes equals .01 inch. A random sample of 25 of its rifle barrels is taken, and the sample standard deviation equals .014 inch. Assuming that the diameters of its rifle barrels are normally distributed, test whether the population standard deviation equals .01 inch. (Let $\alpha = .05$, and use a two-tailed test.)

10. The personnel department of a life insurance company begins to give job applicants a brief aptitude test. The psychologists who devised the test say that the median score for the population of people who apply for jobs of this type is 100, but the personnel manager of the life insurance company suspects that this may not be true for this company's job applicants. Forty of the first fifty job applicants at the life insurance company who take this test score above 100. Assuming that they can be treated as a random sample, test the psychologists' statement. (Let $\alpha = .05$, and use a two-tailed test.)

11. An advertising agency is interested in the median age of the viewers of a particular TV show, since this will determine whether the show attracts the kinds of people who are likely to buy the agency's client's product. According to the TV network, the median age of the viewers is 29 years. The agency draws a random sample of 200 viewers of this program, and finds that their ages are as follows:

Under 14 years	30
14–17 years	41
18–21 years	53
22–25 years	38
26–29 years	22
30–33 years	10
34–37 years	4
Over 37 years	2

Test whether the statement by the TV network is correct. (Let $\alpha = .01$, and use a two-tailed test.)

12. Two television programs, A and B, are being considered by a firm that may decide to sponsor one or the other of them. The firm is interested in obtaining ratings of the two programs from a random sample of television viewers. It draws a random sample of 20 viewers who, after seeing program A, give it the following ratings: 73.1; 74.2; 75.2; 78.0; 78.1; 78.8; 79.1; 80.0; 80.2; 80.9; 81.1; 81.4; 82.0; 82.3; 82.6; 83.1; 83.9; 84.0; 84.1; 84.3. It draws another random sample of 20 viewers who, after seeing program B, give it the following ratings: 76.0; 76.3; 78.4; 78.6; 79.2; 79.4; 80.3; 80.5; 81.0; 81.2; 81.9; 82.5; 82.7; 83.8; 84.2; 84.4; 84.6; 84.8; 85.0; 86.0. Do these data indicate that the population of ratings of program A differs from that of program B? Use the Mann-Whitney test to find out. (Let $\alpha = .05$, and use a two-tailed test.)

13. On a particular day, a canner of tomatoes takes a random sample of 10 cans of its tomatoes shipped out in the morning and 10 cans shipped out in the afternoon. The drained weights of the contents of the 10 cans in each sample were as follows:

Sample taken in morning (ounces)	Sample taken in afternoon (ounces)
22.01	22.58
22.52	19.54
22.53	22.55
24.04	22.02
23.55	21.01
25.04	22.03
25.15	22.14
25.23	21.95
25.52	20.82
24.11	20.21

SOURCE: Some of these data are taken from E. Grant, *Statistical Quality Control.*

Use the Mann-Whitney test to determine whether the population of drained weights of cans shipped out in the morning was different from that of cans shipped out in the afternoon. (Let $\alpha = .05$, and use a two-tailed test.)

14. A sample of 60 residents of each of three federally financed housing projects was asked whether the housing project was run properly. The results were as follows:

	Housing project		
Answer	A	B	C
Yes	39	24	10
No	11	24	36
No opinion	10	12	14
Total	60	60	60

Minitab was used to carry out a χ^2 test to determine whether the residents' opinions on this score differed among the housing projects. Interpret the results, given below.

```
MTB>   READ C5,C6,C7
DATA>   39   24   10
DATA>   11   24   36
DATA>   10   12   14
DATA>   END
        3 ROWS READ
MTB>   CHISQUARE C5,C6,C7
```

Expected counts are printed below observed counts.

	C5	C6	C7	Total
1	39	24	10	73
	24.3	24.3	24.3	
2	11	24	36	71
	23.7	23.7	23.7	
3	10	12	14	36
	12.0	12.0	12.0	
Total	60	60	60	180

ChiSq + 8.84+   0.00+   8.44+
        6.78+   0.00+   6.43+
        0.33+   0.00+   0.33 = 31.17

df = 4

15. A pig farmer wants to test two different vitamin treatments. Each treatment is given to 15 different pigs, and the weight gain (in pounds) for each pig is recorded, the results being as follows:

Treatment A   10.1, 10.8, 11.1, 10.9, 11.2, 10.7, 10.8, 10.9, 11.1,
               10.8, 10.9, 11.1, 10.9, 10.6, 10.7.

Treatment B   10.4, 10.6, 10.8, 10.5, 10.4, 10.5, 10.3, 10.9, 11.1,
               10.8, 10.7, 11.0, 10.8, 10.7, 10.8.

Minitab is used to test whether the median weight gain differs between the two treatments. Interpret the results, given below.

```
MTB>   SET C8
DATA>    10.1    10.8    11.1    10.9    11.2   10.7   10.8   10.9   11.1   10.8
DATA>    10.9    11.1    10.9    10.6    10.7
DATA>   END
MTB    SET C9
DATA>    10.4    10.6    10.8    10.5    10.4   10.5   10.3   10.9   11.1   10.8
DATA>    10.7    11    10.8    10.7    10.8
DATA>   END
MTB>   MANNWHITNEY C8 C9
```

Mann-Whitney Confidence Interval and Test

```
C8          N =    15     MEDIAN =      10.900
C9          N =    15     MEDIAN =      10.700
POINT ESTIMATE FOR ETA1-ETA2 IS    0.2002
95.4 PCT C.I. FOR ETA1-ETA-2 IS (      0.000,      0.399)
W =    278.0
TEST OF ETA1 = ETA2 VS. ETA1 N.E. ETA2 IS SIGNIFICANT AT 0.0620

CANNOT REJECT AT ALPHA = 0.05
```

Answers

Reasons for Component Failure: A Case Study

(a)   The expected frequencies are as follows:

Reason

Position	A	B
I	$(30)(106) \div 200 = 15.9$	$(80)(106) \div 200 = 42.4$
II	$(30)(94) \div 200 = 14.10$	$(80)(94) \div 200 = 37.6$

	C	D
I	$(65)(106) \div 200 = 34.45$	$(25)(106) \div 200 = 13.25$
II	$(65)(94) \div 200 = 30.55$	$(25)(94) \div 200 = 11.75$

Thus,

$$\sum \frac{(f-e)^2}{e} = \frac{(20-15.9)^2}{15.9} + \frac{(32-42.4)^2}{42.4} + \frac{(44-34.45)^2}{34.45} + \frac{(10-13.25)^2}{13.25}$$

$$+ \frac{(10-14.1)^2}{14.1} + \frac{(48-37.6)^2}{37.6} + \frac{(21-30.55)^2}{30.55} + \frac{(15-11.75)^2}{11.75}$$

$$= \frac{16.81}{15.9} + \frac{108.16}{42.4} + \frac{91.2025}{34.45} + \frac{10.5625}{13.25}$$

$$+ \frac{16.81}{14.1} + \frac{108.16}{37.6} + \frac{91.2025}{30.55} + \frac{10.5625}{11.75}$$

$$= 1.057 + 2.551 + 2.647 + .797 + 1.192$$
$$+ 2.877 + 2.985 + .899 = 15.005.$$

Since the number of degrees of freedom is 3, $\chi^2_{.05} = 7.81473$. Since the observed value of the test statistic exceeds this amount, we must reject the hypothesis that the relative frequency of various causes of failure is the same, regardless of the position of the electronic component.

(b)   When the component is in position I, reasons A and C seem to be much more frequently the reasons for failure than when it is in position II. Conversely, when the component is in position II, reasons B and D seem to be much more frequently the reasons for failure than when it is in position I.

(c)   In designing the device, the laboratory can use this information to decide on the steps in preventing failure of the component. For example, if it puts the component in position II, it must be particularly careful to guard against reason B. If it puts the component in position I, it must be more careful to guard against reason C.

Multiple-Choice Questions

1. (b)   2. (d)   3. (c)   4. (a)   5. (d)   6. (a)   7. (d)   8. (d)   9. (e)

Problems and Problem Sets

1. The common proportion defective equals

$$\frac{7+8+9+6+10+11+9+6}{800} = \frac{66}{800},$$

or .0825. Thus, the expected number of defectives in each shipment is 8.25, and the test statistic is

$$\sum \frac{(f-e)^2}{e} = \frac{(7-8.25)^2}{8.25} + \frac{(93-91.75)^2}{91.75} + \frac{(8-8.25)^2}{8.25} + \frac{(92-91.75)^2}{91.75}$$

$$+ \frac{(9-8.25)^2}{8.25} + \frac{(91-91.75)^2}{91.75} + \frac{(6-8.25)^2}{8.25} + \frac{(94-91.75)^2}{91.75}$$

$$+ \frac{(10-8.25)^2}{8.25} + \frac{(90-91.75)^2}{91.75} + \frac{(11-8.25)^2}{8.25} + \frac{(89-91.75)^2}{91.75}$$

$$+ \frac{(9-8.25)^2}{8.25} + \frac{(91-91.75)^2}{91.75} + \frac{(6-8.25)^2}{8.25} + \frac{(94-91.75)^2}{91.75}$$

$$= \frac{(-1.25)^2}{8.25} + \frac{(1.25)^2}{91.75} + \frac{(-0.25)^2}{8.25} + \frac{(0.25)^2}{91.75} + \frac{(0.75)^2}{8.25} + \frac{(-.75)^2}{91.75}$$

$$+ \frac{(-2.25)^2}{8.25} + \frac{(2.25)^2}{91.75} + \frac{(1.75)^2}{8.25} + \frac{(-1.75)^2}{91.75} + \frac{(2.75)^2}{8.25}$$

$$+ \frac{(-2.75)^2}{91.75} + \frac{(0.75)^2}{8.25} + \frac{(-.75)^2}{91.75} + \frac{(-2.25)^2}{8.25} + \frac{(2.25)^2}{91.75}$$

$$= \frac{1}{8.25}(1.5625+.0625+.5625+5.0625+3.0625+7.5625$$

$$+.5625+5.0625) + \frac{1}{91.75}(1.5625+.0625+.5625+5.0625$$

$$+3.0625+7.5625+.5625+5.0625)$$

$$= \left(\frac{1}{8.25} + \frac{1}{91.75}\right)(23.5) = (.1212+.0109)(23.5) = (.1321)(23.5)$$

$$= 3.1044.$$

With 7 degrees of freedom, $\chi^2_{.05} = 14.0671$. Since the observed value of the test statistic does not exceed this amount, we should not reject the hypothesis that the proportion defective is the same in all suppliers' shipments.

2. No. He should have calculated $\Sigma(|f-e| - 1/2)^2 \div e$. See footnote 10 of the text.

3. The common proportion is $\dfrac{7+5+10}{64+64+64} = \dfrac{22}{192} = .115$. Thus, for each brand,

the expected number of cans not in accord with the label is 7.36 (and 56.64 is the expected number that is in accord with the label). The test statistic is

$$\frac{(7-7.36)^2}{7.36} + \frac{(57-56.64)^2}{56.64} + \frac{(5-7.36)^2}{7.36} + \frac{(59-56.64)^2}{56.64}$$

$$+\frac{(10-7.36)^2}{7.36} + \frac{(54-56.64)^2}{56.64}$$

$$= \frac{.1296}{7.36} + \frac{.1296}{56.64} + \frac{5.5696}{7.36} + \frac{5.5696}{56.64} + \frac{6.9696}{7.36} + \frac{6.9696}{56.64}$$

$$= \left(\frac{1}{7.36} + \frac{1}{56.64}\right)(12.6688)$$

$$= (.1359 + .0177)(12.6688) = (.1536)(12.6688) = 1.9459.$$

With 2 degrees of freedom, $\chi^2_{.01} = 9.21034$. Since the observed value of the test statistic does not exceed this amount, we should not reject the hypothesis that the proportion of cans not in accord with the label is the same for one brand as for another.

4. The expected frequencies are as follows:

	Succeeded	*Failed*
Passed test	$(140)(205) \div 500 = 57.4$	$(360)(205) \div 500 = 147.6$
Failed test	$(140)(295) \div 500 = 82.6$	$(360)(295) \div 500 = 212.4$

Thus,

$$\sum\frac{(f-e)^2}{e} = \frac{(103-57.4)^2}{57.4} + \frac{(102-147.6)^2}{147.6} + \frac{(37-82.6)^2}{82.6} + \frac{(258-212.4)^2}{212.4}$$

$$= \frac{(45.6)^2}{57.4} + \frac{(-45.6)^2}{147.6} + \frac{(-45.6)^2}{82.6} + \frac{(45.6)^2}{212.4}$$

$$= (2079.36)(.0174 + .0068 + .0121 + .0047) = 85.25.$$

With 1 degree of freedom $\chi^2_{.05} = 3.8415$. Since the observed value of the test statistic exceeds this amount, we should reject the hypothesis that the test is of no use as a predictor. (If the continuity correction factor is applied, the results remain essentially unchanged.)

5. The expected frequencies are as follows:

	Brittle	*Tough*
30 seconds	$(400)(254) \div 800 = 127$	$(400)(546) \div 800 = 273$
90 seconds	$(400)(254) \div 800 = 127$	$(400)(546) \div 800 = 273$

$$\text{Thus,} \sum\frac{(|f-e|-1/2)^2}{e} = \frac{(20.5)^2}{127} + \frac{(20.5)^2}{127} + \frac{(20.5)^2}{273} + \frac{(20.5)^2}{273}$$

$$= \frac{420.25}{127} + \frac{420.25}{127} + \frac{420.25}{273} + \frac{420.25}{273}$$

$$= 3.309 + 3.309 + 1.539 + 1.539 = 9.696.$$

With 1 degree of freedom $\chi^2_{.01} = 6.6349$. Since the observed value of the test statistic exceeds this amount, it appears that the probability that a nylon bar will be classified as brittle rather than tough is not independent of the length of the heating process.

6. The expected frequencies are as follows:

	Front	Rear
Right	$(240)(180) \div 400 = 108$	$(160)(180) \div 400 = 72$
Left	$(240)(220) \div 400 = 132$	$(160)(220) \div 400 = 88$

Thus, $\sum \dfrac{(|f - e| - 1/2)^2}{e} = \dfrac{(6.5)^2}{108} + \dfrac{(6.5)^2}{132} + \dfrac{(6.5)^2}{72} + \dfrac{(6.5)^2}{88}$

$$= 42.25(.0093 + .0076 + .0139 + .0114)$$
$$= 42.25(.0422) = 1.783.$$

With 1 degree of freedom $\chi^2_{.05} = 3.8415$. Since the observed value of the test statistic does not exceed this amount, we cannot reject the hypothesis that the proportion of left (rather than right) tires that are scrapped is independent of whether the tire is a front or rear tire.

7. The theoretical probability distribution of the number of managers traveling to corporate headquarters is a binomial distribution, with $n = 6$ and $\Pi = .10$. Thus, we can use Appendix Table 1 to obtain the expected frequencies shown below:

Number of managers	Actual frequency	Theoretical frequency
0	45	53.14
1	30	35.43
2 or more	25	11.43

Note that we combine the frequencies corresponding to 2, 3, 4, 5, and 6 managers traveling to corporate headquarters. We must do this if the theoretical frequency is to exceed 5. Based on the above figures,

$$\sum \frac{(f - e)^2}{e} = \frac{(-8.14)^2}{53.14} + \frac{(-5.43)^2}{35.43} + \frac{(-13.57)^2}{11.43}$$

$$= \frac{66.26}{53.14} + \frac{29.48}{35.43} + \frac{184.14}{11.43}$$

$$= 1.2469 + .8321 + 16.1102$$

$$= 18.1892.$$

Since the number of degrees of freedom is 2, $\chi^2_{.01} = 9.21034$. Since the test statistic exceeds this amount, we must reject the hypothesis that the data conform to the theoretical binomial distribution.

8. The theoretical and actual frequency distributions are as follows:

Number of absences	Actual number of workers	Theoretical probability	Theoretical number of workers
0	490	.3679	367.9
1	270	.3679	367.9
2	130	.1839	183.9
3	70	.0613	61.3
4 or more	40	.0190	19.0

The theoretical probabilities come from Appendix Table 3. Based on the above figures,

$$\sum \frac{(f - e)^2}{e} = \frac{(490 - 367.9)^2}{367.9} + \frac{(270 - 367.9)^2}{367.9} + \frac{(130 - 183.9)^2}{183.9}$$

$$+ \frac{(70 - 61.3)^2}{61.3} + \frac{(40 - 19.0)^2}{19.0}$$

$$= \frac{(122.1)^2}{367.9} + \frac{(-97.9)^2}{367.9} + \frac{(-53.9)^2}{183.9} + \frac{(8.7)^2}{61.3} + \frac{(21.0)^2}{19.0}$$

$$= \frac{14,908.41}{367.9} + \frac{9,584.41}{367.9} + \frac{2,905.21}{183.9} + \frac{75.69}{61.3} + \frac{441.00}{19.0}$$

$$= 40.52 + 26.05 + 15.80 + 1.23 + 23.21$$

$$= 106.81.$$

Since no parameters are estimated from the sample, there are 4 degrees of freedom, with the result that $\chi^2_{.01} = 13.2767$. Since the observed value of the test statistic exceeds this amount, we must reject the hypothesis that the number of absences conforms to a Poisson distribution with mean equal to 1.

9. $\frac{(n - 1)s^2}{\sigma_0^2} = \frac{(24)(.014)^2}{.01^2} = \frac{24(.000196)}{.0001} = \frac{.004704}{.0001} = 47.04.$

Since there are 24 degrees of freedom, $\chi^2_{.025} = 39.3641$. Since the observed value of the test statistic exceeds this amount, we must reject the hypothesis that the standard deviation equals 0.01 inch.

10. Using the sign test, the number of pluses is 40. The null hypothesis should be rejected if the number of pluses is less than $n/2 - z_{\alpha/2}\sqrt{n/4}$ or greater than $n/2 + z_{\alpha/2}\sqrt{n/4}$. Since $n = 50$,

$n/2 - z_{\alpha/2}\sqrt{n/4} = 25 - 1.96\sqrt{12.5} = 25 - 1.96(3.536) = 18.07,$

$n/2 + z_{\alpha/2}\sqrt{n/4} = 25 + 1.96\sqrt{12.5} = 25 + 1.96(3.536) = 31.93.$

Since the observed number of pluses exceeds 31.93, we must reject the hypothesis that the median score in the population is 100.

11. The number of pluses is 16. Since $n = 200$,

$$n/2 - z_{\alpha/2}\sqrt{n/4} = 100 - 2.576\sqrt{50} = 100 - 2.576(7.071) = 81.785,$$

$$n/2 + z_{\alpha/2}\sqrt{n/4} = 100 + 2.576\sqrt{50} = 100 + 2.576(7.071) = 118.215.$$

Since the observed number of pluses is less than 81.785, we must reject the hypothesis that the median age is 29 years.

12. The ranking is

73.1; 74.2; 75.2; 76.0; 76.3; 78.0; 78.1; 78.4; 78.6; 78.8; 79.1; 79.2;
A   A   A   B   B   A   A   B   B   A   A   B

79.4; 80.0; 80.2; 80.3; 80.5; 80.9; 81.0; 81.1; 81.2; 81.4; 81.9; 82.0;
B   A   A   B   B   A   B   A   B   A   B   A

82.3; 82.5; 82.6; 82.7; 83.1; 83.8; 83.9; 84.0; 84.1; 84.2; 84.3; 84.4;
A   B   A   B   A   B   A   A   A   B   A   B

84.6; 84.8; 85.0; 86.0.
B   B   B   B

$$R_1 = 1 + 2 + 3 + 6 + 7 + 10 + 11 + 14 + 15 + 18 + 20$$
$$\quad + 22 + 24 + 25 + 27 + 29 + 31 + 32 + 33 + 35$$
$$= 365.$$

$$U = (20)(20) + 20(21)/2 - 365 = 400 + 210 - 365 = 245.$$

$$\frac{U - E_u}{\sigma_u} = \frac{245 - (20)(20)/2}{\sqrt{(20)(20)(41) \div 12}} = \frac{45}{\sqrt{16,400 \div 12}} = \frac{45}{\sqrt{1366.7}} = \frac{45}{36.97}$$

$$= 1.22.$$

Since $z_{.025} = 1.96$, the observed value of the test statistic does not exceed $z_{.025}$; thus, we cannot reject the hypothesis that the population of ratings of program A is the same as the population of ratings of program B.

13. The ranking is

19.54; 20.21; 20.82; 21.01; 21.95; 22.01; 22.02; 22.03; 22.14; 22.52;
A   A   A   A   A   M   A   A   A   M

22.53; 22.55; 22.58; 23.55; 24.04; 24.11; 25.04; 25.15; 25.23; 25.52.
M   A   A   M   M   M   M   M   M   M

$$R_1 = 1 + 2 + 3 + 4 + 5 + 7 + 8 + 9 + 12 + 13$$
$$= 64.$$

$$U = (10)(10) + (10)(11)/2 - 64 = 100 + 55 - 64 = 91.$$

$$\frac{U - E_u}{\sigma_u} = \frac{91 - (10)(10)/2}{\sqrt{(10)(10)(21) \div 12}} = \frac{41}{\sqrt{2100 \div 12}} = \frac{41}{\sqrt{175}} = \frac{41}{13.23} = 3.10.$$

Since $z_{.025} = 1.96$, the observed value of the test statistic exceeds $z_{.025}$; thus, we must reject the hypothesis that the population of drained weights of cans shipped out in the morning was the same as that of cans shipped out in the afternoon.

14. Since there are 4 degrees of freedom, $\chi^2_{.01} = 13.2767$. The observed value of χ^2, which is 31.17, exceeds $\chi^2_{.01}$. Thus, if $\alpha = .01$, we should reject the null hypothesis that the residents' opinions on this score did not differ among the housing projects.

15. If we want α to be greater than .062, we should reject the null hypothesis that the median weight gains are the same for the two treatments. If we want α to be less than .062, we should not reject this hypothesis.

CHAPTER 11

Experimental Design and the Analysis of Variance

Chapter Profile

In designing industrial experiments, one of the most common pitfalls is to *confound* the effect of the variable one wants to estimate with that of some other factor. Sometimes this happens because proper *randomization* did not occur. For example, if an experiment is carried out to determine the difference in the incidence of a disease between a group of people who receive a vaccine and a group who do not, individuals should be assigned to one group or the other at random.

Frequently, the statistician wants to estimate the effect of more than one factor in an experiment. In a *randomized block* design, there are two kinds of effects: *treatment effects* and *block effects.* These terms come from agricultural research where a field may be split into several blocks, and various treatments (for example, different fertilizers) may be assigned at random to plots within each block. If there are replications, more than one observation is obtained concerning the effect of each treatment in each block.

In a *Latin square* design there are three kinds of effects (for example, the effects of various raw materials, types of machines, and types of workers). Each type of raw material is used once with each type of machine and each type of labor. Due to this balance it is possible to estimate the effects of all three factors on the basis of a relatively small number of observations.

The *F distribution* is the probability distribution of the ratio of two independent χ^2 random variables, each divided by its own degrees of freedom. The *one-way analysis of variance* tests whether a number of population means are equal. The total sum of squares in the sample is divided into the *between-group sum of squares* and the *within-group sum of squares.* The ratio of the between-group sum of squares (divided by its degrees of freedom) to the within-group sum of squares (divided by its degrees of freedom) has an F distribution if all population means are equal. Thus, the hypothesis is rejected if this ratio exceeds F_α, where α is the desired significance level.

The *two-way analysis of variance* is appropriate when one observation is taken from each of k treatments and n blocks, the purpose being to determine whether the mean for each treatment is the same, and/or whether the mean for each block is the same. The total sum of squares in the sample is divided into three parts: the *treatment sum of squares,* the *block sum of squares,* and the *error sum of squares.* To test whether the mean for each treatment (or block) is the same, we compute the ratio of the treatment (or block) sum of squares (divided by its degrees of freedom) to the error sum of squares (divided by its degrees of freedom), and we reject the hypothesis that they are the same if this ratio exceeds F_α.

Behavioral Objectives

A. You should be able to define the following key concepts in this chapter:

F distribution	block sum of squares
completely randomized design	confounding
variance ratio	randomization
one-way analysis of variance	randomized block
total sum of squares	experimental error
between-group sum of squares	replication
treatment sum of squares	Latin square
within-group sum of squares	balance
error sum of squares	two-way analysis of variance
analysis-of-variance table	

B. Make sure that you can do each of the following:
1. Indicate how confounding can spoil an experiment, and describe the role that randomization can play in preventing confounding.
2. Describe the advantages and disadvantages of carrying out experiments that vary one factor (holding others fixed) versus varying a number of factors simultaneously.
3. Describe the nature and advantages of randomized blocks (both with and without replication) as an experimental design.
4. Describe the nature and advantages of Latin squares as an experimental design.
5. Describe the conditions under which the *F* distribution arises, and the meaning of its degrees of freedom.
6. Use the one-way analysis of variance to test whether the means of a number of populations are equal.
7. Calculate confidence intervals for the differences among means in a one-way analysis of variance.
8. Use the two-way analysis of variance to test whether the treatment effects and/or the block effects are the same.
9. Calculate confidence intervals for the differences among means in a two-way analysis of variance.

Consumer Preferences: A Case Study

Market-research firm A wants to find out whether a new type of cake mix is preferred by consumers over an older type. It picks at random six persons and asks each to rate the new cake mix on a scale of 1 to 100. Then it picks at random another six persons and asks each to rate the old cake mix on a scale of 1 to 100. Based on the results, it compares the mean score of the new cake mix with the mean score of the old cake mix.

(a) Comment on this experimental design. What problems are likely to arise? What improvements can you suggest?

Market-research firm B also wants to find out whether a new type of cake mix is preferred by consumers over an older type. It picks 500 people who are known to be users of the older type and asks them to compare the new cake mix with the old. It calculates the proportion of these people who say they prefer the new cake mix over the old.

(b) Comment on this experimental design. What problems are likely to arise? What improvements can you suggest?

Market-research firm C is faced with the same problem as market-research firms A and B. It chooses 100 persons at random, all having used neither the old nor the new cake mix. It asks them to eat two small pieces of cake made with the new mix, after which it asks them to eat two small pieces of cake made with the old mix. Then it asks each person whether he or she preferred the first two pieces to the second two pieces, and calculates the proportion of people in the sample who say they do.

(c) Comment on this experimental design. What problems are likely to arise? What improvements can you suggest?

Multiple-Choice Questions

1. If the total sum of squares is 30, the between-group sum of squares is 20, the number of populations is 5, and the number of observations taken from each population is 3, the value of the F ratio is

   (a) 2.
   (b) 3.
   (c) 4.
   (d) 5.
   (e) 6.

2. A firm tested the durability of four types of tires by having a Cadillac outfitted with each type of tire, a Ford outfitted with each type of tire, and a Volkswagen outfitted with each type. Then each of the 12 cars ran over a test track until its tires showed signs of serious wear, and the mean mileage (until signs arose of serious wear) of the three cars using one type of tire was compared with the mean mileage of the three cars using the second type of tire, and so on. This design is

   (a) an example of the use of the one-way analysis of variance.
   (b) biased in favor of the first type of tire.
   (c) a Latin square design.
   (d) a randomized block design.
   (e) none of the above.

3. In the experiment described in the previous question,

   (a) the type of car is the block.
   (b) the type of tire is the treatment.
   (c) there are no replications.
   (d) all of the above are true.
   (e) none of the above are true.

4. In a Latin square design where a statistician wants to estimate the effect of temperature, humidity, and type of raw material on the output of a certain industrial process,

    (a) temperature must be set at three levels.
    (b) humidity must be set at three levels.
    (c) three types of raw materials must be used.
    (d) all the above must be done.
    (e) none of the above must be done.

5. A random variable with an F distribution

    (a) can assume only nonnegative values.
    (b) is the ratio of two χ^2 variables divided by their degrees of freedom.
    (c) has an infinite expected value.
    (d) has both (a) and (b) true.
    (e) has none of the above true.

6. If a random variable has an F distribution with 10 and 12 degrees of freedom, $F_{.05}$ equals

    (a) 2.69.
    (b) 2.98.
    (c) 2.75.
    (d) 2.91.
    (e) none of the above.

7. In a one-way analysis of variance, the between-group sum of squares

    (a) equals the total sum of squares minus the within-group sum of squares.
    (b) must be nonnegative.
    (c) is divided by the within-group sum of squares, and the resulting ratio—multiplied by $k(n - 1) \div (k - 1)$—has an F distribution if the null hypothesis is true and if k is the number of groups and n is the number of observations in each group.
    (d) has both (a) and (b) true.
    (e) has all the above true.

8. In a two-way analysis of variance

    (a) the treatment sum of squares has degrees of freedom equal to the number of treatments minus 1.
    (b) the block sum of squares has degrees of freedom equal to the number of blocks minus 1.
    (c) the total number of degrees of freedom is 1 less than the number of blocks times the number of treatments.
    (d) both (a) and (b) are true.
    (e) all the above are true.

Problems and Problem Sets

1. Fill in the blanks in the following analysis-of-variance table.

Source of variation	Sum of squares	Degrees of freedom	Mean square	F
Between groups	_____	3	1.4	2.8
Within groups	8.0	_____	_____	
Total	_____	_____		

2. Suppose that a firm wants to compare the output rate of three types of machines, and that in the course of this experiment the firm wants to see how the output rate of each type of machine varies depending on whether unskilled or skilled workers are operating it and whether raw material A or B is fed into the machine.

 (a) List the 12 means that the firm must calculate in order to determine the output rate of each type of machine with each type of worker and raw material.

 (b) Can a randomized block design be used to analyze this experiment? Can a Latin-square design be used to analyze this experiment? Why or why not?

3. A firm conducted a study of the factors influencing the lengths of steel bars. The 12 bars were taken from a screw machine, 4 being subjected to W heat treatment, 4 to L heat treatment, and 4 to D heat treatment. The lengths (less 438) were as follows:

Heat treatment		
W	L	D
6	4	7
7	6	9
1	−1	10
6	4	6

(a) Based on this sample of 12, what is the mean effect of each heat treatment on length?

(b) Calculate the between-group sum of squares, the within-group sum of squares, and the total sum of squares.

(c) Construct an analysis-of-variance table, and test the significance of the effect of these heat treatments on length. (Let $\alpha = .05$.)

4. The following yields (in pounds) of a certain chemical were obtained when each of three catalysts (A, B, and C) were used with each of three concentrations of an inert solvent at each of three temperatures. The yields are shown in parentheses:

Temperature (degrees)	Concentration of inert solvent (percent)		
	40	50	60
50	A (47.1)	B (45.6)	C (45.8)
60	C (46.2)	A (48.3)	B (46.1)
70	B (47.7)	C (48.1)	A (49.2)

(a) What kind of an experimental design is being used here?

(b) In what sense is this design balanced?

(c) What is the estimated mean yield at various temperatures?

    (d) What is the estimated mean yield at various concentrations of inert solvent?

    (e) What is the estimated mean yield with each catalyst?

    (f) Write a brief summary of the findings of this experiment.

5. A tire manufacturer wants to test whether the mean diameters of tires produced at its three plants (New York, Illinois, and California) are equal. Last month it took a random sample of tires at each plant, and their diameters (in inches) were as follows:

New York			Illinois			California		
24.2	24.2	24.1	24.4	24.2	24.3	24.4	24.3	24.2
24.1	24.2	24.0	24.3	24.1	24.4	24.5	24.4	24.2
24.3	24.3	24.4	24.3	24.4	24.3	24.4	24.5	24.4

(a) What is the total sum of squares? What is the between-group sum of squares? What is the within-group sum of squares?

(b) What is the number of degrees of freedom for the total sum of squares? For the between-group sum of squares? For the within-group sum of squares?

(c) Construct the analysis-of-variance table and test whether the mean diameter was equal in the three plants. (Let $\alpha = .01$.)

6. A research laboratory in the chemical industry wants to determine the melting point (in degrees centigrade) of hydroquinone. Three analysts (Jones, Smith, and Murphy) carry out the analysis, and each performs it four times, once with thermometer A, once with thermometer B, once with thermometer C, and once with thermometer D. The results are as follows:

Analyst	Thermometer (degrees centigrade)			
	A	B	C	D
Jones	174.0	173.0	171.5	173.5
Smith	173.0	172.0	171.0	171.0
Murphy	173.5	173.0	173.0	172.5

SOURCE: With slight modifications, from G. Wernimont, "Quality Control in the Chemical Industry," *Industrial Quality Control.*

(a) If the treatment effects are the effects of various thermometers, and the block effects are the effects of various analysts, what is the total sum of squares? The treatment sum of squares? The block sum of squares? The error sum of squares?

(b) What is the number of degrees of freedom for the total sum of squares? The treatment sum of squares? The block sum of squares? The error sum of squares?

(c) Construct the analysis-of-variance table, and test whether the thermometers differ significantly with regard to their indications of the melting point, and whether the analysts differ significantly in their perceptions of the melting point. (Let $\alpha = .05$.)

7. A study is carried out of three different methods of training workers in an auto plant. A group of 30 employees of equal aptitude is divided into three groups. Each group is trained according to one of the three methods. At the end of the training period, each of the students is graded on his or her performance, the results being as shown below:

Method A	Method B	Method C
62	81	89
68	83	78
84	76	84
82	78	63
90	94	69
76	95	77
78	68	87
93	94	91
52	86	65
86	79	74

Minitab is used to test the hypothesis that all three training methods are equally effective.

(a) Interpret the results, part of which are given below.

(b) What part of the printout is missing?

```
MTB>   SET C10
DATA>   62  68  84  82  90  76  78  93  52  86
DATA>   END
MTB>   SET C11
DATA>   81  83  76  78  94  95  68  94  86  79
DATA>   END
MTB>   SET C12
DATA>   89  78  84  63  69  77  87  91  65  74
DATA>   END
MTB>   AOVONEWAY  C10,C11,C12
```

ANALYSIS OF VARIANCE

SOURCE	DF	SS	MS	F
FACTOR	2	242	121	1.05
ERROR	27	3123	116	
TOTAL	29	3365		

8. Four male workers and four female workers were chosen at random, and divided at random into pairs (or a man and a woman). Each such pair received one of four training programs aimed at reducing the number of clerical errors they made per day, the results being as follows:

	Program A	Program B	Program C	Program D
	(Reduction in number of errors per day)			
Men	15	21	14	6
Women	8	9	6	3

Minitab is used to test whether there is any difference among the training programs in their effectiveness.

(a) Interpret the results, part of which are shown below.

(b) What part of the printout is missing?

```
MTB>   READ INTO C13,C14,C15
DATA>  15  1  1
DATA>  21  1  2
DATA>  14  1  3
DATA>  6  1  4
DATA>  8  2  1
DATA>  9  2  2
DATA>  6  2  3
DATA>  3  2  4
DATA>  END
        8 ROWS READ
MTB>   TWOWAY ANALYSIS, OBS IN C13, BLOCKS IN C14,
        TREATMENTS IN C15

ANALYSIS OF VARIANCE C13
```

SOURCE	DF	SS	MS
C14	1	112.50	112.50
C15	3	114.50	38.17
ERROR	3	20.50	6.83
TOTAL	7	247.50	

Answers

Consumer Preferences: A Case Study

(a) It might be preferable to have the same people rate both cake mixes. The variation among individuals in the score given to a particular mix may be substantial.

(b) The results may be biased because all the people in the sample are known to use the old cake mix. The frame might be extended to include all consumers.

(c) There are at least two problems: (1) the results may be biased because they pertain only to people who have used neither cake mix. (2) The results may be biased because the new mix is always eaten before the old mix. It would be preferable to enlarge the frame to include all consumers and to control the order in which the cake mixes are given. In half of the cases, the old mix might be eaten first; in the other half, the new mix might be eaten first.

Multiple-Choice Questions

1. (d)   2. (d)   3. (d)   4. (d)   5. (d)   6. (c)   7. (e)   8. (e)

Problems and Problem Sets

1. The complete table is:

Source of variation	Sum of squares	Degrees of freedom	Mean square	F
Between groups	4.2	3	1.4	2.8
Within groups	8.0	16	0.5	
Total	12.2	19		

2. (a) It must calculate the mean output rate of

   (1) type 1 machine with unskilled labor and raw material A,
   (2) type 1 machine with unskilled labor and raw material B,
   (3) type 1 machine with skilled labor and raw material A,
   (4) type 1 machine with skilled labor and raw material B,
   (5) type 2 machine with unskilled labor and raw material A,
   (6) type 2 machine with unskilled labor and raw material B,
   (7) type 2 machine with skilled labor and raw material A,
   (8) type 2 machine with skilled labor and raw material B,
   (9) type 3 machine with unskilled labor and raw material A,
   (10) type 3 machine with unskilled labor and raw material B,
   (11) type 3 machine with skilled labor and raw material A, and
   (12) type 3 machine with skilled labor and raw material B.

   (b) Yes. No, because each of the three factors would have to have three possible levels. (In this case, two of them—skill and raw material—have two possible levels.)

3. (a) The mean for each heat treatment:

   W: 5.00
   L: 3.25
   D: 8.00

(b) $BSS = 4[(5.00 - 5.417)^2 + (3.25 - 5.417)^2 + (8.00 - 5.417)^2]$
$= 4[.417^2 + 2.167^2 + 2.583^2] = 4(.1739 + 4.6959 + 6.6719)$
$= 4(11.5417) = 46.167.$

$$TSS = \sum_i \sum_j x_{ij}^2 - \bar{x}.. \sum_i \sum_j x_{ij}$$

$= (36 + 49 + 1 + 36 + 16 + 36 + 1 + 16 + 49 + 81 + 100 + 36)$
$\quad - 5.417(6 + 7 + 1 + 6 + 4 + 6 - 1 + 4 + 7 + 9 + 10 + 6)$
$= 457 - 5.417(65) = 457 - 352.105 = 104.895.$

$WSS = 104.895 - 46.167 = 58.728.$

(c) The table is:

Source of variation	Sum of squares	Degrees of freedom	Mean square	F
Between groups	46.167	2	23.084	3.538
Within groups	58.728	9	6.525	
Total	104.895	11		

Since the numbers of degrees of freedom are 2 and 9, $F_{.05} = 4.26$. Since the observed value of F does not exceed 4.26, we do not reject the hypothesis that these heat treatments result in no difference in mean length.

4. (a) Latin square.
   (b) Each catalyst is used once and only once with each concentration and temperature. Each concentration is used once and only once with each catalyst and temperature. Each temperature is used once and only once with each concentration and catalyst.
   (c) The means are
       50°: 46.17,
       60°: 46.87,
       70°: 48.33.
   (d) The means are
       40 percent: 47.00,
       50 percent: 47.33,
       60 percent: 47.03.
   (e) The means are
       A: 48.20,
       B: 46.47,
       C: 46.70.
   (f) The yield seems highest with catalyst A and when the temperature is 70°, but without carrying out a formal test, we cannot say whether these differences are due to chance.

5. (a) The means are
       New York: 24.200000,
       Illinois: 24.300000,
       California: 24.36667,
       Overall: 24.28889.

$$TSS = 24.0^2 + 3(24.1)^2 + 6(24.2)^2 + 7(24.3)^2 + 8(24.4)^2 + 2(24.5)^2$$

$$- \frac{1}{27}[24.0 + 3(24.1) + 6(24.2) + 7(24.3) + 8(24.4) + 2(24.5)]^2$$

$$= 576.00 + 1742.43 + 3513.84 + 4133.43 + 4762.88 + 1200.50$$

$$- \frac{1}{27}[24.0 + 72.3 + 145.2 + 170.1 + 195.2 + 49.0]^2$$

$$= 15{,}929.080 - \frac{1}{27}(655.8)^2 = 15{,}929.080 - 15{,}928.653$$

$$= 0.427.$$

$$BSS = 9[(24.2 - 24.28889)^2 + (24.3 - 24.28889)^2$$
$$+ (24.36667 - 24.28889)^2]$$
$$= 9(.08889^2 + .01111^2 + .07778^2)$$
$$= 9(.0079014 + .0001234 + .0060497)$$
$$= 9(.0140745) = .127.$$

$$WSS = .427 - .127 = .300.$$

(b) 26.

2.

24.

(c) The table is:

Source of variation	Sum of squares	Degrees of freedom	Mean square	F
Between groups	.127	2	.0635	5.08
Within groups	.300	24	.0125	
Total	.427	26		

Since there are 2 and 24 degrees of freedom, $F_{.01} = 5.61$. Since the observed value of F is less than 5.61, we do not reject the hypothesis that the mean diameter is equal in the three plants.

6. (a) In this case, let's use the formulas in Appendix 11.2:

$$TSS = \sum_i \sum_j x_{ij}^2 - \frac{1}{kn}T^2,$$

$$BSS = \frac{1}{n}\sum_j T_j^2 - \frac{1}{kn}T^2,$$

$$RSS = \frac{1}{k}\sum_i T_i^2 - \frac{1}{kn}T^2,$$

where T is the sum of all observations, T_j is the sum for the jth treatment, and T_i is the sum for the ith block. Clearly,

T	= 2071.0,	T_A	= 520.5,
T_{Jones}	= 692.0,	T_B	= 518.0,
T_{Smith}	= 687.0,	T_C	= 515.5,
T_{Murphy}	= 692.0,	T_D	= 517.0.

Thus,

$$TSS = 174.0^2 + 173.0^2 + 173.5^2 + 173.0^2 + 172.0^2 + 173.0^2$$
$$+ 171.5^2 + 171.0^2 + 173.0^2 + 173.5^2 + 171.0^2 + 172.5^2$$
$$- 1/12(2071)^2$$
$$= 30,276 + 29,929 + 30,102.25 + 29,929 + 29,584 + 29,929$$
$$+ 29,412.25 + 29,241 + 29,929 + 30,102.25 + 29,241$$
$$+ 29,756.25 - 1/12(4289041)$$
$$= 357,431 - 357,420.083 = 10.917,$$
$$BSS = 1/3(520.5^2 + 518^2 + 515.5^2 + 517^2) - 357,420.083$$
$$= 1/3(270,920.25 + 268,324 + 265,740.25 + 267,289) - 357,420.083$$
$$= 1/3(1,072,273.5) - 357,420.083$$
$$= 357,424.5 - 357,420.083 = 4.417,$$
$$RSS = 1/4(692^2 + 687^2 + 692^2) - 357,420.083$$
$$= 1/4(478,864 + 471,969 + 478,864) - 357,420.083$$
$$= 1/4(1,429,697) - 357,420.083$$
$$= 357,424.25 - 357,420.083 = 4.167,$$
$$ESS = 10.917 - 4.417 - 4.167 = 10.917 - 8.584 = 2.333.$$

(b) 11.

   3.

   2.

   6.

(c) The table is:

Source of variation	Sum of squares	Degrees of freedom	Mean square	F
Treatments	4.417	3	1.472	3.78
Blocks	4.167	2	2.084	5.36
Error	2.333	6	0.389	
Total	10.917	11		

With 3 and 6 degrees of freedom, $F_{.05} = 4.76$. Since the observed value of F is less than this amount, the treatment effects (that is, the differences among thermometers) are not statistically significant. With 2 and 6 degrees of freedom, $F_{.05} = 5.14$. Since the observed value of F is greater than this amount, the block effects (that is, the differences among analysts) are statistically significant.

7. (a) Let $\alpha = .05$. Given that there are 2 and 27 degrees of freedom, Appendix Table 9 shows that $F_{.05}$ equals 3.35. Since the observed value of F is only 1.05, there is no reason to reject the null hypothesis that all three training methods are equally effective.

   (b) The p-statistic is missing.

8. (a) Let the programs be treatments and the sexes be blocks. The ratio of the treatment mean square to the error mean square is $38.17 \div 6.83 = 5.59$. Since there are 3 and 3 degrees of freedom, $F_{.05} = 9.28$, according to Appendix Table 9. Thus, if $\alpha = .05$, there is no reason to reject the null hypothesis that there is no difference among programs in effectiveness, since the observed value of $F(5.59)$ is less than $F_{.05}$.

   (b) The values of F and the p-statistics are missing.

PART V

Regression and Correlation

Regression and Correlation

Chapter Profile

If the expected value of a dependent variable (Y_i) is a linear function of an independent variable (X_i), the method of *least squares* is used to estimate the parameters, or constants, of this linear function. This method dictates that we choose the value of each parameter that minimizes the sum of the squared deviations of the points in the sample from the estimated regression line. According to the *Gauss-Markov theorem*, the method of least squares results in the most efficient linear unbiased estimates of the parameters.

The least-squares estimate of B, the slope of this linear function, is

$$b = \sum_{i=1}^{n} (X_i - \overline{X})(Y_i - \overline{Y}) \div \sum_{i=1}^{n} (X_i - \overline{X})^2 ,$$

and the least-squares estimate of A, the intercept of this linear function, is

$$a = \overline{Y} - b\overline{X} .$$

The line, $\hat{Y} = a + bX$, is called the sample regression line. The *standard error of estimate*, which is a measure of the amount of variation about the regression line, equals

$$s_e = \sqrt{\sum_{i=1}^{n} (Y_i - \hat{Y}_i)^2 \div (n-2)} ,$$

where $\hat{Y}_i$ is the estimate of Y_i from the regression.

If we are trying to predict the conditional mean of Y when the independent variable equals X^*, the confidence interval is

$$(a + bX^*) \pm t_{\alpha/2} s_e \sqrt{\frac{1}{n} + \frac{(X^* - \overline{X})^2}{\sum_{i=1}^{n} X_i^2 - n\overline{X}^2}} .$$

If we are trying to predict the value of the dependent variable that will occur if the independent variable is set at X^*, the prediction interval is

$$(a + bX^*) \pm t_{\alpha/2} s_e \sqrt{\frac{n+1}{n} + \frac{(X^* - \overline{X})^2}{\sum_{i=1}^{n} X_i^2 - n\overline{X}^2}} .$$

In both cases, the confidence coefficient is $(1 - \alpha)$ if Y_i is normally distributed.

The *coefficient of determination* shows how well the regression line fits the data. It equals the ratio of the variation in the dependent variable explained by the regression to the total variation. Its square root, *r*, is called the *correlation coefficient:*

$$r = \left\{ n\sum_{i=1}^{n} X_i Y_i - \sum_{i=1}^{n} X_i \sum_{i=1}^{n} Y_i \right\} \div \sqrt{\left[n\sum_{i=1}^{n} X_i^2 - \left(\sum_{i=1}^{n} X_i\right)^2 \right]\left[n\sum_{i=1}^{n} Y_i^2 - \left(\sum_{i=1}^{n} Y_i\right)^2 \right]}.$$

If *r* equals +1, there is a perfect *direct* relationship between X_i and Y_i; if *r* equals −1, there is a perfect *inverse* relationship between them. If X_i and Y_i are independent, the population correlation coefficient is zero. Based on the sample correlation coefficient, we can test whether the population correlation coefficient, ρ, is zero. If

$r \div \sqrt{(1 - r^2)/(n - 2)}$ is greater than $t_{\alpha/2}$ or less than $-t_{\alpha/2}$, the null hypothesis (that $\rho = 0$) should be rejected.

    Multiple regression assumes that the expected value of the dependent variable is a linear function of more than one independent variable. As in the case of simple regression (where there is only one independent variable), the method of least squares can be used to obtain most efficient linear unbiased estimates of the parameters, or constants, of this linear relationship. Also, it is possible to construct confidence intervals for these parameters. The *multiple coefficient of determination* or the *multiple correlation coefficient* is used to measure how well the estimated multiple regression fits the data.

Behavioral Objectives

A. You should be able to define the following key concepts in this chapter:

scatter diagram	variation explained by regression
intercept	variation unexplained by regression
slope	*dummy variable
method of least squares	*serial correlation
Gauss-Markov theorem	*Durbin-Watson test
regression line	*multiple coefficient of determination
standard error of estimate	*multiple regression
regression coefficient	*multiple correlation coefficient
coefficient of determination	extrapolation
correlation coefficient	*multicollinearity
total variation	

*These items pertain to Chapter 13.

B. Make sure that you can do each of the following:
  1. Plot the relationship between an independent variable (X_i) and a dependent variable (Y_i) in a scatter diagram.
  2. Calculate the least-squares estimates of A and B, the intercept and slope of the population regression line.
  3. Compute and interpret the standard error of estimate.
  4. Calculate a confidence interval for the conditional mean of Y.
  5. Calculate a prediction interval for a prediction of Y, based on the regression line.
  6. Calculate a confidence interval for B, the slope of the true (or population) regression line.
  7. Compute and interpret the sample coefficient of determination.
  8. Test whether the population correlation coefficient equals zero.
  *9. Calculate the least-squares estimates of the intercept A and slopes B_1, $B_2, \ldots, B_k$ of a multiple regression with k independent variables.
  *10. Compute and interpret the multiple coefficient of determination.
  *11. Understand the use of dummy variables.
  *12. Understand the problems caused by multicollinearity, serial correlation of the error terms, and other departures from the assumptions underlying regression techniques.

Experimentation in the Textile Industry: A Case Study[1]

In the manufacture of cloth, the weft packages should not disintegrate unduly during weaving. A direct measure of the tendency to disintegrate exists, but it is very laborious and uneconomical to carry out. In addition, there are indirect measures based on laboratory tests. A textile firm would like to determine the extent to which one of these indirect measures is correlated with the direct measure. If the correlation is high enough, the firm believes that it may be able to use the indirect measure instead of the direct measure.

An experiment was carried out in which both the direct and indirect measures of the tendency to disintegrate were calculated for 18 lots of packages. The results were as shown on the following page:

---

*These items pertain to Chapter 13.
1. This case is adapted from a section in L. Tippett, *Technological Applications of Statistics*.

| | Measure | |
Lot	Direct	Indirect
1	31	6.2
2	31	6.2
3	21	10.1
4	21	8.4
5	57	2.9
6	80	2.9
7	35	7.4
8	10	7.3
9	0	11.1
10	0	10.7
11	35	4.1
12	63	3.5
13	10	5.0
14	51	4.5
15	24	9.5
16	15	8.5
17	80	2.6
18	90	2.9

(a) What is the correlation coefficient between the two measures?

(b) What is the linear regression line which you would use to predict the value of the direct measure on the basis of knowledge of the indirect measure?

(c) Plot the scatter diagram between the direct and indirect measures in the graph below:

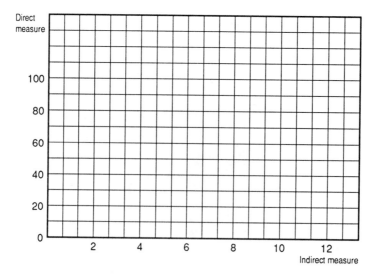

(d) Based on your findings in (a) to (c), write a brief report indicating the factors to be weighed in deciding whether to substitute the indirect measure for the direct measure.

Multiple-Choice Questions

1. A statistician calculates a correlation coefficient based on a sample of 11 observations. To test whether the population correlation coefficient equals zero, the statistician carries out a t test. If the sample correlation coefficient equals .8,

    (a) $t = 4$ and the number of degrees of freedom is 9.
    (b) $t = 4$ and the number of degrees of freedom is 11.
    (c) $t = 5$ and the number of degrees of freedom is 9.
    (d) $t = 5$ and the number of degrees of freedom is 11.
    (e) none of the above.

2. Suppose that $Y = 1$ when $X = 0$, that $Y = 2$ when $X = 1$, and that $Y = 3$ when $X = 2$. In this case, the least-squares estimate of B is

    (a) 0.
    (b) .05.
    (c) 1.
    (d) 1.5.
    (e) none of the above.

3. Based on the data in the previous question, the least-squares estimate of A is

    (a) −1.
    (b) 0.
    (c) 1.
    (d) 2.
    (e) none of the above.

4. Based on the data in question 2, the standard error of estimate is

    (a) 0.
    (b) 1.
    (c) 2.
    (d) 3.
    (e) none of the above.

5. Based on the data in question 2, the sample correlation coefficient is

    (a) −1.
    (b) 0.
    (c) .5.
    (d) 1.
    (e) none of the above.

6. The most efficient linear unbiased estimates

    (a) are the ones with minimum interquartile range.

    (b) are the ones with minimum variance among those which are unbiased.

    (c) are the ones with minimum variance among those which are unbiased and which are linear functions of the dependent variable.

    (d) are the ones with minimum interquartile range among those which are unbiased and which are linear functions of the dependent variable.

    (e) are none of the above.

7. Holding constant the number of observations and the standard error of estimate, increases in the sample variance of the independent variable result in

    (a) increases in the width of the confidence interval for B.

    (b) no change in the width of the confidence interval for B.

    (c) decreases in the width of the confidence interval for B.

    (d) decreases in the width of the confidence interval for B, if $B > 0$.

    (e) none of the above.

8. If the sample correlation coefficient is .5, this means that

    (a) none of the variation in the dependent variable is explained by the regression.

    (b) 25 percent of the variation in the dependent variable is explained by the regression.

    (c) 50 percent of the variation in the dependent variable is explained by the regression.

    (d) 75 percent of the variation in the dependent variable is explained by the regression.

    (e) none of the above.

9. If the sample correlation coefficient is .4, this means that

    (a) the dependent variable is inversely related to the independent variable.

    (b) the dependent variable increases at an increasing rate with increases in the independent variable.

    (c) the dependent variable increases at a decreasing rate with increases in the independent variable.

    (d) the dependent variable is directly related (in the sample) to the independent variable.

    (e) the dependent variable is directly related (in the population) to the independent variable.

*10. A multiple regression is calculated with output of wheat (in tons per year) as the dependent variable, and with input of land (in acres) and of labor (in years) as the independent variables. If the regression coefficient of the labor variable is 10.1, this indicates that

    (a) the annual output of wheat per year of labor equals 10.1 tons.

    (b) the number of years of labor required, on the average, to produce a ton of wheat is 10.1.

    (c) an extra year of labor is associated with an extra 10.1 tons of wheat per year.

    (d) an extra ton of wheat per month is associated with an extra input of 10.1 years of labor.

    (e) none of the above are true.

*11. In the previous question, suppose that the standard error of the regression coefficient described is 2.0. Then, if the regression is based on a very large number of observations, the 95 percent confidence interval for the true (or population) regression coefficient is

    (a) 8.13 to 12.14.

    (b) 6.18 to 14.02.

    (c) 6.81 to 13.42.

    (d) 6.10 to 14.13.

    (e) none of the above.

Problems and Problem Sets

1. Robert Klitgaard, in his book, *Data Analysis for Development* (Oxford: Oxford University Press, 1985), estimated the following correlation coefficients, based on data for 71 countries:

	Per capita gross domestic product	*Calories*	*Population density*	*Urban population (percentage)*
Life expectancy	0.71	0.55	0.32	0.76
Per capita gross domestic product		0.53	0.25	0.74
Calories			0.18	0.61
Population density				0.47

Interpret his results.

2. A market research firm is asked by a client to provide information regarding year-to-year changes in the sales of kitchen appliances. This client is particularly interested in what happened during 1983–84 because it feels (rightly or wrongly) that the period is similar to the current situation. According to the *Statistical Abstract of the United States,* the retail value of shipments of major kitchen appliances in the United States in 1983 and 1984 (in millions of dollars) was:

Appliance	1983	1984
Refrigerators	3,607	4,001
Microwave ovens	2,586	3,362
Ranges, electric	1,299	1,477
Dishwashers	1,205	1,368
Freezers	568	545
Ranges, gas	695	785
Disposers	395	466

Regress the 1984 value of shipments of an appliance on its 1983 value of shipments. Interpret your results.

3. A statistician is interested in the relationship between a firm's expenditure on typewriters and its expenditure on paper clips. To correct for the fact that some firms are much bigger than others, the statistician divides both a firm's expenditure on typewriters and its expenditure on paper clips by its sales. Having done this, the statistician finds that there is a fairly close relationship between a firm's expenditure on typewriters (divided by its sales) and its expenditure on paper clips (divided by its sales). Comment on this procedure.

4. A retail outlet for air conditioners believes that its weekly sales are dependent upon the average temperature during the week. It picks at random 12 weeks in 1994 and finds that its sales are related to the average temperature in these weeks as follows:

Mean temperature (degrees)	Sales (number of air conditioners)
72	3
77	4
82	7
43	1
31	0
28	0
81	8
83	5
76	5
60	4
50	4
55	5

(a) Plot these data in a scatter diagram below:

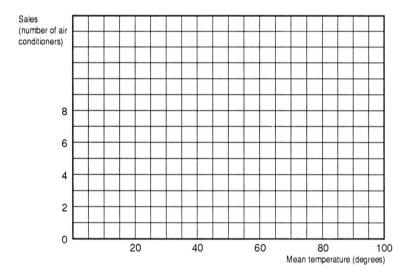

(b) Calculate the intercept and slope of the sample regression line, where sales is the dependent variable and temperature is the independent variable. If a software package is available, use it; otherwise calculate the regression by hand.

(c) Compute the standard error of estimate.

(d) Assuming that (holding temperature constant) sales are normally distributed, calculate a 90 percent confidence interval for the slope of the population regression line.

(e) Calculate a 90 percent confidence interval for the point on the true regression line corresponding to a temperature of 80°. Indicate why the retail outlet might find such a confidence interval useful.

(f) Based on weather forecasts indicating that next week's mean temperature will be 80°, the retail outlet uses the regression to forecast its sales next week. What will be its forecast? Compute a 90 percent prediction interval for the outlet's sales next week?

(g) Calculate the correlation coefficient between the mean temperature and the retail outlet's sales. Test whether the population correlation coefficient equals zero. (Let $\alpha = .05$.)

5. An executive at a Wall Street securities firm wants to determine the relationship between the U.S. national output and the profits (after taxes) of the General Electric Corporation. Her research assistant provides her with the following data for 12 years concerning each variable:

National output (billions of dollars)	General Electric's profits (millions of dollars)
688	355
753	339
796	361
868	357
936	278
982	363
1,063	510
1,171	573
1,306	661
1,407	705
1,529	688
1,706	931

(a) Plot the scatter diagram between General Electric's profits and the U.S. national output below:

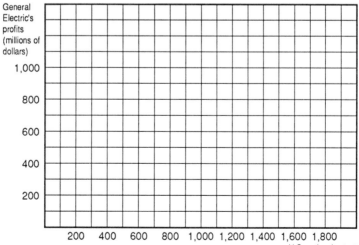

(b) The Minitab printout of the regression of General Electric's profits on U.S. national output is shown below. (C2 is General Electric's profits; C1 is U.S. national output.) What is the regression equation?

```
MTB>      READ INTO C1, C2
DATA>     688    355
DATA>     753    339
DATA>     796    361
DATA>     868    357
DATA>     936    278
DATA>     982    363
DATA>     1063   510
DATA>     1171   573
DATA>     1306   661
DATA>     1407   705
DATA>     1529   688
DATA>     1706   931
DATA>     END
          12 ROWS READ
MTB>      REGRESS C2 ON 1 PREDICTOR IN C1
```

THE REGRESSION EQUATION IS
C2 = −135 + 0.586 C1

PREDICTOR	COEF	STDEV	T-RATIO	P
CONSTANT	−134.54	71.67	−1.88	0.090
C1	0.58580	0.06265	9.35	0.000

S = 67.81   R − SQ = 89.7%   R − SQ(ADJ) = 88.7%

ANALYSIS OF VARIANCE

SOURCE	DF	SS	MS	F	
REGRESSION	1	402044	402044	87.43	0.0
ERROR	10	45985	4599		
TOTAL	11	448029			

(c) What is the standard error of estimate?

(d) On the average, what effect does a $1 increase in national output seem to have on the profits of General Electric? Calculate a 90 percent confidence interval for the size of this effect.

(e) If the Wall Street executive feels that next year's national output will be $2 trillion, what forecast of General Electric's profits will she make on the basis of the regression? Calculate a 90 percent confidence interval for this forecast. Does this forecast involve extrapolation? If so, is this hazardous?

(f) What is an estimate of the conditional mean of General Electric's profits if the national output equals $2 trillion? Calculate a 90 percent confidence interval for this mean.

(g) What is the correlation coefficient between national output and General Electric's profits? Test the hypothesis that the population correlation coefficient equals zero. (Set α = .05, and use a one-tailed test.)

(h) Do the results obtained in previous parts of this problem prove that changes in General Electric's profits are caused by changes in U.S. national output? Can we be sure that the expected value of General Electric's profits is a linear function of the U.S. national output? What other kinds of functions might be as good or better?

(i) What other independent variables would you expect to influence General Electric's profits?

(j) After completing the foregoing analysis, the financial executive is informed by her research assistant that the data on page 215 pertain to 1965–76. If you were the financial executive, would you feel that this regression line was an adequate model to forecast General Electric's profits? Why or why not?

*6. Suppose that a firm calculates a multiple regression where the dependent variable is the firm's monthly sales (in millions of dollars) and the independent variables are (1) the firm's expenditures on advertising during the relevant month (in millions of dollars) and (2) the amount spent by its competitor on advertising during that month (in millions of dollars). Based on the computer printout of the results of the multiple regression, the firm's statistician finds that the value of the Durbin-Watson statistic is 1.25.

(a) If the regression is based on 50 observations, what are the implications of this result?

*This question pertains to Chapter 13.

(b) The computer printout shows that the correlation between this firm's monthly advertising expenditures and its competitor's monthly advertising expenditures equals .98. What are the implications of this result?

(c) The statistician instructs a staff member to obtain data concerning each variable that the staff member thinks may be a determinant of the firm's sales and carry out a stepwise multiple regression. What dangers may exist in this procedure?

*7. Suppose that the retail outlet in problem 4 suspects that its sales depend on the price of its air conditioners as well as on the mean temperature. For the randomly chosen 12 weeks, it obtains data regarding the price of an air conditioner as well as the mean temperature and its sales. The results are as follows:

Mean temperature (degrees)	Price of air conditioner (hundreds of dollars)	Sales (number of air conditioners)
72	2	3
77	2	4
82	1	7
43	2	1
31	2	0
28	2	0
81	1	8
83	2	5
76	2	5
60	1	4
50	1	4
55	1	5

*This question pertains to Chapter 13.

The Minitab printout of the regression of sales ($C5$) on mean temperature ($C3$) and price ($C4$) is as follows:

```
MTB>    READ INTO C3, C4, C5
DATA>  72    2   3
DATA>  77    2   4
DATA>  82    1   7
DATA>  43    2   1
DATA>  31    2   0
DATA>  28    2   0
DATA>  81    1   8
DATA>  83    2   5
DATA>  76    2   5
DATA>  60    1   4
DATA>  50    1   4
DATA>  55    1   5
DATA>  END
        12 ROWS READ
MTB>    REGRESS C5 ON 2 PREDICTORS IN C3 AND C4
```

THE REGRESSION EQUATION IS
$C5 = 1.66 + 0.0960 \, C3 - 2.35 \, C4$

PREDICTOR	COEF	STDEV	T-RATIO	P
CONSTANT	1.6592	0.9566	1.73	0.117
C3	0.095959	0.009928	9.67	0.000
C4	−2.3541	0.3854	−6.11	0.000

$S = 0.6473$ $R - SQ = 94.6\%$ $R - SQ(ADJ) = 93.4\%$

ANALYSIS OF VARIANCE

SOURCE	DF	SS	MS	F	P
REGRESSION	2	65.896	32.948	78.63	0.000
ERROR	9	3.771	0.419		
TOTAL	11	69.667			

(a) What is the regression equation?

(b) How much of an increase in weekly sales can be expected if the mean temperature goes up by 1° and the price of an air conditioner is held constant?

(c) How much of an increase in weekly sales can be expected if the price of an air conditioner goes down by $1 and the mean temperature remains constant?

(d) Suppose that the retail outlet is convinced that the price elasticity of demand for its air conditioners is constant when the price of an air conditioner is between $100 and $300. If this is true, is this regression equation of the right mathematical form? If not, what alternative form would you suggest?

Answers

Experimentation in the Textile Industry: A Case Study

(a) Let Y be the direct measurement, and let X be the indirect measurement. If you must do the calculations by hand, they are as follows:

Y	X	Y²	X²	XY
31	6.2	961	38.44	192.2
31	6.2	961	38.44	192.2
21	10.1	441	102.01	212.1
21	8.4	441	70.56	176.4
57	2.9	3249	8.41	165.3
80	2.9	6400	8.41	232.0
35	7.4	1225	54.76	259.0
10	7.3	100	53.29	73.0
0	11.1	0	123.21	0
0	10.7	0	114.49	0
35	4.1	1225	16.81	143.5
63	3.5	3969	12.25	220.5
10	5.0	100	25.00	50.0
51	4.5	2601	20.25	229.5
24	9.5	576	90.25	228.0
15	8.5	225	72.25	127.5
80	2.6	6400	6.76	208.0
90	2.9	8100	8.41	261.0

Sum	654	113.8	36,974	864.00	2970.2
Mean	36.3333	6.3222			

$$\Sigma(Y_i - \overline{Y})^2 = 36,974 - (654)(36.3333) = 36,974 - 23,762 = 13,212.$$

$$\Sigma(X_i - \overline{X})^2 = 864 - (113.8)(6.3222) = 864 - 719.4664 = 144.5336.$$

$$\Sigma(X_i - \overline{X})^2(Y_i - \overline{Y}) = 2970.2 - 654(6.3222) = 2970.2 - 4134.719 = -1164.519.$$

These three equations are based on the fact that

$$\Sigma(Y_i - \overline{Y})^2 = \Sigma Y_i^2 - (\Sigma Y_i)\overline{Y},$$
$$\Sigma(X_i - \overline{X})^2 = \Sigma X_i^2 - (\Sigma X_i)\overline{X},$$
$$\Sigma(X_i - \overline{X})(Y_i - \overline{Y}) = \Sigma X_i Y_i - (\Sigma Y_i)\overline{X}.$$

Still another formula for r is

$$\frac{\Sigma(x_i - \overline{x})(y_i - \overline{y})}{\sqrt{\Sigma(y_i - \overline{y})^2}\sqrt{\Sigma(x_i - \overline{x})^2}}.$$

Using this formula,

$$r = \frac{-1164.519}{\sqrt{13,213}\sqrt{144.5336}} = \frac{-1164.519}{(114.95)(12.02)}$$

$$= \frac{-1164.519}{1381.699} = -.84.$$

(b) Based on equation (12.2a) in the text,

$$b = \frac{-1164.519}{144.5336} = -8.057,$$

$$a = 36.3333 - (-8.057)(6.3222) = 36.333 + 50.937$$

$$= 87.27.$$

Thus, the sample regression line is

$$\hat{Y} = 87.27 - 8.057X.$$

(c)

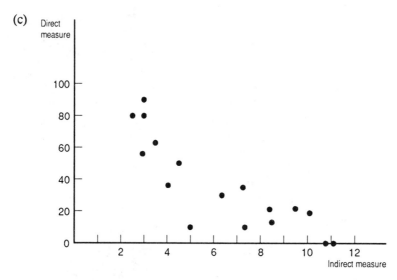

(d) The two measures seem to be correlated reasonably well. Variation in the indirect measure can explain $(.84)^2$, or about 70 percent, of the variation in the direct measure. The relationship between them is inverse, not direct. On the average, the direct measure equals 87.27 minus 8.057 times the indirect measure.

Multiple-Choice Questions

1. (a)   2. (c)   3. (c)   4. (a)   5. (d)   6. (c)   7. (c)   8. (b)   9. (d)
10. (c)   11. (b)

Problems and Problem Sets

1. There seems to be a direct relationship between all pairs of these variables. The highest correlation (about 0.75) is between life expectancy and per capita GDP, life expectancy and percentage of population that is urban, and per capita GDP and percent of population that is urban. Of course, correlations of this sort do not indicate the lines of causation.

2. The regression equation is $\hat{Y} = -25 + 1.18X$, where Y is the 1984 sales of an appliance and X is its 1983 sales. To estimate an appliance's sales, one can use this equation. Since r^2 is about 0.985, this equation seems to fit very well. However, it would be very hazardous to apply this equation to the current situation.

3. One possible problem with this procedure is that one can create a spurious correlation by dividing both the independent and dependent variables by the same quantity (in this case, the firm's sales). This is illustrated in the text by *To Err Is Human . . . But Costly: The Case of Copper and Lead.*

4. (a)

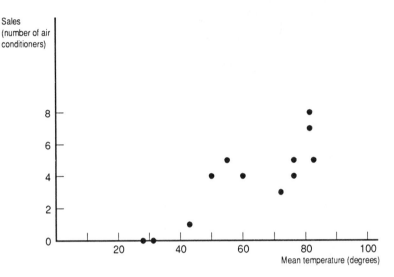

(b) If the calculations must be done by hand, they are as follows:

	X	Y	X²	Y²	XY
	72	3	5184	9	216
	77	4	5929	16	308
	82	7	6724	49	574
	43	1	1849	1	43
	31	0	961	0	0
	28	0	784	0	0
	81	8	6561	64	648
	83	5	6889	25	415
	76	5	5776	25	380
	60	4	3600	16	240
	50	4	2500	16	200
	55	5	3025	25	275
Sum	738	46	49,782	246	3299
Mean	61.5	3.8333			

$$b = \frac{12(3299) - (738)(46)}{12(49,782) - 738^2} = \frac{39,588 - 33,948}{597,384 - 544,644} = \frac{5,640}{52,740} = 0.1069.$$

$$a = 3.8333 - (.1069)(61.5) = 3.8333 - 6.5743 = -2.741.$$

Thus, the sample regression is

$$\hat{Y} = -2.741 + .1069X.$$

(c) $$s_e = \sqrt{\frac{246 + (2.741)(46) - (.1069)(3299)}{10}}$$

$$= \sqrt{\frac{246 + 126.086 - 352.663}{10}}$$

$$= \sqrt{1.9423} = 1.39.$$

Thus, the standard error of estimate equals 1.39 air conditioners.

(d) To begin with, we calculate s_b, the standard error of b.

$$s_b = s_e \sqrt{\frac{1}{\Sigma X_i^2 - n\overline{X}^2}}$$

$$= 1.39 \sqrt{\frac{1}{4395}} = 1.39\left(\frac{1}{66.29}\right) = .021.$$

Since there are 10 degrees of freedom, $t_{.05} = 1.812$. Thus, the 90 percent confidence interval is

$$.1069 \pm (1.812)(.021),$$

or $$.1069 \pm .0381.$$

That is, the confidence interval is .0688 to .1450.

(e) The confidence interval is

$$-2.741 + 1.069(80) \pm t_{.05}(1.39)\sqrt{\frac{1}{12} + \frac{(80 - 61.5)^2}{4395}},$$

$$5.811 \pm (1.812)(1.39)\sqrt{\frac{1}{12} + \frac{342.25}{4395}}$$

or $$= 5.811 \pm 2.5187\sqrt{.0833 + .0779}.$$

Thus, the confidence interval is $5.811 \pm (2.5187)(.4015)$, or 5.811 ± 1.011. In other words, the interval is 4.800 to 6.822.

This confidence interval may be useful because it is an estimate of the mean number of air conditioners the retail outlet will sell in weeks when the temperature is 80°.

(f) Its forecast is

$$-2.741 + .1069(80) = -2.741 + 8.552 = 5.811.$$

The 90 percent prediction interval is

$$5.811 \pm t_{.05}(1.39)\sqrt{\frac{13}{12} + \frac{(80-61.5)^2}{4395}}$$

$$= 5.811 \pm (1.812)(1.39)\sqrt{\frac{13}{12} + \frac{342.25}{4395}}$$

$$= 5.811 \pm 2.5187\sqrt{1.0833 + .0779}.$$

Thus, the prediction interval is 5.811 ± 2.714. In other words, the interval is 3.097 to 8.525.

(g) $r^2 = \dfrac{[12(3299) - (46)(738)]^2}{[12(49,782) - 738^2][12(246) - 46^2]}$

$$= \frac{(39,588 - 33,948)^2}{(597,384 - 544,644)(2952 - 2116)}$$

$$= \frac{5640^2}{(52,740)(836)} = \frac{31,809,600}{44,090,640} = .7214.$$

Thus, the correlation coefficient r equals $\sqrt{.7214}$, or .8494.

$$t = \frac{r}{\sqrt{(1-r^2)/(n-2)}} = \frac{.8494}{\sqrt{(.2786) \div 10}} = \frac{.8494}{\sqrt{.02786}}$$

$$= .8494 \div .1669 = 5.089.$$

Since there are 10 degrees of freedom, $t_{.025} = 2.228$. Because the observed value of t exceeds this value, we must reject the hypothesis that the population correlation coefficient equals zero.

5. (a)

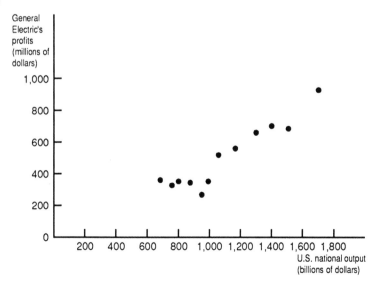

(b) $C2 = -134.54 + .5858C1$

(c) 67.81 millions of dollars.

(d) On the average, a $1 increase in national output seems to be associated with a $.000586 increase in General Electric's profits (recalling that national output is measured in billions of dollars, while General Electric's profits are measured in millions of dollars).

The confidence interval is

$$.586 \pm t_{.05}(.0626),$$

or $$.586 \pm (1.812)(.0626),$$

or $$.586 \pm .113, \text{ or } .473 \text{ to } .699.$$

That is, a $1 increase in national output seems to be associated with a $.000473 to $.000699 increase in General Electric's profits.

(e) The forecast equals $-135 + .586(2,000) = -135 + 1,172 = 1,037$. That is, it equals 1,037 millions of dollars.

The prediction interval equals

$$1,037 \pm t_{.05}(67.81)\sqrt{13/12 + (2,000 - 1,100.42)^2 / 1,171,497}$$

$$= 1,037 \pm (1.812)(67.81)\sqrt{1.083 + 899.58^2 / 1,171,497}$$

$$= 1,037 \pm 122.87\sqrt{1.083 + 809,244 / 1,171,497}$$

$$= 1,037 \pm 122.87\sqrt{1.083 + .691}$$

$$= 1,037 \pm 122.87\sqrt{1.774} = 1,037 \pm (122.87)(1.332)$$

$$= 1,037 \pm 163.66.$$

That is, the prediction interval is 873.34 to 1,200.66 millions of dollars.

This forecast is an extrapolation. For reasons given in the text, this is a hazardous procedure.

(f) The estimate is the same as in part (e), that is, 1,037 millions of dollars.

The confidence interval equals

$$1,037 \pm 122.87\sqrt{1/12 + .691}$$

$$= 1,037 \pm 122.87\sqrt{.083 + .691}$$

$$= 1,037 \pm 122.87\sqrt{.774} = 1,037 \pm (122.87)(.88)$$

$$= 1,037 \pm 108.13.$$

That is, the confidence interval is 928.87 to 1,145.13 millions of dollars.

(g) $r = \sqrt{.897} = .947$.

$$t = .947 \div \sqrt{(1 - .947^2)/10} = .947 \div \sqrt{.002809/10}$$

$$= .947 \div \sqrt{.0002809} = .947 \div .0168 = 56.37.$$

Since $t_{.05} = 1.812$, t exceeds $t_{.05}$. Thus, the null hypothesis (that $\rho = 0$) should be rejected.

(h) No. No. A nonlinear relationship, such as those taken up in Appendix 12.1, might be as good or better.

(i) The size of General Electric's output, the prices General Electric has to pay for inputs, the prices of General Electric's products, and many others.

(j) No. The most recent data should be used for this purpose.

6. (a) Since there are 50 observations and 2 independent variables, $n = 50$ and $k = 2$. If we set $\alpha = .05$ and use a two-tailed test, we should reject the hypothesis of zero serial correlation of the error terms in the regression if the Durbin-Watson statistic is less than 1.38 or greater than 2.62. (See Appendix Table 11.) Since the observed value of this statistic is 1.25, there is evidence of serial correlation in the error terms.

(b) This result indicates that there exists considerable multicollinearity, and that it may be difficult to sort out the effects of the individual independent variables.

(c) It is important that the staff member have good *a priori* reasons for including each of the independent variables. Using stepwise multiple regression, it is not very difficult to find some set of independent variables that "explain" much of the variation in practically any dependent variable, even if these independent variables really have little or no effect on the dependent variable.

7. (a) If we let Y equal sales, X_1 equal mean temperature, and X_2 equal price, the multiple regression equation is

$$\hat{Y} = 1.659 + 0.096\,X_1 - 2.354\,X_2.$$

(b) A sales increase of 0.096 air conditioners.

(c) A sales increase of 0.0235 air conditioners. (Recall that X_2 is measured in hundreds of dollars.)

(d) No. If the price elasticity of demand is constant, it may be better to assume that

$$\log Y_i = A + B_1 \log X_{1i} + B_2 \log X_{2i} + e_i.$$

(See Appendix 12.1.)

PART VI

Time Series and Index Numbers

CHAPTER 14

Introduction to Time Series

Chapter Profile

Attempts are often made to estimate the *trend* of a time series, which is the general long-term movement over time of the series. In some cases, a trend is estimated by regressing the series against time; that is, by calculating a least-squares regression of the series on time. If a nonlinear trend is appropriate, an exponential curve or a quadratic curve may be estimated. If an exponential curve is chosen, the logarithm of each observation should be regressed on time. If a quadratic curve is chosen, each observation should be regressed on both time and the square of time. Another way to find a trend is to calculate a *moving average* of the observations. The basic idea underlying the use of moving averages is that, if the time series contains certain fluctuations or cycles which tend to recur, the effect of these cycles can be eliminated by taking a moving average, where the number of years in the average is equal to the period of the cycle. Another technique that can be used is *exponential smoothing.*

In monthly (or quarterly) time series, *seasonal variation* is likely to be present. To estimate a *seasonal index,* one begins by taking a 12-month moving average of the time series. Since the period of the seasonal cycle is 12 months, a moving average of this sort should deseasonalize the data. To center this moving average on the middle of the month, the moving average centered at the beginning of the month and the one centered at the end of the month should be averaged. Then the ratio of the actual value for each month to the moving average should be computed, and multiplied by 100. For a given month, the seasonal index is the median of these ratios for the month in question (scaled up or down so that the sum of the seasonal indexes is 1200).

Economic time series frequently exhibit certain *cyclical fluctuations,* often termed *the business cycle.* These fluctuations are by no means as regular as the word *cycle* seems to imply. Each cycle can be divided into four phases: *trough, expansion, peak,* and *recession.* Leading indicators, which are certain economic series that go down or up before most others do, are sometimes used to forecast a peak or a trough. Unfortunately, although these indicators are not worthless, they are not very reliable forecasting devices.

Forecasting is one of the most difficult and most important tasks for statisticians. One very simple forecasting device is the extrapolation of a trend computed from past values of the time series. If one is forecasting monthly (or quarterly) values, this forecast should be corrected for seasonal variation. To do this, one can multiply the trend extrapolation by the seasonal index (divided by 100) for the relevant month. Going a step further, one might attempt to modify the resulting forecast for expected cyclical fluctuations. Leading indicators or econometric models may be used to forecast cyclical fluctuations. An econometric model is a system of equations (or a single equation) estimated from past data that is used to forecast economic and business variables.

Behavioral Objectives

A. You should be able to define the following key concepts in this chapter:

time series	seasonal variation
trend	deseasonalized data
linear trend	seasonal index
exponential trend	cyclical variation
quadratic trend	trough
moving averages	expansion
trend extrapolation	peak
leading indicators	recession
serial correlation	exponential smoothing
econometric model	

B. Make sure that you can do each of the following:
1. Describe the nature of a trend, and use the least-squares method to derive a linear trend.
2. Use the least-squares method to calculate an exponential trend.
3. Calculate a moving average to smooth a time series.
4. Use exponential smoothing to smooth a time series.
5. Describe the nature of seasonal variation, and construct a seasonal index.
6. Use a seasonal index to deseasonalize data.
7. Describe the nature of cyclical variation, and describe the four phases of the "business cycle."
8. Use simple trend extrapolation to forecast an economic time series, and use seasonal indexes to include seasonal variation.
9. Describe the nature and usefulness of leading indicators.
10. Describe the nature and purpose of econometric models.

Interest Rates and Monetary Growth: A Case Study

The following chart is a modification of that published by the Council of Economic Advisers in the 1976 *Economic Report of the President:*

(a) If you had to represent the general movement of interest rates during late 1974 and 1975, would you expect a linear regression to fit as well as a quadratic regression (where time is the independent variable)?

(b) M_1 and M_2 are alternative measures of the money supply, M_2 being somewhat more inclusive than M_1. If someone were to regress the growth rate of M_1 (in the chart) on time during the period from the beginning of 1975 to mid-1975, do you think the regression coefficient would be positive or negative?

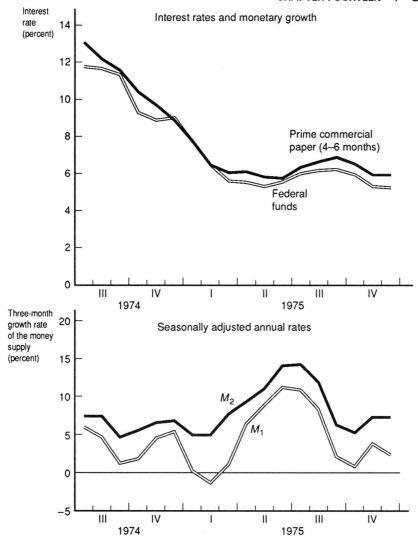

(c) Suppose that someone were to regress the growth rate of M_2 on time during the entire period in the chart. Suppose that the same person were to regress the growth rate of M_1 on time during the entire period in the chart. Do you think the residuals from the former regression would be positively or negatively correlated with the residuals from the latter regression?

Multiple-Choice Questions

1. A statistician calculates a least-squares linear trend based on data for 1962 to 1994. The statistician lets $t' = -16$ for 1962, ..., $t' = 0$ for 1978, ..., $t' = 16$ for 1994. He computes the mean value of the time series (for 1962 to 1994) and finds that it is 12. For 1978, the trend value of the time series is

   (a) 0.

   (b) −16.

   (c) 16.

    (d) 12.
    (e) none of the above.

2. Suppose that the time series of the sales of the Amber Corporation is essentially a purely random sequence of numbers. The Amber Corporation's statistician calculates a five-year moving average of the firm's sales. This moving average is likely to

    (a) exhibit cyclical fluctuations.
    (b) have a different timing of peaks and troughs than the original series.
    (c) be a horizontal line.
    (d) do both (a) and (b).
    (e) do none of the above.

3. The Amber Corporation calculates a seasonal index for its sales. For September, this index equals 90. If the firm's actual sales for September of this year are $90 million, the deseasonalized value of its sales is

    (a) $81 million.
    (b) $100 million.
    (c) $90 million.
    (d) $109 million.
    (e) none of the above.

4. In the case of the Amber Corporation, the sum of the 12 seasonal indexes for the months of the year is

    (a) 100.
    (b) 120.
    (c) 1000.
    (d) 1200.
    (e) none of the above.

5. A 12-month average of the Amber Corporation's sales from June 1994 to May 1995 is centered at

    (a) the beginning of December 1994.
    (b) the middle of December 1994.
    (c) the end of December 1994.
    (d) the middle of November 1994.
    (e) none of the above.

6. For the U.S. economy, late 1981 was a period of

    (a) a trough.
    (b) a recession.
    (c) a peak.
    (d) an expansion.
    (e) none of the above.

7. The Blue Corporation's statistician estimates a least-squares regression of the firm's annual sales on time, the result being $S = 25 + 3t$, where S is the firm's

sales (in millions of dollars) and t is the year minus 1988. Based on the extrapolation of this regression, the firm's sales (in millions of dollars) in 1998 are forecasted to be

(a) 30.
(b) 25.
(c) 55.
(d) 60.
(e) none of the above.

8. Leading indicators

(a) include stock prices.
(b) include business failures.
(c) turn downward in some cases, whereas the economy does not do so subsequently.
(d) do both (a) and (b).
(e) do all the above.

9. A firm extrapolates a quadratic trend of its sales to October 1997, the result being $80 million. The firm knows from past experience that its sales are subject to seasonal variation, and that the seasonal index for October is 104. The firm's forecast of its October 1997 sales is

(a) $80 million ÷ 104.
(b) $80 million × 104.
(c) $80 million ÷ 1.04.
(d) $80 million × 1.04.
(e) none of the above.

Problems and Problem Sets

1. The President's Council of Economic Advisers has published the following graph:

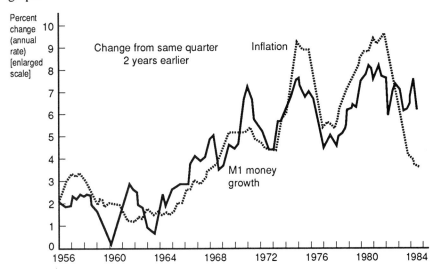

(a) During this 28-year period, was there a close relationship between money growth and the rate of inflation?

(b) Was there a trend in money growth? In inflation? If so, were these trends similar?

(c) Would you expect cyclical variation in money growth? In inflation? Why or why not?

2. A retail store has sales of $2.8 million in November and $3.1 million in December. For this firm's sales, the seasonal index is 95 in November and 110 in December. A local newspaper runs a story saying that the store's sales were depressed in November because of a recession, but that they bounced back in December, and thus indicate that a recovery was under way. Do you agree? Why or why not?

3. Suppose that you were an executive at General Electric in 1977, and that you wanted to calculate the trend in General Electric's sales. The firm's sales during 1950–76 were as follows:

Year	Sales (billions of dollars)	Year	Sales (billions of dollars)
1950	2.2	1964	4.9
1951	2.6	1965	6.2
1952	3.0	1966	7.2
1953	3.5	1967	7.7
1954	3.3	1968	8.4
1955	3.5	1969	8.4
1956	4.1	1970	8.8
1957	4.3	1971	9.6
1958	4.2	1972	10.5
1959	4.5	1973	11.9
1960	4.2	1974	13.9
1961	4.5	1975	14.1
1962	4.8	1976	15.7
1963	4.9		

(a) Using the method of least squares, derive a linear trend. Use a computer software package, if available; otherwise, do the calculations by hand.

(b) Plot General Electric's sales in the graph below. Also, plot the trend line derived in (a).

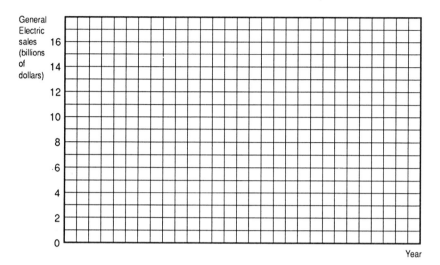

(c) Does a visual inspection of how well the linear trend fits suggest that an exponential trend would do better? That a quadratic trend would do better?

(d) Calculate a five-year moving average of General Electric's sales.

(e) Calculate a seven-year moving average of General Electric's sales.

(f) Calculate a nine-year moving average of General Electric's sales.

4. (a) Following up on the previous problem, suppose that in 1977 you had been asked to use the linear trend in problem 3(a) to forecast General Electric's 1995 sales by trend extrapolation. What would your forecast have been?

(b) With the advantages of hindsight, indicate whether you see anything questionable about this forecast. If so, what?

5. The Morse Corporation, a hypothetical producer of landing gear, had the following monthly sales:

Month	Sales (millions of dollars)		
	1992	*1993*	*1994*
January	2	3	3
February	3	4	5
March	4	5	4
April	5	6	6
May	6	7	7
June	7	8	8
July	8	8	9
August	7	7	8
September	6	6	7
October	5	5	6
November	4	3	5
December	3	4	3

(a) Calculate a 12-month moving average of this firm's sales.

(b) Using the results from (a), center the moving average at the middle of each month.

(c) Calculate a seasonal index for the Morse Corporation's sales, based on the results from (a) and (b).

(d) In 1995, the Morse Corporation's sales increased from $7 million in April to $8 million in May. Allowing for the seasonal variation, did sales increase from April to May?

6. Suppose that the Acme Corporation finds that a linear trend for its sales is

$$S = 5 + 0.1t,$$

where S is the firm's monthly sales (in millions of dollars) and t is measured in months from January 1989.

(a) Based on this trend alone, what are the forecasted sales for the firm in February 1997?

(b) Based on past experience, the Acme Corporation estimates that the seasonal index for February is 109. How can this information be used to modify the forecast in (a)? What assumptions underlie this modification? Once this modification is made, what is the forecast of the Acme Corporation's sales in February 1997?

7. The Alpha Corporation wants to calculate an exponentially smoothed time series from the following data:

1986	2	1991	28
1987	4	1992	38
1988	8	1993	50
1989	12	1994	70
1990	20	1995	90

(a) Calculate an exponentially smoothed time series, letting the smoothing constant equal 1/4.

(b) Calculate an exponentially smoothed time series, letting the smoothing constant equal 1/2.

(c) Calculate an exponentially smoothed time series, letting the smoothing constant equal 3/4.

Answers

Interest Rates and Monetary Growth: A Case Study
(a) No, the relationship looks curvilinear rather than linear.
(b) Positive, since the chart shows that the M_1 growth rate tended to increase during the period from the beginning of 1975 to mid-1975.
(c) Based on an inspection of the chart, it appears that the residuals would tend to be positively correlated.

Multiple-Choice Questions
  1. (d)   2. (d)   3. (b)   4. (d)   5. (a)   6. (b)   7. (c)   8. (e)   9. (d)

Problems and Problem Sets
1. (a) Yes. However, there is debate over the line of causation.
   (b) For most of this period, there were upward trends in both the rate of growth of the money supply and the rate of increase of the price level.
   (c) Yes, since both play a major role in business fluctuations.
2. From seasonal variation alone we would expect December's sales to be $110 \div 95 = 1.158$ times November's sales. In fact, December's sales were $3.1 \div 2.8 = 1.107$ times November's sales. Thus, allowing for seasonal variation, sales fell from November to December.
3. (a) If you must calculate the trend by hand, the calculations are as follows: Let $t' = 0$ when $t = 1963$. Let y be General Electric's sales.

t'	y	$(t')^2$	y^2	$t'y$
−13	2.2	169	4.84	−28.6
−12	2.6	144	6.76	−31.2
−11	3.0	121	9.00	−33.0
−10	3.5	100	12.25	−35.0
−9	3.3	81	10.89	−29.7
−8	3.5	64	12.25	−28.0
−7	4.1	49	16.81	−28.7
−6	4.3	36	18.49	−25.8
−5	4.2	25	17.64	−21.0
−4	4.5	16	20.25	−18.0
−3	4.2	9	17.64	−12.6
−2	4.5	4	20.25	−9.0
−1	4.8	1	23.04	−4.8
0	4.9	0	24.01	0.0
1	4.9	1	24.01	4.9

t'	y	$(t')^2$	y^2	$t'y$
2	6.2	4	38.44	12.4
3	7.2	9	51.84	21.6
4	7.7	16	59.29	30.8
5	8.4	25	70.56	42.0
6	8.4	36	70.56	50.4
7	8.8	49	77.44	61.6
8	9.6	64	92.16	76.8
9	10.5	81	110.25	94.5
10	11.9	100	141.61	119.0
11	13.9	121	193.21	152.9
12	14.1	144	198.81	169.2
13	15.7	169	246.49	204.1

Sum	0	180.9	1638	1,588.79	734.8
Mean	0	6.7			

$$b = \frac{734.8 - (180.9)(0)}{1638 - (0)(0)} = \frac{734.8}{1638} = .449.$$

$$a = 6.7 - (.449)(0) = 6.7.$$

Thus, the trend is $6.7 + .449t'$.

(b)

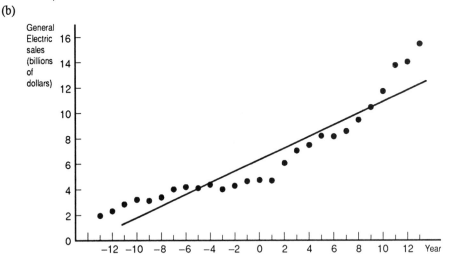

(c) It appears from the graph that the trend may be curvilinear, and that an exponential or quadratic trend might do better.

(d) (e) and (f)

Year	G.E.'s sales (billions) of dollars)	5-year moving total	7-year moving total	9-year moving total	5-year moving average	7-year moving average	9-year moving average
					(millions of dollars)		
1950	2.2						
1951	2.6						
1952	3.0	14.6			2.92		
1953	3.5	15.9	22.2		3.18	3.17	
1954	3.3	17.4	24.3	30.7	3.48	3.47	3.41
1955	3.5	18.7	25.9	33.0	3.74	3.70	3.67
1956	4.1	19.4	27.4	34.6	3.88	3.91	3.84
1957	4.3	20.6	28.1	36.1	4.12	4.01	4.01
1958	4.2	21.3	29.3	37.4	4.26	4.19	4.16
1959	4.5	21.7	30.6	39.0	4.34	4.37	4.33
1960	4.2	22.2	31.4	40.4	4.44	4.49	4.49
1961	4.5	22.9	32.0	42.5	4.58	4.57	4.72
1962	4.8	23.3	34.0	45.4	4.66	4.86	5.04
1963	4.9	25.3	36.7	48.9	5.06	5.24	5.43
1964	4.9	28.0	40.2	52.8	5.60	5.74	5.87
1965	6.2	30.9	44.1	57.0	6.18	6.30	6.33
1966	7.2	34.4	47.7	61.3	6.88	6.81	6.81
1967	7.7	37.9	51.6	66.1	7.58	7.37	7.34
1968	8.4	40.5	56.3	71.7	8.10	8.04	7.97
1969	8.4	42.9	60.6	78.7	8.58	8.66	8.74
1970	8.8	45.7	65.3	86.4	9.14	9.33	9.60
1971	9.6	49.2	71.5	93.3	9.84	10.21	10.37
1972	10.5	54.7	77.2	101.3	10.94	11.03	11.26
1973	11.9	60.0	84.5		12.00	12.07	
1974	13.9	66.1			13.22		
1975	14.1						
1976	15.7						

4. (a) 6.7 + .449(32)= 6.7 + 14.4 = 21.1 Thus, the forecast is $21.1 billions.
   (b) This forecast is below General Electric's sales in 1985, which were about $27.9 billions. Thus, this forecast seems much too low. (In 1992, its sales were about $59 billions.)

5. (a) and (b)

	12-month moving sum of sales	*12-month moving average (millions of dollars)*	*Centered 12-month moving average*
June			
July	60	5.000	5.042
August	61	5.083	5.125
September	62	5.167	5.208
October	63	5.250	5.292
November	64	5.333	5.375
December	65	5.417	5.458
January	66	5.500	5.500
February	66	5.500	5.500
March	66	5.500	5.500
April	66	5.500	5.500
May	66	5.500	5.458
June	65	5.417	5.458
July	66	5.500	5.500
August	66	5.500	5.542
September	67	5.583	5.542
October	66	5.500	5.500
November	66	5.500	5.500
December	66	5.500	5.500
January	66	5.500	5.542
February	67	5.583	5.625
March	68	5.667	5.708
April	69	5.750	5.792
May	70	5.833	5.916
June	72	6.000	5.958
July	71	5.917	

(c) The calculation of each month's actual sales as a ratio of the centered moving average is shown below:

Month	Actual sales	Centered moving average	Ratio
		(millions of dollars)	
July	8	5.042	1.587
August	7	5.125	1.366
September	6	5.208	1.152
October	5	5.292	0.945
November	4	5.375	0.744
December	3	5.458	0.550
January	3	5.500	0.545
February	4	5.500	0.727
March	5	5.500	0.909
April	6	5.500	1.091
May	7	5.458	1.282
June	8	5.458	1.466
July	8	5.500	1.455
August	7	5.542	1.263
September	6	5.542	1.083
October	5	5.500	0.909
November	3	5.500	0.545
December	4	5.500	0.727
January	3	5.542	0.541
February	5	5.625	0.889
March	4	5.708	0.701
April	6	5.792	1.036
May	7	5.916	1.183
June	8	5.958	1.343

The computation of the seasonal index is as follows:

Month	Ratios		Median	Index[1]
January	0.545	0.541	0.543	54.2
February	0.727	0.889	0.808	80.7
March	0.909	0.701	0.805	80.4
April	1.091	1.036	1.064	106.3
May	1.282	1.183	1.232	123.0
June	1.466	1.343	1.404	140.2
July	1.587	1.455	1.521	151.9
August	1.366	1.263	1.314	131.2
September	1.152	1.083	1.117	111.5
October	0.945	0.909	0.927	92.6
November	0.744	0.545	0.644	64.3
December	0.550	0.727	0.638	63.7
Sum			12.017	1200.0

1. To obtain the index, we multiply each figure in the previous column by 12.000/12.017, and multiply the results by 100.

(d) Between April and May we would expect an increase of $(123.0/106.3 - 1)100$, or 15.7 percent. Thus, this increase of 14.3 percent in 1995 is somewhat less than would be expected. Allowing for seasonal variation, sales decreased between April and May in 1995.

6. (a) If January 1989 is $t = 0$, then February 1997 is $t = 97$. Thus, the forecasted value of sales is

$$5 + 0.1(97) = 5 + 9.7 = 14.7.$$

That is, the forecast is $14.7 million.

(b) Using this information, we can try to include seasonal factors as well as trend in the forecast. If we are willing to assume that the seasonal variation in the future will be like that in the past, the forecast is

$$(1.09)(14.7) = 16.02.$$

That is, the forecast is $16.02 million.

7. (a) $S_0 = 2$.
$S_1 = (1/4)(4) + (3/4)(2) = 2.50$.
$S_2 = (1/4)(8) + (3/4)(2.50) = 3.88$.
$S_3 = (1/4)(12) + (3/4)(3.88) = 5.91$.
$S_4 = (1/4)(20) + (3/4)(5.91) = 9.43$.
$S_5 = (1/4)(28) + (3/4)(9.43) = 14.07$
$S_6 = (1/4)(38) + (3/4)(14.07) = 9.50 + 10.55 = 20.05$.
$S_7 = (1/4)(50) + (3/4)(20.05) = 12.50 + 15.04 = 27.54$.
$S_8 = (1/4)(70) + (3/4)(27.54) = 17.50 + 20.66 = 38.16$.
$S_9 = (1/4)(90) + (3/4)(38.16) = 22.50 + 28.62 = 51.12$.

(b) $S_0 = 2$.
$S_1 = (1/2)(4) + (1/2)(2) = 3.00$.
$S_2 = (1/2)(8) + (1/2)(3.00) = 5.50$.
$S_3 = (1/2)(12) + (1/2)(5.50) = 8.75$.
$S_4 = (1/2)(20) + (1/2)(8.75) = 14.38$.
$S_5 = (1/2)(28) + (1/2)(14.38) = 21.19$.
$S_6 = (1/2)(38) + (1/2)(21.19) = 29.60$.
$S_7 = (1/2)(50) + (1/2)(29.60) = 39.80$.
$S_8 = (1/2)(70) + (1/2)(39.80) = 54.90$.
$S_9 = (1/2)(90) + (1/2)(54.90) = 72.45$.

(c) $S_0 = 2$.
$S_1 = (3/4)(4) + (1/4)(2) = 3.50$.
$S_2 = (3/4)(8) + (1/4)(3.50) = 6.88$.
$S_3 = (3/4)(12) + (1/4)(6.88) = 10.72$.
$S_4 = (3/4)(20) + (1/4)(10.72) = 17.68$.
$S_5 = (3/4)(28) + (1/4)(17.68) = 25.42$.
$S_6 = (3/4)(38) + (1/4)(25.42) = 28.50 + 6.36 = 34.86$.
$S_7 = (3/4)(50) + (1/4)(34.86) = 37.50 + 8.72 = 46.22$.
$S_8 = (3/4)(70) + (1/4)(46.22) = 52.50 + 11.56 = 64.06$.
$S_9 = (3/4)(90) + (1/4)(64.06) = 67.50 + 16.02 = 83.52$.

CHAPTER 15

Index Numbers

Chapter Profile

Index numbers are often used to measure changes in prices, quantities, and other items. Every index number that measures changes over time refers to some *base period,* which is the period from which all changes are measured. Each such index number also refers to a *given period,* which is the period that is compared with the base period. To illustrate the various types of index numbers, let's focus on an index of prices. Suppose that the prices of m commodities will be included in the index, and that P_{01} is the price of the first commodity in the base period, P_{11} is its price in the given period, P_{02} is the price of the second commodity in the base period, P_{12} is its price in the given period, and so on.

The *simple aggregative price index* is $100 \left(\sum_{i=1}^{m} P_{1i} \div \sum_{i=1}^{m} P_{0i} \right)$. One major

difficulty with an index of this sort is that the result depends on the units in which the commodities are expressed. The *average of relatives* gets around this difficulty:

It is equal to $100 \left(\sum_{i=1}^{m} \frac{P_{1i}}{P_{0i}} \div m \right)$. However, an unweighted index of this sort has the

disadvantage that the prices are not equally important. In order to remedy this deficiency, statisticians generally use weighted index numbers.

One important kind of weighted index number is the *Laspeyres index.* Its formula is

$$100 \left(\sum_{i=1}^{m} Q_{0i} P_{1i} \div \sum_{i=1}^{m} Q_{0i} P_{0i} \right),$$

where Q_{0i} is the amount consumed in the ith commodity in the base period, and Q_{1i} is the amount consumed of this commodity in the given period. Another important kind of weighted index number is the *Paasche index.* Its formula is

$$100 \left(\sum_{i=1}^{m} Q_{1i} P_{1i} \div \sum_{i=1}^{m} Q_{1i} P_{0i} \right).$$

The Paasche index has the disadvantage that, if the index is a series calculated repeatedly over time, fresh data have to be obtained for each period concerning the weights (that is, concerning the Q_{1i}).

It is also possible to use weights that pertain to some period other than the base period or the given period. Frequently, the weights refer to an average of several years. Chain index numbers—index numbers that measure changes from one period to the next—are often used also.

Probably the most famous price index calculated by the government is the Consumer Price Index, which is issued monthly by the Bureau of Labor Statistics. An important output index is the Index of Industrial Production, which is computed monthly by the Federal Reserve Board.

Behavioral Objectives

A. You should be able to define the following key concepts in this chapter:

base period   Paasche index
given period   fixed-weight aggregative index
unweighted index number   reference base
simple aggregative index   chain index numbers
average of relatives   Consumer Price Index
weighted index number   real wages
Laspeyres index   Index of Industrial Production

B. Make sure that you can do each of the following:
   1. Construct a simple aggregative index, and indicate the very substantial disadvantages in such an index.
   2. Construct a simple average of relatives, and indicate the disadvantages of such an index.
   3. Construct a Laspeyres index of prices (or output).
   4. Construct a Paasche index of prices (or output).
   5. Discuss the choice of a period to which the weights should pertain, and discuss the choice of a base period.
   6. Describe the nature and uses of chain index numbers.
   7. Describe the purposes, nature, and construction of the Consumer Price Index.
   8. Discuss the application of the Consumer Price Index to the measurement of inflation and to escalator clauses.
   9. Describe the purposes, nature, and construction of the Index of Industrial Production.

The Index of Industrial Production: A Case Study

The following is a quotation from the Federal Reserve Board's 1972 book concerning its Index of Industrial Production:[1]

The effects on the total index of the use of alternative weight years for the separate periods beginning in 1954 are presented in Table One. The top figure in the first column indicates a rise of 11.7 per cent from 1954 to 1958 if 1954 weights are used. The figures below indicate that for the same time period the total index would rise by 10.5 per cent with 1958 weights, 10.0 with 1963 weights, and 9.4 with 1967 weights. For the whole period 1954–70, the increases ranged from a high of 110.0 per cent using 1954 weights to a low of 96.5 using 1967 weights. As the table shows, the changes in the monthly index

---

1. Federal Reserve Board, *Industrial Production* (Washington, D.C.: U.S. Government Printing Office, 1972), p. 56.

differ slightly from these percentages in each of the first three periods, and as a result the increase shown by the monthly index from 1954 to 1970 is 105.4 per cent rather than the 106.6 per cent that would be obtained by combining the changes shown in the circled blocks. Changes from 1954 to 1970 that might have been calculated by averaging the weights for 1954 to 1967 or by using weights for the single year 1958 over the whole period would have differed little from the changes shown by the monthly linked index.

TABLE 1
Effects of Alternative Weight Periods

	Time period				
Weight periods	1954 to 1958	1958 to 1963	1963 to 1967	1967 to 1970	1954 to 1970
	Percentage increase				
1954	11.7	32.1	31.5	8.4	110.0
1958	10.5	32.2	31.3	7.4	106.1
1963	10.0	31.4	31.1	7.0	102.7
1967	9.4	30.8	28.7	6.6	96.5
					106.6
Monthly index	11.6	32.1	30.7	6.7	103.4
	Annual rates compounded				
1954	2.8	5.7	7.1	2.7	4.7
1958	2.5	5.7	7.1	2.4	4.6
1963	2.4	5.6	7.0	2.3	4.5
1967	2.3	5.5	6.5	2.2	4.3
					4.6
Monthly index	2.8	5.7	6.9	2.2	4.6

(a) In general, do later-year weights yield smaller or larger increases in the index?
(b) What do you think accounts for the fact that later-year weights result in this difference?

Multiple-Choice Questions

1. The *Economic Report of the President* reported that in 1981 the Consumer Price Index for medical care was 294.5 and the Consumer Price Index for food was 274.6(1967 = 100). Thus, the percentage increase in the price of medical care during 1967–81 divided by the percentage increase in the price of food was about

   (a) $294.5 \div 274.6 = 1.072$.
   (b) $274.6 \div 294.5 = 0.932$.
   (c) $194.5 \div 174.6 = 1.114$.
   (d) $174.6 \div 194.5 = 0.898$.
   (e) none of the above

2. According to the *Economic Report of the President,* the Producer Price Index equaled 178.7 in December 1975, and 49.1 in 1929. Thus, producer prices, on the average were

    (a) more than three times as high in 1929 as in December 1975.
    (b) between two and three times as high in 1929 as in December 1975.
    (c) about as high in 1929 as in December 1975.
    (d) between two and three times as high in December 1975 as in 1929.
    (e) more than three times as high in December 1975 as in 1929.

3. In December 1975, the Producer Price Index for farm products equaled 186.0, and the Producer Price Index for industrial commodities equaled 176.1. From this we can be sure that

    (a) the price of farm products was higher than the price of industrial commodities in December 1975.
    (b) the price of farm products was lower than the price of industrial commodities in December 1975.
    (c) the price of farm products was equal to the price of industrial commodities in December 1975.
    (d) the base year was 1929.
    (e) we can be sure of none of the above.

4. During the base period, an index number

    (a) equals 100, and this is the only time when it equals 100.
    (b) is greater than 100.
    (c) is less than 100.
    (d) equals 100, and this is not necessarily the only time when it equals 100.
    (e) is undefined.

5. According to the Department of Agriculture, the prices (in dollars per hundred pounds) received by farmers for hogs, cattle, and lambs were as follows in 1960, 1970, and 1974:

Year	Hogs	Cattle	Lambs
1960	15.30	20.40	17.90
1970	22.70	27.10	26.40
1974	34.20	35.60	37.00

    If 1960 is the base period and 1974 is the given period, a simple aggregative index of these three prices would equal

    (a) 201.6.
    (b) 192.4.
    (c) 196.5.
    (d) 199.3.
    (e) 194.5.

6. If 1969 is the base period and 1974 is the given period, a simple average of relatives of the three prices in question 5 would equal

   (a) 201.6.
   (b) 192.4.
   (c) 196.5.
   (d) 199.3.
   (e) 194.5.

7. Suppose that the number of pounds of hogs sold in 1960 equaled the number of pounds of lamb sold, but equaled one-half the number of pounds of cattle sold. Under these circumstances, if 1960 is the base period and 1974 is the given period, the Laspeyres index of the three prices in question 5 would equal

   (a) 201.6.
   (b) 192.4.
   (c) 196.5.
   (d) 199.3.
   (e) 194.5.

8. Suppose that the number of pounds of hogs sold and the number of pounds of lamb sold increased by 50 percent between 1960 and 1974, whereas the number of pounds of cattle sold was the same in 1974 as in 1960. Under these circumstances (and those described in the previous question), if 1960 is the base period and 1974 is the given period, the Paasche index of the three prices in question 5 would equal

   (a) 201.6.
   (b) 192.4.
   (c) 196.5.
   (d) 199.3.
   (e) 194.5.

9. Irving Fisher's "ideal" index (see Exercise 15.5 in the text) is the _____ of the Laspeyres index and the Paasche index.

   (a) mean
   (b) median
   (c) greater
   (d) lesser
   (e) geometric mean

10. According to the 1993 *Economic Report of the President,* the gross domestic product—in real terms—decreased by about 1.2 percent between 1990 and 1991. In money terms, the gross domestic product increased by about 2.8 percent between 1990 and 1991. Thus, between 1990 and 1991 the general price level must have

    (a) increased by about 7 percent.
    (b) increased by about 5 percent.

(c) increased by about 4 percent.

(d) increased by about 2 percent.

(e) decreased.

11. If a Laspeyres output index is constructed, in which the given year is 1994 and the base year is 1980, the weights are

(a) 1980 outputs.

(b) 1994 outputs.

(c) 1980 prices.

(d) 1994 prices.

(e) none of the above.

Problems and Problem Sets

1. According to the 1993 *Economic Report of the President,* output per hour of labor in the business sector of the U.S. economy was 113.5 in the third quarter of 1992, where 1982 = 100.

(a) Is 113.5 an index number?

(b) If it is an index number, what is the base period? What is the given period?

(c) Did output per hour of labor grow by about 2 percent per year during 1982–92?

2. According to *Business Week,* July 7, 1986, the *Business Week* production index equaled 156.1 then, as compared with 155.1 a year before.

   (a) By what percentage did production change during the previous year, based on this index?

   (b) According to *Business Week,* this index averaged 100.0 in 1967. By what percentage did production change between 1967 and mid-1985, based on this index?

3. In 1993, Betsy Bunker spent $300 a week, half on food and half on housing. (For simplicity, we suppose that she purchases only these two goods.) Between 1993 and 1994, the price of food increased by 6 percent and the price of housing increased by 4 percent. Calculate a Laspeyres price index for the things she buys, where 1993 is the base year and 1994 is the given year.

4. An economist is asked to compare the present rate of change of wages with those during 1960–75. He begins by obtaining relevant data for 1960–75. According to the Bureau of Labor Statistics, average hourly earnings in manufacturing, contract construction, and retail trade were as follows in 1960, 1965, 1970, and 1975:

Average hourly earnings (dollars)

Year	Manufacturing	Construction	Retail trade
1960	2.26	3.08	1.52
1965	2.61	3.70	1.82
1970	3.36	5.24	2.44
1975	4.81	7.24	3.33

(a) Using 1960 as the base period, calculate a simple average of relatives to represent the changes over time in average hourly earnings in these industries during 1960–75.

(b) According to the Bureau of Labor Statistics, the number of workers in manufacturing, contract construction, and retail trade was (approximately) as follows in 1960, 1965, 1970, and 1975:

Number of workers (millions)

Year	Manufacturing	Construction	Retail trade
1960	17	3	11
1965	18	3	13
1970	19	4	15
1975	18	3	17

Using 1960 as the base period, calculate a Laspeyres index of average hourly earnings in these industries in 1960, 1965, 1970, and 1975.

(c) Calculate a Paasche index of average hourly earnings in these industries, where 1960 is the base year and 1975 is the given year.

(d) Suppose that 1965 is regarded as a much more normal year than 1960 or 1975. Calculate a fixed-weight aggregative index for average hourly earnings in these industries where the weights pertain to 1965.

(e) Write a short paragraph summarizing your findings in (a) to (d) concerning the extent to which average hourly earnings increased between 1960 and 1975. To what extent do your findings depend on the type of index number used? What are the relative advantages and disadvantages of the various index numbers you computed?

5. It frequently is necessary to change the base period of an index number series. This generally is accomplished by dividing each value of the index number (based on the *old* base period) by the value of the index number for the new base period (based on the *old* base period), and then multiplying the result by 100. For example, if one wanted to shift the base of a price index from 1990 to 1993, one would divide all the old index numbers by the old value of the index in 1993 and then multiply the resulting numbers by 100. The Producer Price Index for selected years was as follows:

1950	81.8
1960	94.9
1970	110.4
1975	174.9

These index numbers are based on a base period of 1967. Compute these index numbers with a base period of 1970 rather than 1967.

6. The Consumer Price Index (with a base year of 1967) was as follows during the early 1970s:

1971	121.3
1972	125.3
1973	133.1
1974	147.7
1975	161.2

An economic historian wants to shift the base to 1973. In other words, he wants to compute these index numbers with a base period of 1973 rather than 1967. Can you help him out?

7. The economic historian in the previous problem is also interested in average hourly earnings during the 1970s. For Los Angeles, the Consumer Price Index equaled 129.2 in 1973 and 142.5 in 1974. Suppose that average weekly earnings in Los Angeles were $250 in 1973 and $300 in 1974. Expressed in 1973 dollars, how large were average weekly earnings in Los Angeles in 1974?

8. Index numbers can be used to represent spatial or international differences as well as differences over time. The economic historian in the previous two problems is concerned with unemployment during the 1970s. The adjusted unemployment rate of six major countries in the first quarter of 1976 were as follows:

Country	Percent
Canada	6.8
United States	7.5
Japan	2.1
France	4.2
Germany	3.9
Italy	3.6

Letting the U.S. unemployment rate equal 100, calculate an index number for each of the other countries' unemployment rates during the first quarter of 1976.

9. The economic historian discussed above is also concerned with production during the 1960s and 1970s. The amounts of copper, lead, and zinc produced in the United States in 1960, 1970, and 1974 were as follows:

Year	Copper (millions of pounds)	Lead (thousands of tons)	Zinc (thousands of tons)
1960	2,286	229	334
1970	3,439	572	534
1974	3,194	669	500

SOURCE: *World Almanac.*

(a) Using 1960 as the base period, calculate a simple average of relatives to represent the changes over time in the overall production of these three metals.

(b) The prices of copper, lead, and zinc in the United States in 1960, 1970, and 1974 were approximately as follows:

Year	Copper (cents per pound)	Lead (dollars per ton)	Zinc (dollars per ton)
1960	32	240	260
1970	58	320	300
1974	77	460	720

Using 1960 as the base period, calculate a Laspeyres index of the overall production of these three metals, where 1974 is the given year.

(c) Calculate a Paasche index of overall production of these three metals where the given year is 1974 and the base year is 1960.

    (d) Calculate Fisher's "ideal" index of overall production of these three metals, where the given year is 1974 and the base year is 1960. (See Exercise 15.5.)

    (e) Summarize your findings in (a) to (d) in a short paragraph. Compare the results based on different types of production indexes and describe the advantages and disadvantages of each type.

10. It sometimes is necessary to "splice" two or more series of index numbers. For example, suppose that one index number series represents the output of steel in Pennsylvania from 1930 to 1960 and another index number series represents the output of steel in Pennsylvania from 1960 to 1990. In particular, suppose that the two index number series are as follows:

Year	Index I (1930 = 100)	Index II (1960 = 100)
1930	100	
1940	110	
1950	120	
1960	125	100
1970		115
1980		130
1990		140

(a) Using these two separate series, form a single index number series that goes from 1930 to 1990 with a base period of 1930.

(b) Form a single index number series for steel production in Pennsylvania from 1930 to 1990 with a base of 1960.

(c) Form a single index number series that goes from 1930 to 1990 with a base period of 1990.

Answers

The Index of Industrial Production: A Case Study

(a) Later-year weights yield smaller increases in the index.

(b) The Federal Reserve Board explains this fact as follows: "As has been noted many times in the literature of index numbers, relatively large increases in production series from one weight year to another are likely to be accompanied by relatively small increases in prices (in this case value-added prices). Consequently when weights are updated, the relative importance of industries that have been growing rapidly (but may not continue to do so in the next period) is reduced, and that of industries that have been growing slowly is increased."[2]

Multiple-Choice Questions

1. (c)   2. (e)   3. (e)   4. (d)   5. (d)   6. (a)   7. (b)   8. (c)   9. (e)
10. (c)   11. (c)

Problems and Problem Sets

1. (a) Yes.
   (b) 1982 is the base period; the third quarter of 1992 is the given period.
   (c) No.
2. (a) .6 percent.
   (b) There was a 55.1 percent increase.
3. Let Q_{01} and P_{01} be the amount she purchased and the price she paid for food in 1993, Q_{02} and P_{02} be the amount she purchased and the price she paid for housing in 1993, Q_{11} and P_{11} be the amount she purchased and the price she paid for food in 1994, and Q_{12} and P_{12} be the amount she purchased and the price she paid for housing in 1994. Then the Laspeyres price index equals

$$100 \left(\frac{Q_{01}P_{11} + Q_{02}P_{12}}{Q_{01}P_{01} + Q_{02}P_{02}} \right) = 100 \left[\frac{Q_{01}P_{01}}{Q_{01}P_{01} + Q_{02}P_{02}} \left(\frac{P_{11}}{P_{01}} \right) + \frac{Q_{02}P_{02}}{Q_{01}P_{01} + Q_{02}P_{02}} \left(\frac{P_{12}}{P_{02}} \right) \right]$$

$$= 100 [.50(1.06) + .50(1.04)]$$

$$= 105.$$

4. (a) The relatives (times 100) are:

Year	Manufacturing	Construction	Retail trade
1960	100.0	100.0	100.0
1965	115.5	120.1	119.7
1970	148.7	170.1	160.5
1975	212.8	235.1	219.1

The average of relatives (times 100) are:

1960: 100.0
1965: 118.4
1970: 159.8
1975: 222.3

2. *Ibid.*, pp. 56–57.

(b) For 1965, $\Sigma Q_{0i}P_{1i} = 17(2.61) + 3(3.70) + 11(1.82) = 75.49$, and $\Sigma Q_{0i}P_{0i} = 17(2.26) + 3(3.08) + 11(1.52) = 64.38$. Thus, the index for 1965 equals 100 times $75.49 \div 64.38 = 117.3$.

For 1970, $\Sigma Q_{0i}P_{1i} = 17(3.36) + 3(5.24) + 11(2.44) = 99.68$. Thus, the index for 1970 equals 100 times $99.68 \div 64.38 = 154.8$.

For 1975, $\Sigma Q_{0i}P_{1i} = 17(4.81) + 3(7.24) + 11(3.33) = 140.12$. Thus, the index for 1975 equals 100 times $140.12 \div 64.38 = 217.6$.

Finally, the index for 1960 must equal 100.0.

(c) $\Sigma Q_{1i}P_{1i} = 18(4.81) + 3(7.24) + 17(3.33) = 164.91$.
$\Sigma Q_{1i}P_{0i} = 18(2.26) + 3(3.08) + 17(1.52) = 75.76$.
Thus, the index for 1975 equals 100 times $164.91 \div 75.76 = 217.7$.

(d) For 1960, the index must equal 100.0.

For 1965, $\Sigma Q_{Wi}P_{1i} = 18(2.61) + 3(3.70) + 13(1.82) = 81.74$, and $\Sigma Q_{Wi}P_{0i} = 18(2.26) + 3(3.08) + 13(1.52) = 69.68$. Thus, the index for 1965 equals 100 times $81.74 \div 69.68 = 117.3$.

For 1970, $\Sigma Q_{Wi}P_{1i} = 18(3.36) + 3(5.24) + 13(2.44) = 107.92$. Thus, the index for 1970 equals 100 times $107.92 \div 69.68 = 154.9$.

For 1975, $\Sigma Q_{Wi}P_{1i} = 18(4.81) + 3(7.24) + 13(3.33) = 151.59$. Thus, the index for 1975 equals 100 times $151.59 \div 69.68 = 217.6$.

(e) A comparison of the results of (a) to (d) is given below:

Year	Simple average of relatives	Laspeyres	Paasche	1965 weights
1960	100.0	100.0	100.0	100.0
1965	118.4	117.3	—	117.3
1970	159.8	154.8	—	154,9
1975	222.3	217.6	217.7	217.6

The results of the various indexes are reasonably similar. They all indicate an increase of about 18 percent during 1960–65, an increase of about 55–60 percent during 1960–70, and an increase of about 118–122 percent during 1960–75.

5. The index number for 1950 equals 100 times $81.8 \div 110.4 = 74.1$.
The index number for 1960 equals 100 times $94.9 \div 110.4 = 86.0$.
The index number for 1970 equals 100 times $110.4 \div 110.4 = 100.0$.
The index number for 1975 equals 100 times $174.9 \div 110.4 = 158.4$.

6. The index number for 1971 equals 100 times $121.3 \div 133.1 = 91.1$.
The index number for 1972 equals 100 times $125.3 \div 133.1 = 94.1$.
The index number for 1973 equals 100 times $133.1 \div 133.1 = 100.0$.
The index number for 1974 equals 100 times $147.7 \div 133.1 = 111.0$.
The index number for 1975 equals 100 times $161.2 \div 133.1 = 121.1$.

7. $\$300 \div 142.5/129.2 = \$300 \div 1.103 = \$272$.

8. Canada: $100(6.8/7.5) = 90.7$.
United States: $100(7.5/7.5) = 100.0$.
Japan: $100(2.1/7.5) = 28.0$.
France: $100(4.2/7.5) = 56.0$.
Germany: $100(3.9/7.5) = 52.0$.
Italy: $100(3.6/7.5) = 48.0$.

9. (a) The relatives (times 100) are:

	Copper	Lead	Zinc
1960	100.0	100.0	100.0
1970	150.4	249.8	159.9
1974	139.7	292.1	149.7

The averages of relatives are:

1960: 100.0
1970: 186.7
1974: 193.8

(b) $\dfrac{\Sigma P_{0i}Q_{1i}}{\Sigma P_{0i}Q_{0i}} = \dfrac{640(1,597,000) + 240(669,000) + 260(500,000)}{640(1,143,000) + 240(229,000) + 260(334,000)}$

after converting the copper output and price into tons. (For example, since there are 2,000 pounds in a ton, a price of 32 cents per pound in 1960 amounts to $640 per ton, and an output of 2,286 million pounds amounts to 1,143,000 tons.) This equals

$$\frac{1,022,080,000 + 160,560,000 + 130,000,000}{731,520,000 + 54,960,000 + 86,840,000} = \frac{1,312,640,000}{873,320,000}$$

$$= 1.503.$$

Thus, the index equals 1.503 times 100, or 150.3.

(c) $\dfrac{\Sigma P_{1i}Q_{1i}}{\Sigma P_{1i}Q_{0i}} = \dfrac{(1,540)(1,597,000) + (460)(669,000) + (720)(500,000)}{(1,540)(1,143,000) + (460)(229,000) + (720)(334,000)}$

$$= \frac{2,459,380,000 + 307,740,000 + 360,000,000}{1,760,220,000 + 105,340,000 + 240,480,000}$$

$$= \frac{3,127,120,000}{2,106,040,000}$$

$$= 1.485,$$

so the index equals 148.5.

(d) Fisher's ideal index equals $\sqrt{(\text{Laspeyres index})(\text{Paasche index})}$, so it

equals $\sqrt{(150.3)(148.5)} = \sqrt{22,319.55} = 149.4$.

(e) The average of relatives has the serious disadvantage that it does not weight the outputs by their prices. The other three indexes result in quite similar results. They indicate that the output of these metals increased by about 48.5 to 50.3 percent between 1960 and 1974.

10. (a) 1930: 100
1940: 110
1950: 120
1960: 125
1970: 115(1.25) = 143.8
1980: 130(1.25) = 162.5
1990: 140(1.25) = 175.0.

(b) 1930: $100(100 \div 125) = 80.0$
1940: $100(110 \div 125) = 88.0$
1950: $100(120 \div 125) = 96.0$
1960: 100
1970: 115
1980: 130
1990: 140.

(c) 1930: $100(100 \div 175) = 57.1$
1940: $100(110 \div 175) = 62.9$
1950: $100(120 \div 175) = 68.6$
1960: $100(125 \div 175) = 71.4$
1970: $100(143.8 \div 175) = 82.2$
1980: $100(162.5 \div 175) = 92.9$
1990: 100.0

U.S. Consumer Demand for Dairy Products*

R. Haidacher, J. Blaylock, and L. Myers

Trends in Dairy Product Consumption

Consumption of dairy products measured on a milk-equivalent milkfat basis and including donations increased sharply in the 1980s from 12.3 billion pounds to 14.2 billion pounds (Table 1). Consumption rose steadily in 1974–81 after declining roughly .5 percent per year in 1965–74 (Figure 1). Consumption continued to increase at an average rate of 3.3 percent per year from 1981–84 before slowing to a 1 percent growth in 1985–86. But some of this increase resulted from expanded donations. While consumption rose, stock levels also grew rapidly from 8.6 billion pounds in 1980 to 22.6 billion pounds by January 1, 1984, and put added pressure on donation programs.

Although consumed, dairy product donations are not purchased in the market and their exclusion from the disappearance data provides a better indication of how consumer purchases have changed (Figure 1). In 1965–74, the annual drop in consumption, excluding donations, averages closer to 0.25 percent than the 0.50 percent with donations. In 1974–84, the average increase drops

from over 1 percent with donations to about 0.8 percent without donations. In 1981–85, the average increase in consumption of 3.3 percent with donations drops to about 2.3 percent without donations. But the average increase of less than 1 percent in 1985–86 with donations is smaller than the 2.6 percent increase without donations because donations actually fell.

This dairy product consumption picture changes again when described in per capita terms using July 1 estimates of the U.S. civilian population. While total consumption fell less than 0.5 percent per year during 1965–74, consumption per capita decreased on average 1.5 percent per year (Figure 2). Per capita consumption excluding donations increased in 1983 after generally falling from the mid-1960s through the early 1980s. Per capita consumption including donations increased 0.1 percent during 1974–81 while per capita consumption excluding donations dropped 0.25 percent.

This declining trend for per capita consumption without donations continued to 1983 while per capita consumption including donations shows a sharp upward trend beginning in 1981. Per capita consumption excluding donations increased at an average annual rate of about 2.1 percent in 1983–86 while per capita consumption including donations increased about 1.3

*This is an excerpt from *Consumer Demand for Dairy Products* (Washington, D.C.: U.S. Department of Agriculture, 1988).

percent. Moreover, per capita consumption including donations remained almost unchanged in 1985–86. Excluding donations, per capita consumption increased more than 1.6 percent in 1985–86.

Table 1
Supply and Utilization of All Dairy Products*

	Supply					Utilization					
									Domestic disappearance		
										Civilian§	
Years	Production	Imports	Beginning stocks†	Total supply	Total use	Exports‡	Shipments	Fed to calves	Military	Total	Per capita
					Million pounds						Pounds
1965	124,180	923	5,290	130,393	125,937	1,836	522	2,061	2,819	118,699	619.5
1966	119,912	2,791	4,456	127,159	122,300	778	430	1,980	2,376	116,736	603.6
1967	118,732	2,908	4,859	126,499	118,247	363	461	1,891	2,117	113,415	580.7
1968	117,225	1,780	8,252	127,257	120,550	1,185	586	1,821	3,295	113,663	576.7
1969	116,108	1,621	6,707	124,436	119,092	921	498	1,745	2,696	113,232	568.7
1970	117,007	1,874	5,245	124,126	118,293	522	438	1,702	2,419	113,212	560.7
1971	118,566	1,346	5,803	125,715	120,611	2,458	568	1,635	2,031	113,919	556.0
1972	120,025	1,694	5,104	126,823	121,325	1,470	677	1,624	1,671	115,883	558.5
1973	115,491	3,860	5,498	124,849	119,641	654	638	1,584	1,257	115,508	551.1
1974	115,586	2,923	5,208	123,717	117,831	582	576	1,558	1,137	113,978	538.6
1975	115,398	1,669	5,886	122,953	119,110	550	496	1,566	1,075	115,423	539.9
1976	120,180	1,943	3,843	125,966	120,257	507	520	1,567	1,013	116,650	540.3
1977	122,654	1,968	5,709	130,331	121,750	465	527	1,541	996	118,176	541.8
1978	121,461	2,310	8,626	132,397	123,668	376	602	1,497	977	120,216	545.2
1979	123,350	2,305	8,729	134,384	125,785	400	620	1,442	1,163	122,160	547.8
1980	128,406	2,109	8,599	139,114	126,155	426	562	1,395	1,067	122,705	543.9
1981	132,770	2,329	12,959	148,058	129,680	3,197	586	1,418	1,019	123,460	541.7
1982	135,505	2,477	18,378	156,360	136,306	5,095	516	1,521	1,369	127,805	555.4
1983	139,672	2,616	20,054	162,342	139,696	3,188	577	1,527	1,307	133,097	573.0
1984	135,450	2,741	22,646	160,837	144,113	3,600	634	2,134	1,361	136,404	581.7
1985	143,147	2,776	16,704	162,627	148,932	4,805	566	1,747	1,128	140,686	594.1
1986‖	144,080	2,674	13,695	160,449	147,582	1,971	546	1,870	1,128	142,067	594.4

*Milk-equivalent, milkfat basis.
†Excludes cream and bulk condensed milk, starting 1970.
‡Government and commercial.
§Includes donations.
‖Preliminary.

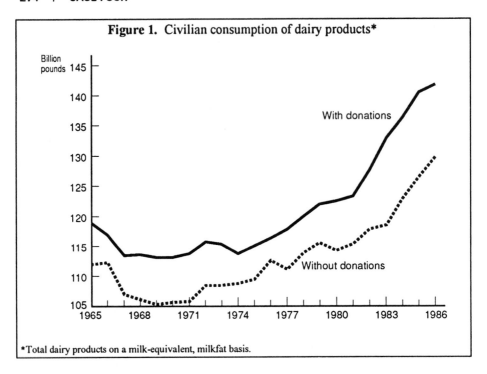

Figure 1. Civilian consumption of dairy products*

*Total dairy products on a milk-equivalent, milkfat basis.

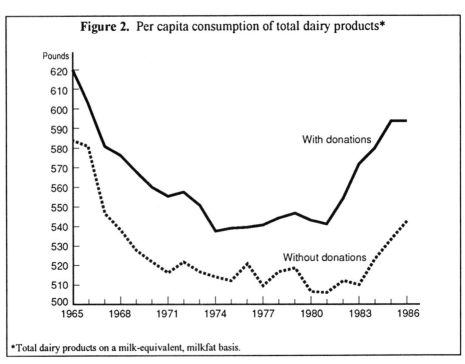

Figure 2. Per capita consumption of total dairy products*

*Total dairy products on a milk-equivalent, milkfat basis.

Because trade in dairy products is limited, imports and exports have minimal impact on the per capita dairy product total (Table 1). As a percentage of total disappearance, imports ranged from a low of 0.7 percent to a high of 3.2 percent over the last 20 years. Exports were also limited and fluctuated from a low of 0.3 percent to a high of 3.7 percent (Figure 3). Subtracting annual imports from annual exports to measure net trade indicates that imports exceeded exports in most of the last two decades and by as much as 3.2 billion pounds in 1973. However, exports exceeded imports from 1981 through 1985.

These aggregate dairy product statistics are useful for evaluating total milk utilization. But consumers purchase and use individual dairy products. The following section shows how consumption trends differ substantially across the individual dairy product categories.

Cheese

The consumption pattern for cheese (excluding cottage cheese) contrasts sharply with other dairy products. Cheese is one of the few dairy products whose per capita consumption rose steadily, more than doubling over the last two decades. Per capita cheese consumption rose an average of 4.2 percent from 9.8 pounds in 1966 to 23.2 pounds in 1986. Throughout this period, per capita consumption declined only once—a decrease of a little over 0.1 pound in 1974–75 (Figure 4).

Cheese donations increased significantly during the early 1980s. Donations accounted for more than 10 percent of 1983 per capita consumption. But total per capita cheese consumption continued its rise in the 1980s, at or near the pre-1981

trend, even with donations factored out.

Consumption of American-type cheese, the largest component of the cheese total, increased 3.5 percent per year from 6.2 pounds per person in 1966 to 12.2 pounds in 1985 but slipped to 12.1 pounds in 1986 (Figure 4). Donations of American cheese increased significantly in the early 1980s, especially in 1983–86. However, consumption of American cheese still increased after donations are excluded, at about the pre-1980s rate of growth.

Per capita consumption of Italian-type cheese increased an average of 8 percent per year from about 1.5 pounds per capita in 1966 to over 7 pounds in 1986. Donations constituted a small portion of Italian cheese, averaging about 0.12 pound per capita per year during 1980–86. Miscellaneous cheese consumed per capita doubled from about 2 pounds in 1966 to about 4 pounds in 1986, averaging about a 3.6 percent increase per year.

Fluid Milk and Cream

Although per capita fluid milk consumption increased in 1983–86, the 3.5-pound increase was only large enough to push consumption back up to the 1981 level of 245 pounds (Figure 5). Per capita consumption of fluid milk and cream declined steadily from 292 pounds in 1965 to 242 pounds in 1982, or slightly less than 1 percent per year. But this slow decline in fluid milk and cream products masks rather significant changes in its components: lowfat milk is steadily replacing whole milk. Per capita consumption of whole milk declined about 3 percent per year from 246 pounds in 1965 to 118 pounds in 1986. Other milk, mostly lowfat milk, increased at an average

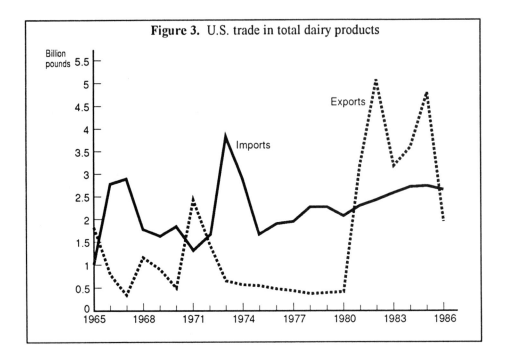

Figure 3. U.S. trade in total dairy products

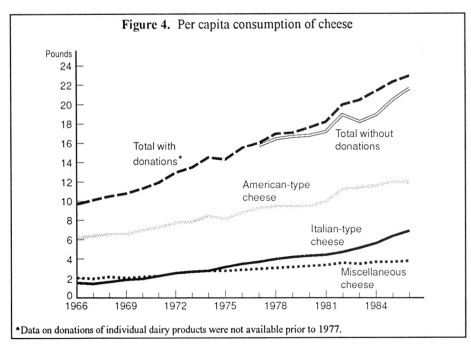

Figure 4. Per capita consumption of cheese

*Data on donations of individual dairy products were not available prior to 1977.

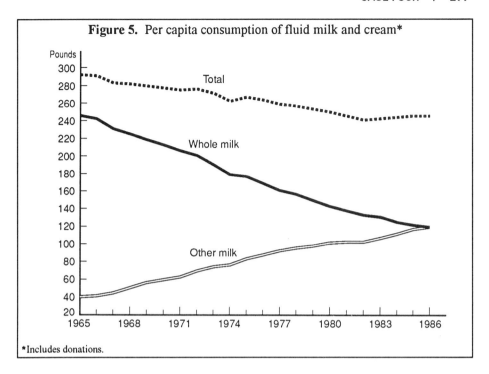

Figure 5. Per capita consumption of fluid milk and cream*

Pounds

Total

Whole milk

Other milk

1965 1968 1971 1974 1977 1980 1983 1986

*Includes donations.

annual rate of over 5 percent, from 39 pounds per capita in 1965 to over 119 pounds in 1986. Changes in fluid milk and cream consumption are important contributors to aggregate dairy product consumption since fluid use represented 36 percent of total 1985 marketings, milk-equivalent basis.

Fluid milk consumption hit a low of 241.9 pounds per capita in 1982, increased to 245.1 pounds in 1985, and did not change in 1986. Cream and specialty products (included in the total but not shown separately in Figure 5) decreased from about 7 pounds per capita in 1965 to a low of 5.3 pounds in 1971 before increasing slowly back to about 7.5 pounds in 1986.

Despite the recent increase, per capita fluid milk consumption has declined over the long run even with lowfat products substituted for whole milk products (Figure 5). Whether or not the last few years represent a leveling off in fluid milk consumption

or a change in direction is, at this point, unclear. It should be noted that the fluid milk and cream data include donations and food assistance quantities.

Butter

Per capita consumption of butter, excluding donations, has stabilized at about 4 pounds per person after posting small increases in 1977–79 (Figure 6). Based on unpublished data, butter donations doubled in 1983, remained at about that level until 1985, and then dropped slightly in 1986 (Figure 6).

Evaporated, Condensed, and Dry Milk Products

Per capita consumption of condensed, evaporated, and dry milk products declined from 1965 to 1980–81, leveled off, and then increased slightly through 1986 (Figure 7). Consumption of evaporated and condensed milk products declined about 3 percent per year, from about 16 pounds in 1965 to a low of about 7 pounds in 1980 where it remained until 1984 before increasing to 7.9 pounds in 1986. Consumption of dry milk products declined slowly (less than 1 percent) from about 7 pounds in 1965 to a low of 5.6 pounds in 1981–82. Per capita consumption rose to 7.2 pounds in 1986. Without donations, consumption would have increased to 6.6 pounds.

Frozen Dairy Products

Per capita consumption of frozen dairy products has been relatively stable at 27 to 28 pounds during 1965–86 (Figure 8). Per capita consumption of ice cream remained relatively stable during 1965–86, varying less than 1.5 pounds per year. People consumed about 18.5 pounds of ice cream in 1965. Consumption dropped slightly to 17.3 pounds per person in 1972, returned to 18.5 pounds in 1975, gradually dropped to 17.1 in 1979, and returned to 18.3 pounds in 1986.

Other frozen dairy products have a similar per capita consumption pattern, but at only about half the quantity of ice cream (Figure 8). Although both product categories showed higher per capita consumption in 1986, there is little evidence to indicate a change in the historic pattern of per capita consumption, given the small magnitude of variation during 1965–86.

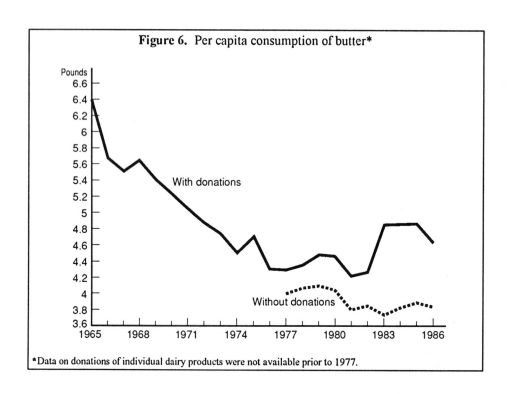

Figure 6. Per capita consumption of butter*

*Data on donations of individual dairy products were not available prior to 1977.

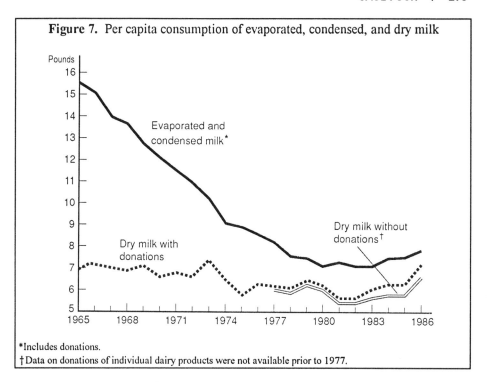

Figure 7. Per capita consumption of evaporated, condensed, and dry milk

*Includes donations.
†Data on donations of individual dairy products were not available prior to 1977.

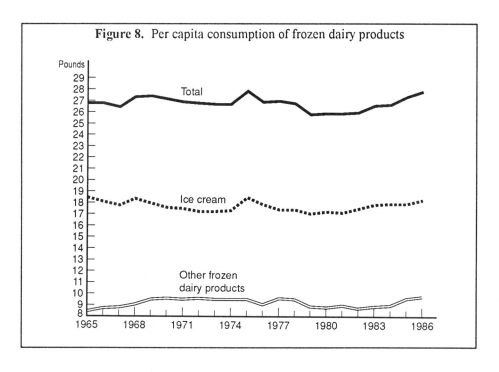

Figure 8. Per capita consumption of frozen dairy products

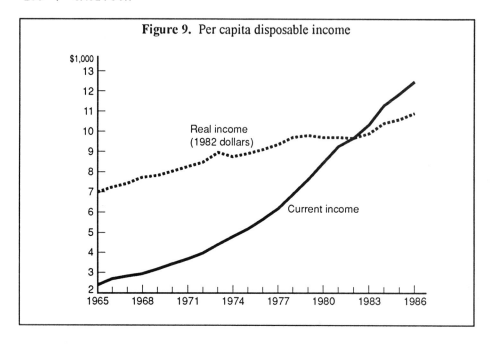

Figure 9. Per capita disposable income

Prices and Income Are Major Determinants in Demand for Dairy Products

Our analysis indicates that changes in relative prices and income are the most important factors influencing annual changes in per capita consumption of dairy products. The effects of income and prices are first discussed separately, followed by an analysis of all prices and income.

Income

Quantitative analysis of the link between income and consumption has traditionally focused on measuring elasticities using real per capita disposable income. Real per capita income increased an average of 2.2 percent per year over the past 20 years but accelerated to more than 3 percent per year in the mid-1980s (Figure 9).

The responsiveness of dairy product consumption or expenditures to changes in real per capita disposable income can be measured

using either time-series or household data. . . . Time-series estimates of income elasticities are generally referred to as short run, while elasticities from household data show a longer-run response. It is difficult to isolate the separate effects of time trends and income on consumption in time-series demand models because of generally increasing income levels. As Brandow stated, "It is virtually impossible to separate statistically the effects of income and trend in the postwar period because real incomes per capita rose almost linearly and because prices and undeflated income were highly correlated." Recognizing that the income elasticities may embody trend effects, time-series income elasticity estimates should be interpreted accordingly. Elasticity estimates from household data are free from this limitation, but they pertain only to at-home expenditures, which is not a limitation if a product is mostly consumed at home.

Income elasticities from time-series data show the percentage change in the quantity consumed for a given percentage change in income. . . . Estimates based on time-series disappearance data suggest that a 10 percent increase in income increases per capita consumption of total dairy products 1.8 percent and increases per capita cheese consumption 5.9 percent. But a 10 percent increase in income decreases per capita consumption of fluid milk and evaporated and condensed milk by 2.2 and 2.7 percent, respectively. Income hardly affects consumption of butter and frozen and other dairy products (both coefficients were small and not significant).

The large magnitude of the time-series income elasticities for fluid milk; evaporated, condensed, and dry milk; and cheese are probably influenced by time trends. Ward and Dixon obtained a 0.39 income elasticity for fluid milk, based on monthly data for 1978–86. Even though their model includes a time trend, the elasticity appears high and may overstate the effect of income changes on fluid milk consumption.

The wide disparity in income elasticities from time-series data leads us to rely on estimates from household surveys. At-home fluid milk consumption, about 69 percent of total fluid milk use, has an expenditure elasticity of about zero according to most cross-section demand studies. This appears to be the most reasonable estimate of the income elasticity for fluid milk. As previously noted, at-home and away-from-home cheese consumption are about equal, each at approximately 38 percent of total use. Therefore, the income elasticity for cheese probably lies somewhere between the 0.3 estimate from household (at-home) data and the 0.6 time-series estimate.

We have seen that income elasticities from household survey data can provide insight into consumer response to income changes, even though the data reflect only at-home expenditure on dairy products. At-home per capita spending on fluid milk is not very responsive to income changes. However, some dairy items, such as cheese, show a marked response to income changes. For example, a 10 percent increase in income raises at-home per capita expenditures on cheese 3.2 percent. A further breakdown of individual product income elasticities suggests that a 10 percent increase in income lowers at-home expenditures on fresh whole milk about 1 percent. Most studies using household data agree with these findings, with respect to both the sign and magnitude of the elasticities.

A 10 percent increase in income increases at-home expenditures on total dairy products 1.4 percent. A 10 percent increase in income affects at-home per capita expenditures on individual dairy products differently:

- It has little or no effect on per capita fluid milk expenditures.
- It lowers per capita expenditures on canned milk 1.2 percent.
- It raises per capita expenditures on frozen and other dairy products about 2 percent.
- It raises per capita expenditures on butter and cheese over 3 percent each.

Prices[1]

Changes in relative prices are also major determinants of changes in per capita consumption for individual dairy products. Consumer Price Indexes (CPIs, which measure prices of goods and services) show the relative price change from the base year for a product category. The

1. Unless otherwise noted, prices refer to CPI price indices.

average increase in retail prices was lower for dairy products than for other foods since the mid-1970s (Figure 10). But prices of dairy products rose even slower relative to prices of all foods and all goods and services during 1981–86, meaning that relative dairy product prices declined. Although linked to support and farm-level prices, retail dairy product price indexes exhibit different patterns because of marketing costs, product transformations, and competitive conditions.

The economic theory of consumer demand assumes that if all prices and incomes increase by the same proportion, consumers will not alter their behavior by acting as if they had become wealthier. This assumption means that changes in relative prices, not changes in nominal prices, determine changes in consumption behavior. Recall that per capita dairy consumption increased during the same period that relative dairy product prices decreased (Table 1, Figures 2 and 10).

Per capita consumption of all dairy products moves in the opposite direction as relative dairy product prices. A 10 percent increase (decrease) in the own price of total dairy products decreases (increases) per capita consumption of total dairy products 3.1 percent. The responses to a 10 percent increase in individual dairy product prices are 2.6 percent for fluid milk, 8.3 percent for evaporated and dry milk, 1.7 percent for butter, 1.2 percent for frozen and other dairy products, and 3.3 percent for cheese. Consumption of total and individual dairy products also responds to changes in the prices of other dairy products and other foods.

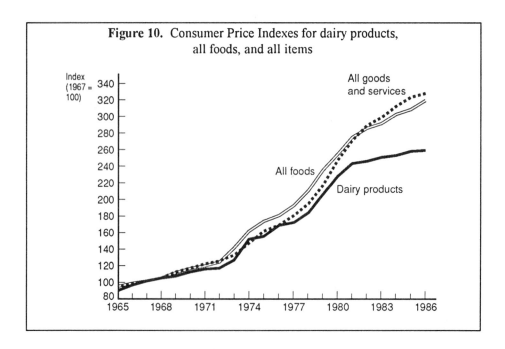

Figure 10. Consumer Price Indexes for dairy products, all foods, and all items

Total Dairy Products. A 10 percent increase in the price of total dairy products reduces per capita consumption by 3.1 percent, all else held constant. . . . Estimated relationships from a complete demand system showed that other foods are economically interdependent with dairy products. Fish, eggs, fresh fruit and vegetables, cereal and bakery products, and nonalcoholic beverages appear to be substitutes for dairy products. Consumers will tend to substitute dairy products for those foods when prices of dairy products fall and do the opposite when dairy product prices rise. Poultry, fats, processed fruit and vegetables, and sugar appear to be complements with dairy products. Decreases in the price of any complement increases consumption of all of them because changes in per capita consumption of complements move in the same direction.

Fluid Milk and Evaporated and Dry Milk Fluid milk comprises whole milk and other milk beverages (mainly lowfat milk). Other factors held constant, a 10 percent increase in the price of fluid milk reduces per capita consumption 2.6 percent. Fluid milk's −0.26 price elasticity is quite similar to those found by Ward and Dixon (−0.25), Brandow (−0.29), and George and King (−0.35). A 10 percent increase in the price of evaporated and dry milk reduces its per capita consumption 8.3 percent. A cross-price elasticity between two commodities shows interdependence; it tells how much a change in the price of a particular food affects consumption of another food. A 10 percent increase in the price of evaporated and dry milk increases the quantity of fluid milk demanded by 0.7 percent (Table 2). However, with

a cross-price elasticity of 0.71, per capita consumption of evaporated and dry milk increases 7.1 percent with a 10 percent increase in fluid milk prices. These results indicate that fluid milk and evaporated and dry milk are substitutes (both have positive coefficients). The cross-price elasticities between fluid milk, cheese, and margarine and those between evaporated and dry milk and frozen and other dairy products show rather strong substitution relationships. On the other hand, the cross-price elasticities between fluid milk and frozen and other dairy products, for example, indicate that these products are complements (both have negative coefficients).

Fluid milk also appears to have significant substitutes outside the dairy group, in such foods as carrots, celery, tomatoes, grapefruit, and chicken. Substitutes for evaporated and dry milk include foods such as chicken, eggs, apples, lettuce, carrots, and cabbage. Some complementary relationships outside the dairy group also exist. Evaporated and dry milk appear to be complements with grapefruit, bananas, other fruit, turkey, and pork. Fluid milk appears to be a complement with pork, turkey, fish, eggs, potatoes, bananas, and carrots.

Butter. Changing butter's price hardly affects the consumption of butter. Although butter has a price elasticity of −0.17, we are not confident that the elasticity is different from zero because of its relatively large standard error (0.17). Margarine responds more to changes in its own price than does butter, with a −0.27 elasticity. George and King found butter to be more responsive to price changes than did Huang, partly because George and King's data

Table 2
Price Elasticities for Dairy Products and Margarine

			Price elasticity for—				
Quantities	*Fluid milk*	*Evaporated and dry milk*	*Frozen dairy products*	*Cheese*	*Butter*	*Margarine*	*Income elasticity**
			Coefficient				
Fluid milk	−0.259 (.120)	0.074 (.041)	−0.090 (.028)	0.103 (.024)	0.002 (.021)	0.017 (.011)	−0.221 (0.069)
Evaporated and dry milk	.713 (.395)	−.826 (.264)	.274 (.138)	−.140 (.101)	.089 (.113)	−.051 (.083)	−.266 (.223)
Frozen and other dairy products	−.253 (.079)	.079 (.040)	−.121 (.085)	.021 (.037)	−.045 (.043)	.028 (.019)	.011 (.058)
Cheese	.453 (.109)	−.068 (.048)	.031 (.061)	−.332 (.117)	−.241 (.058)	.040 (.021)	.593 (.120)
Butter	.032 (.170)	.080 (1.03)	−.144 (.137)	−.460 (.110)	−.167 (.175)	.048 (.067)	.023 (.192)
Margarine	.201 (.139)	−.066 (.105)	.125 (.082)	.110 (.057)	.067 (.093)	−.267 (.137)	.111 (.107)

NOTE: The upper numbers are elasticity estimates. The numbers in parentheses are the standard errors.
*See discussion of income elasticities estimated using time series data.

covered 1955–65, which is before the large subsequent shift toward more away-from-home eating.

The estimated cross-price elasticities between butter and margarine are 0.05 and 0.07, respectively (Table 2). Although these estimates indicate that the two products may be substitutes, the elasticities are not significant because their magnitudes are smaller than their standard errors..

Significant negative cross-price elasticities between butter and cheese of −0.46 and −0.24, respectively, indicate a complementary relationship in consumption but for unknown reasons. Although it is a complement with fish and certain fruit and vegetables, and a substitute for other vegetables, other fruit, and chicken, butter has few strong

relationships with foods outside the dairy group.

Frozen and Other Dairy Products. An own price change hardly affects per capita consumption of frozen and other dairy products. A 10 percent increase (decrease) in its price, decreases (increases) its consumption 1.2 percent (Table 2). Frozen and other dairy products are apparently complements with fluid milk, coffee, beef, and pork. Apparent substitutes include evaporated and dry milk, margarine, chicken, fish, eggs, bananas, grapefruit, celery, and cabbage.

Cheese.   Cheese is perhaps the most complicated dairy product because of the many varieties that may be classified according to degree of hardness, structure, or the type of organisms responsible for ripening the product.

Cheese is often broadly classified into American cheese (including cheddar, colby, washed curd, stirred curd, and Monterey jack) and other cheese (including a wide variety of Italian cheeses, Swiss cheese, brick, Muenster, and miscellaneous cheeses).

The estimated price elasticity for cheese is –0.33 (Table 2), which is similar to George and King's –0.46 elasticity estimate. Cheese appears to be a strong substitute for fluid milk and a strong complement with butter. Cheese shows some significant relationships with nondairy foods. The cross-price elasticity of cheese with beef and veal prices is –0.26, a complementary relationship that may partially reflect popular complementary preparations, such as cheeseburgers. Cheese also seems to be a complement with other fats, grapes, grapefruit, tomatoes, and onions. Apparent cheese substitutes include margarine, apples, celery, cabbage, canned tomatoes, and sugar.

Questions

1. What sort of an equation would you use to represent the trend in:

(a) per capita consumption of cheese?

(b) per capita consumption of whole milk?

(c) per capita consumption of butter?

(d) per capita consumption of evaporated, condensed, and dry milk?

(e) per capita consumption of ice cream?

2. Is multicollinearity a problem in estimated income elasticities of dairy products from time-series data? Why or why not?

3. The authors say that: "The large magnitude of the time-series income elasticities for fluid milk, evaporated, condensed and dry milk, and cheese are probably influenced by time trends." What do they mean by this? Explain.

4. Based on Table 2, construct a 95 percent confidence interval for the price elasticity of demand for:

(a) fluid milk.

(b) evaporated and dry milk.

(c) cheese.

5. Based on Table 2, can you reject the hypothesis that the price elasticity of demand for the following products is zero? Explain.

(a) Frozen and other dairy products

(b) Butter

(c) Margarine

How Large Are Economic Forecast Errors?*

Stephen K. McNees

Virtually everyone follows some forecaster's views, analyzing each pronouncement and eagerly awaiting the next. Opinion about the reliability of economic forecasts ranges widely, however—some argue that they are literally worthless, even though most forecasters typically can point to a sequence of predictions that virtually replicates the eventual outcome. How much confidence should one place in economic forecasts?

The answer would seem straight-forward: To measure a forecast's reliability, one need simply compare it with what "actually" occurs. The diversity of opinion on reliability indicates the answer is not so simple. Two problems arise immediately, one philosophical and one practical. The philosophical problem is one of induction: Forecast accuracy cannot be measured until what actually happened is known, but the main interest typically lies in the accuracy of current forecasts for which, necessarily, no actual outcome is available. Despite many attempts to make headway with this problem, some form of assumption must be made that the future will resemble the present. Neither logic nor econometrics can provide assurance that this assumption will hold. In fact, the future is almost certain to differ at

least somewhat from previous experience. Nevertheless, no alternative exists to blithely assuming that the reliability of today's forecasts will resemble the reliability of previous forecasts—that some forecaster (or model) has captured the essential lasting features of past and future behavior.

The practical problem in measuring the accuracy of past forecasts is that so many different forecasts are available—and, in some cases, so many different measures of what actually happened—that millions of different errors can be calculated, and this varied experience can be summarized in many different ways. The problem, in other words, is not the paucity of measures of reliability but their multiplicity or, more precisely, their variety. The errors vary with many factors, including (1) the economic series or variable predicted, (2) the forecaster, (3) the time period being forecast, (4) the horizon of the forecast, and (5) the choice of "actual" data to measure what really happened.

Much attention focuses on the first three factors—the economic variable, the forecaster, and the forecast period. To illustrate the importance of the fourth and fifth factors, consider the accuracy of one prominent forecaster's predictions over the last 10 years of real GNP growth in the current quarter. The top panel of Table 1 describes the accuracy of the predictions as measured against the

*This article appeared in the *New England Economic Review*, July–August 1992. The appendices have been omitted.

first official estimate of real growth ("preliminary actual data," or "advance" actual data); the bottom panel, the accuracy of the predictions when measured against the final revised estimate of real growth (prior to the benchmark revision). The first column shows the accuracy of forecasts made late in the first month of each quarter, just after the preliminary estimate of the prior quarter became available; these are called "early-quarter" forecasts. The second column shows "midquarter" forecasts, those made in the middle month of each quarter. The final column shows the errors of the forecasts made in the last month of the quarter, or "late-quarter" forecasts. These forecasts are customarily the expectations against which the press and financial market participants judge the preliminary GNP data release.

The table documents two obvious points: (1) The forecasts are much more accurate predictions of the preliminary data, which are based largely on information also available to the forecaster, than they are of the final revised data, which are based on information that does not become available until much later. (2) Forecasts made later in the quarter, when the forecaster has more information, are more accurate than earlier forecasts. Note, however, that

Table 1
Accuracy of Current Quarter Forecasts of Annual Growth Rate of Real GNP, 1981:III to 1991:III

Percentage Points unless Otherwise Specified

Relative to PRELIMINARY actual data	Early (first month of quarter)	Mid (second month of quarter)	Late (third month of quarter)
RANGE	−5.2 to 4.7	−3.2 to 2.8	−2.1 to 1.9
>1	59%	41%	29%
>2	15%	17%	2%
>3	10%	5%	0%
MAE	1.4	1.0	.8
RMSE	1.8	1.4	.9
MEAN	−.2	−.1	−.1
Relative to REVISED actual data			
RANGE	−5.8 to 4.4	−4.0 to 3.8	−4.0 to 4.2
>1	61%	51%	68%
>2	37%	34%	24%
>3	22%	20%	15%
MAE	1.9	1.6	1.5
RMSE	2.4	2.0	1.9
MEAN	−.4	−.3	−.3

NOTE: Preliminary actual data are the first estimates released in the month immediately following each quarter's end and are equivalent to what the U.S. Department of Commerce terms "advance" actual data. Revised actual data are the last estimates made prior to the benchmark revision. MAE = Mean Absolute Error, RMSE = Root Mean Squared Error, MEAN = Mean Error.

the improvement in forecast accuracy is much greater compared to the preliminary than to the revised actual data. For example, 10 percent of the forecasts of real growth made in the first month of the quarter were off the mark by more than 3 percentage points while none of the forecasts made during the last month of the quarter missed the preliminary estimate by more than 2.1 percentage points. The elimination of the large outliers, through the incorporation of incoming high-frequency data, cuts the root mean square error (RMSE) in half between the first and third months. In contrast, relative to the revised actuals, the proportion of errors exceeding 3 percentage points

falls only from 22 percent of the forecasts made in the first month of the quarter to 15 percent of the forecasts made in the last month of the quarter; the proportion of forecast errors exceeding 1 percentage point was actually somewhat larger for the forecasts made in the last month of the quarter. The RMSE falls only by about 20 percent over the quarter. Thus, while the incoming high-frequency data shed a lot of light on what the preliminary estimate of real GNP will be, they provide relatively little new information on what the final revised number will be.

Table 2 presents comparable information for forecasts of the current-quarter rate of growth of the

Table 2
Accuracy of Current Quarter Forecasts of Annual Growth Rate of CPI, 1980:I to 1992:I

Percentage Points unless Otherwise Specified

Relative to PRELIMINARY actual data	Early (first month of quarter)	Mid (second month of quarter)	Late (third month of quarter)
RANGE	−5.0 to 4.8	−2.7 to 2.2	−3.5 to 1.2
>1	35%	20%	4%
>2	22%	8%	2%
>3	12%	0%	2%
MAE	1.2	.7	.3
RMSE	1.8	1.0	.6
MEAN	.1	.1	−.0
Relative to REVISED actual data			
RANGE	−5.2 to 4.0	−2.9 to 2.8	−1.7 to 2.1
>1	39%	22%	14%
>2	22%	10%	2%
>3	10%	0%	0%
MAE	1.2	.8	.5
RMSE	1.7	1.1	.7
MEAN	.1	.1	−.0

NOTE: See Table 1.

consumer price index (CPI). Note first that little difference can be seen in the accuracy of the predictions whether compared to the preliminary or the revised data. Unlike real GNP, where additional information is collected to improve the estimates, the CPI is based on a survey conducted each month, which cannot be repeated; all revisions come solely from changing the seasonal adjustment factors. Note also that the timing of the forecast is even more important for the CPI than for real GNP; this reflects the fact that CPI data are collected and released monthly so that by the time the late-quarter forecast is made, forecasters know the actual outcome for two of the three months of the quarter.

Forecasters have often been accused of bias. However, none of these forecasts shows a systematic tendency to either overestimate or underestimate the actual outcome. The mean errors are essentially zero, whatever the forecast horizon and whichever actual data are used.

Should forecast accuracy be assessed relative to the preliminary or to the revised actuals? The answer depends entirely on the purposes of the forecast. if the objective is to understand what influences behavior at the time—for example, if one is interested in the reaction of investors in financial markets—the preliminary data are the obvious choice, as the revised data are not available until much later. However, if the objective is to measure how close the forecast comes to what actually occurred—what nonfinancial decision makers, model builders, and policymakers presumably would want to know—it is equally clear that the revised data, based on the most complete information set, provide a better estimate of reality.

This is particularly true for comparative evaluations: If forecaster A provides the most accurate predictions of what was initially thought to have happened (preliminary data), but forecaster B provides the best forecasts of what turns out to have actually occurred, once all the facts are in, it would seem odd to call A the better forecaster of the economy, even though forecaster A clearly is a superior forecaster of the social accountants who produce GNP estimates. Fortunately, the distinction between preliminary and revised data becomes less important for forecasts of longer time spans, such as one-year-ahead forecasts, and for variables other than the National Income and Product Accounts and the monetary aggregates, such as the CPI and the unemployment rate. For example, prices in financial markets (stock prices and interest and exchange rates) are measured precisely and thus are not subject to revision.

Variations in Forecast Accuracy over Time

A crucial determinant of the size of forecast errors is the forecast period; some periods are very difficult to predict while others are relatively easy. Figure 1 shows the errors of one-quarter-ahead and four-quarter-ahead forecasts, made by one prominent forecaster, of growth in real GNP from 1971:I to 1991:III. The errors for the different time spans follow different patterns: The four-quarter-ahead forecasts are dominated by the overestimates of the two major recessions, 1974–75 and 1981–82, and the underestimates of the early recoveries from the 1980 and

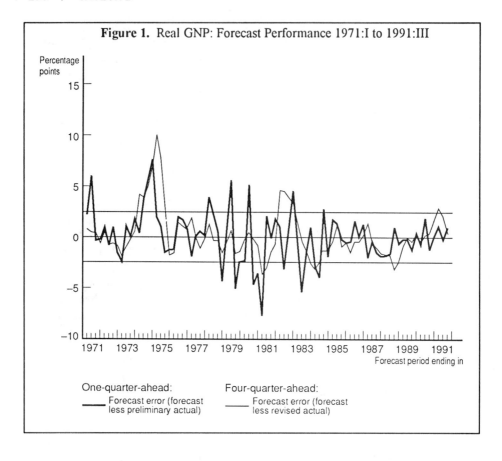

Figure 1. Real GNP: Forecast Performance 1971:I to 1991:III

One-quarter-ahead:
_____ Forecast error (forecast
less preliminary actual)

Four-quarter-ahead:
_____ Forecast error (forecast
less revised actual)

1981–82 recessions. The only other errors in the four-quarter-ahead forecasts that exceeded 2½ percentage points were a 3.2 percentage point underestimate of the rate of real growth in the year after the October 1987 stock market crash and a 2.9 percentage point overestimate for the 1990:I to 1991:I period, which included the 1990–91 recession.

The one-quarter-ahead forecasts are not so clearly linked to business cycle turning points, even though the largest errors were the overestimates in 1974 and the underestimates of the early recovery from the 1980 recession. In addition, large errors occurred in 1978, 1979, 1983, and 1984. But because the one-quarter-ahead errors, although large, were offsetting, the errors of forecasts covering multiquarter time spans were not especially great.

Forecasters' reputations probably reached the nadir in 1979–80, when for six quarters in a row virtually all one-quarter-ahead forecasts were in the wrong direction—when forecasts expected positive real growth, it was negative and vice versa. And in the only quarter (1980:II) when everyone's forecast was of the correct algebraic sign, the size of the decline was vastly underestimated.

Figure 2 shows corresponding information for CPI forecast errors. By far the largest errors were the sustained underestimations of the acceleration of inflation in 1973–75 and again in 1978–80. From these experiences forecasters gained the reputation of systematically

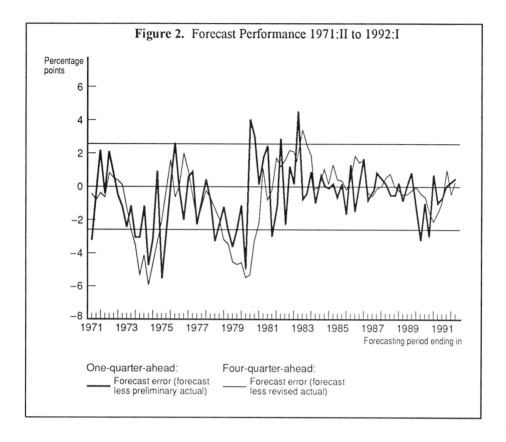

Figure 2. Forecast Performance 1971:II to 1992:I

Percentage points

Forecasting period ending in

One-quarter-ahead:
_____ Forecast error (forecast less preliminary actual)

Four-quarter-ahead:
_____ Forecast error (forecast less revised actual)

underestimating inflation. These shortfalls were followed by large overestimates of the rate of inflation in 1983, which was undoubtedly associated with the underestimation of the severity of the 1981–82 recession. Since 1983, the record of forecasting the CPI has been much improved. The one-quarter-ahead forecast errors have exceeded 2 percentage points only in 1990:I and in 1990:III, when the forecasts were made just prior to the sharp increase in oil prices associated with Iraq's invasion of Kuwait. These errors resulted in the 2.1 percentage point underestimate of the inflation rate for the year 1990, the first error that large since the overestimates in 1983. The fact that CPI forecasting errors have declined in absolute terms does not necessarily indicate that

forecasting ability has improved, however. The variability of the inflation rate has also been much smaller in the last 10 years. Relative to the 1970s, the 1980s have been an easy time to forecast inflation.

Large variations in forecast accuracy over time have several important implications. First, in terms of comparing different forecasters, it is critically important to compare identical forecast periods. The best forecaster's errors in the 1970s would be far larger, in absolute terms, than an inferior forecaster's errors in the 1980s. More fundamentally, the fact that accuracy varies over time poses a challenge to the constancy assumption needed to make inferences about future periods. Is it possible to know whether the current "easy" period will last or whether we will revert to the hectic 1970s? In the former case, only recent experience would be relevant for estimating the accuracy of current forecasts. But in the latter case, recent experience would be deceptive; it will be important to look at a longer sweep of history to remind us of how much uncertainty there can be.

Has Forecast Accuracy Improved?

The figures clearly suggest forecast accuracy has improved over the past 20 years. Since the four-quarter period ending in 1984:I, no four-quarter real GNP forecast error has exceeded 3¼ percentage points and only two have exceeded 2½ percentage points. The record for inflation forecasts has been more impressive: Since the four-quarter period ending in 1983:IV, no four-quarter-ahead CPI forecast error has exceeded 2¼ percentage points and only one (1989:I to 1990:I) has

exceeded 2 percentage points.

These facts undoubtedly overstate the degree of improvement that has been achieved. History shows a close association between business cycle turning points and the size of forecast errors. Much of the improvement merely reflects the fact that no turning point occurred for the 92 months between November 1982 and July 1990. Forecast errors did increase during the 1990–91 recession, when real growth was overestimated by nearly 3 percentage points and inflation underestimated by about 2 percentage points. Even errors this large, far larger than average, pale in comparison with those from earlier recessions.

In order to try to distinguish genuine improvement from a string of good luck, it is helpful to examine a longer time period. Table 3 summarizes the longest consistent forecasting record available—the forecasts of real GNP growth in the following year made each November since 1952 by the Research Seminar in Quantitative

---

Table 3

Accuracy of RSQE Forecasts of Real GNP, 1953 to 1991

Percentage Points unless Otherwise Specified

Years	MEAN (1)	MAE (2)	MAE/N4 (3)	RMSE (4)	RMSE/SD actual (5)
All	–.1	1.3	.51	2.0	.70
1953–71	–.8	1.4	.62	2.2	.84
1972–91	.5	1.2	.43	1.6	.57
1950s	–1.5	2.1	.59	3.2	.90
1960s	–.7	1.0	.71	1.4	.85
1970s	.6	1.4	.39	1.9	.55
1980s	.2	.9	.44	1.3	.51

NOTE: MEAN = Mean Error, MAE = Mean Absolute Error, RMSE = Root Mean Squared Error, N4 = naive "same as four-year average" forecast, SD actual = standard deviation of actual real growth in forecast period.
SOURCE: Forecasts: Research Seminar in Quantitative Economics, University of Michigan, *The Economic Outlook for 1992*, Table 1, p. 4.

Economics (RSQE) at the University of Michigan. The distribution of errors has been fairly stable over time: About half of the errors were less than 1 percentage point, ranging only from a low of 40 percent in the 1970s to 60 percent in the 1960s and 1980s; about one-fifth of the errors exceeded 2 percentage points, ranging only from a low of 10 percent in the 1980s to a high of nearly 30 percent in the 1950s. In absolute terms, the largest errors, underestimates of the first years of expansions, occurred in the 1950s. Errors were far smaller in the relatively tranquil 1960s but rose somewhat in the turbulent 1970s; errors in the 1980s were about the same as the 1960s. The 1990s are off to a poor start: The errors for 1990 and 1991 are both larger than the average for the entire period, nearly double the average error in the 1980s.

A long-term trend toward greater accuracy is more apparent when the errors are judged relative to standards, in order to account for varying degrees of difficulty over time. Column 3 in the table compares the MAE of the RSQE forecast with that of a naive rule of thumb that predicts real growth each year to be equal to its average rate in the four previous years. (This rule is more accurate than the simple rule that predicts next year's growth will be the same as this year's growth.) The RSQE errors were 40 to 30 percent smaller than those of the naive rule in the 1950s and 1960s, respectively, and improved to a level nearly 60 percent smaller in the 1970s and 1980s. Column 5 shows that the RMSE of the Michigan forecast has declined steadily relative to the standard deviation of real GNP in each forecast period. The standard deviation of real GNP is a direct measure of the difficulty of forecasting in each period. Alternatively, it can be viewed as the RMSE of a forecaster who knew in advance the average actual growth rate in the forecast period but knew nothing about the yearly deviations from that true average. The Michigan forecasts have improved steadily relative to that hypothetical straw man.

Thus, forecast accuracy seems to have improved, whether viewed from the perspective of several decades or by comparing the recent performance with the rather dismal record in the 1970s and early 1980s. Continuing improvement is not inevitable; the performance in the 1990–91 recession was distinctly worse than average. Future improvement (deterioration) depends on whether forecasting techniques improve more rapidly (slowly) than changes occur in the structure of the economy.

Variations in Accuracy among Variables

It is commonly asserted that particular economic variables are "unpredictable." Because it is easy to find someone who will gladly predict anything, such statements are intended to refer to the accuracy of predictions and not the difficulty of making some prediction, no matter how reliable. It is obvious that some variables can be predicted more accurately than others, but not at all obvious how to compare errors in forecasts of different variables. Is a $10 billion error in GNP better or worse than a 50 basis point error in interest rates? Is a 1 percentage point error for the CPI the same as a 1 percentage point error for the unemployment rate? Clearly, forecast errors for different variables cannot simply be added up. Some kind of standardization is required if a comparison of different variables is even to be attempted.

Although perfection is the goal of forecasting, we know that the future is unknown and we do not expect forecasts to eliminate all uncertainty. A forecast is useful if it can reduce uncertainty. But to measure a reduction presumes some estimate of the level of uncertainty that prevailed initially. Forecast evaluation cannot be done in absolute terms but only relative to some standard, because no unique estimate of the level of uncertainty exists, no totally obvious standard of comparison. The only sensible standard of comparison is some alternative forecasting technique. Traditionally, forecasts have been evaluated relative to simple rule-of-thumb forecasts, such as no change or same change (as in some past period). A no-change standard of comparison is a sensible, even a surprisingly stringent, standard of comparison for several variables—primarily ratios of two variables, such as unemployment rates, profit rates, foreign exchange rates, and interest rates. Most economic variables, however, grow exponentially over time. For these variables, a same-change standard is a more stringent and sensible basis of comparison.

Variations in the difficulty of predicting different variables can be illustrated by examining the forecasts published twice a year in the *Wall Street Journal* from a survey conducted by Tom Herman. Interest rate forecasts for the next six months have been collected since 1982, and for the next year since 1984; forecasts of real GNP, the CPI, and the unemployment rate have been collected since 1986. Although 68 different individuals have submitted at least one forecast, more than half

(36) of these have participated in fewer than 10 of the surveys, and only three have participated in all surveys. We have already seen that forecast accuracy varies over time, so that the infrequent forecasters would benefit from skipping difficult periods and suffer if they missed the easy periods. In order to try to control for these missing forecasts, each forecaster's performance is compared not with those of the other forecasters but with a straw man—a no-change forecast for interest rates and the unemployment rate, and a same-change forecast for the CPI and the real GNP growth rate. Difficult (easy) periods presumably would also be more (less) difficult for the straw man, so that individuals' performances relative to the straw man would be affected less by missing forecasts or gaps.

The results, summarized in Table 4, show drastic differences among variables in the forecasters' ability to outperform the straw man. At one extreme, none of the forecasters could predict the long-term interest rate a half-year into the future as well as the simple assumption that the rate would not change; 83 percent (10 of the 12 forecasters) were more than 20 percent *less* accurate than the naive straw man. Only one forecaster, a different individual for the half-year and the full-year horizons, could predict short-term interest rates more accurately than the straw man, and neither forecaster was more than 5 percent more accurate.

At the other extreme, everyone could predict the CPI better than the simple straw man forecast, which predicted that future changes will be the same as the most recent change. Only 14 percent (4 of 29 forecasters) were unable to beat the straw man by more than 20 percent in forecasting CPI growth over the next year.

Table 4
Mean Absolute Errors of Forecasts Relative to Naive Straw Man

Variable (straw man) Forecast	High	Low (ratio)	Median	>1.2	>1.1	>1 (percent)	>.9	>.8
	(1)	(2)	(3)	(4)	(5)	(6)	(7)	(8)
Short-term interest rate								
Next half-year	1.48	.97	1.28	67	92	92	100	100
Next year	1.67	.95	1.20	50	67	92	100	100
Long-term interest rate								
Next half-year	1.59	1.04	1.28	83	83	100	100	100
Next year	1.57	.89	1.20	50	75	83	92	100
Unemployment rate								
Next half-year	2.26	.57	.84	3	14	28	31	55
Next year	2.71	.63	.97	14	24	31	62	76
CPI growth rate								
Next half-year	.98	.59	.72	0	0	0	7	21
Following half-year	1.02	.56	.68	0	0	7	10	14
Next year	1.11	.38	.54	0	3	3	10	14
GNP(lag*)								
Next half-year	2.05	.63	.86	21	31	34	48	72
Following half-year	1.21	.56	.75	3	3	7	17	34
Next year	1.54	.56	.69	3	3	7	14	31
GNP(lead†)								
Next half-year	3.25	1.00	1.30	69	86	93	100	100
Following half-year	1.49	.74	.96	17	28	38	66	76
Next year	2.09	.78	.99	28	38	48	69	97

NOTE: Short-term interest, long-term interest, and unemployment rates are relative to a no-change straw man. CPI and GNP growth rates are relative to a same-change straw man.
*Lag: Last observed half-year growth rate prior to forecast.
†Lead: Next half-year growth rate after forecast.
SOURCE: Twelve individual forecasters' interest rate forecasts, 1982–91; other variables, 29 individual forecasts, 1986–91, as published in the *Wall Street Journal*.

The real GNP growth and unemployment rates are more difficult to estimate than the CPI but not as difficult as interest rates. Only about one-third of the forecasters were unable to outperform the no-change straw man for the unemployment rate. Nearly half of the forecasters could beat the straw man by more than 20 percent for the half-year horizon, and almost 25 percent of the forecasters were over 20 percent more accurate in the year-ahead forecast.

Real GNP forecasts are compared to two straw men. The first, GNP lag, is the simple idea that real GNP will continue to grow at the same rate as it grew in the last observed half-year. One-third of the forecasters could not improve upon this forecast of the next half-year, while all but one could improve upon this forecast of the following half-year and of the entire year after the forecast is made.

The forecasts were made during the first few days of January and July, a few weeks before the initial estimate of actual growth in the prior quarter was released. Although they did not yet know the preliminary official estimate of the previous quarter, the forecasters had a considerable amount of information on that quarter. A second straw man—GNP lead—compares the forecasts with the preliminary estimate of real GNP growth in the half-year before the forecasts, which is released a few weeks after the forecasts were made. Only a few forecasters slightly outperformed this straw man for the first half-year period, but a majority were more accurate in forecasting real growth in the subsequent half-year and in the full year after the forecast.

This contrast reinforces the earlier observation concerning the importance of forecast release dates. It also illustrates the importance of the choice of a straw man as a standard of comparison. Although the no-change and same-change standards applied here seem reasonable, other standards could alter the results. These results are not sensitive, however, to the summary error measure or the actual data employed. Similar results hold for the RMSE instead of the MAE, or for revised actual data in place of the preliminary actual data used in the table.

Variations in Forecast Accuracy among Forecasters

Much of the interest in forecast accuracy stems from the wish to know "Who is the best forecaster?" . . . [My results show] that no single forecaster dominates all outliers for all, or even most, of the variables. In light of the importance of the time within the quarter when the forecast was made, consider only the early-quarter forecasts, those made in the first month. For most variables, the most accurate forecaster varies depending on the horizon of the forecast. Even for the few exceptions (gross domestic final sales, housing starts, state and local government purchases, and the unemployment rate), three different forecasters were "the best." One of the two remaining forecasters was best in predicting the GNP deflator up through seven quarters ahead. However, different forecasters have different interests; to deem one of these forecasters the best, based on a few variables, runs the risk of misleading those forecast users whose primary interest is in some other variable.

Suppose attention is confined to the concept of the inflation rate; [my results show] one forecaster who excels for the CPI measure while a different forecaster excels for the GNP deflator. Assume a forecast user cares only about one specific variable and one specific horizon. [My results] can be used to determine which forecaster has been the most accurate for that particular variable and horizon, but this does not imply that this particular forecaster will continue to be the most accurate in the future. The reason is that the *differences* in accuracy are typically fairly small; the "best" forecaster's errors were, on average, less than 10 percent smaller than those of the second best forecaster. These differences are of doubtful economic or statistical significance.

The fact that the accuracy of the most prominent group of forecasters is similar does not imply that *all* forecasters are equally accurate. A few of the individuals whose performance was summarized in Table 4 commonly made errors that were large multiples of the simple straw man used as a standard of comparison. It is as easy to make poor forecasts as it is difficult to consistently make the best forecasts.

Conclusion

With so much variability in forecasting accuracy, it is easier to disprove any generalization than to offer a valid one. Nevertheless, it seems clear that a major factor in forecast accuracy is the time period to be forecast. Errors were enormous in the severe 1973–75 and 1981–82 recessions, much smaller in the 1980 and 1990–91 recession, and generally quite minimal apart from business cycle turning points. Because turning points also tend to be periods when simple rule-of-thumb forecasts fare poorly, the moral for the forecast user seems to be not to ignore the forecasts but rather to think carefully about plausible outcomes far from the consensus view.

Clearly, accuracy also varies among variables. For good theoretical reasons, it is difficult to forecast a financial variable where genuinely unique knowledge presents an opportunity to profit. These reasons do not hold as forcefully for standard nonfinancial variables—real GNP, inflation, and unemployment rates—where the opportunities for profit are less apparent. Nevertheless, some nonfinancial variables are also extremely difficult to predict. A prominent example is the change in business inventories, where forecasts are often inferior to a no-change rule of thumb.

The interplay between forecast accuracy and the length or span of the forecast is also important. Forecast accuracy obviously tends to improve as the horizon of the forecast declines. But, at least for real GNP, the improvement is relatively slow over time until the forecast period actually starts, when some actual high-frequency data can be incorporated into the forecast. At the same time, longer time spans are often easier to forecast, as aberrations in the economy and/or noise in the measurement procedures "average out." The variability of four-quarter or eight-quarter cumulative changes is generally smaller than that of quarterly changes.

Finally, the importance of the forecaster, as a determinant of accuracy, is often exaggerated, perhaps by the forecasters themselves. Some forecasters have much to fear from a clear statement of the accuracy of their forecasts. But the vast majority of prominent forecasters, including those who have invited public scrutiny of their performance, have much to gain from disclosure of how accurate their forecasts have been. First, although it may be disappointing to learn that others' performances have been similar, it must be comforting to learn that others cannot document a clearly superior performance. Second, and more importantly, there has been much disillusionment with macroeconomic forecasting. Some of this is justified, but some of it may reflect forecasters' failure to educate forecast users in how much (little) confidence to place in their forecasts. In forecasting, an explanation of how much (little) the forecaster knows can be more useful to the user than a single best guess of what the future will be. Only with some understanding of how large forecast errors are likely to be does the forecaster's message become valuable.

Questions

1. Why has "there been much disillusionment with macroeconomic forecasting"? Does this mean that macroeconomic forecasts are useless?

2. According to McNees, "History shows a close association between business cycle turning points

[i.e., peaks and troughs] and the size of forecast errors." Why?

3. What variables are particularly hard to forecast? Which ones are relatively easy to forecast?

4. Is it always true that forecast accuracy tends to get better as the horizon of the forecast is reduced? Why or why not?

5. Is there substantial evidence that forecasters are biased? If so, what is this evidence?

PART VII

Quality Improvement and Statistical Decision Theory

CHAPTER 16

How Top Managers Use Statistical Methods: The Case of Quality Improvement

Chapter Profile

One key aspect of product quality is uniformity. Many leading statisticians argue that the lack of uniformity frequently is due to factors outside the control of the workers—defective equipment, materials that are not of uniform quality, poor organization, and so on—and that it may do little good to exhort workers producing many defects to do better or to praise and grant pay increases to workers producing few defects.

To enhance and maintain quality, many firms use *statistical process control*. A *control chart* is a technique employed to distinguish variation in a process due to *common causes* from variation due to *special causes*. A control chart ordinarily consists of three lines, as well as points plotted on the graph. If a point falls outside the control limits, or if the rules in Figure 16.3 of the textbook indicate that the process is unstable, attempts should be made to determine the special causes that are responsible.

$\overline{X}$ and R charts are based on variable data; p charts and c charts are based on attribute data. For any control chart to be successful, it is very important that the subgroups be chosen in such a way that each subgroup is as homogeneous as possible and that there is maximum opportunity for variation from one subgroup to another.

At Harley-Davidson, the adoption of statistical quality control techniques is given considerable credit for the firm's turnaround. Each machine operator at Harley-Davidson has his or her own set of charts pertaining to his or her own outputs. Basically, the operator is trying to see whether the process is stable.

In recent years, there has been less reliance on inspection to improve quality. Rather than looking primarily to inspection of the final product as a means of improving and controlling quality, firms now are focusing more attention on how their product is designed and made. The objective is to design and make the product in such a way as to prevent the production of poor-quality output, and thus eliminate the need for intensive inspection of the final product.

To get the most out of statistical methods, a firm (or other organization) must pay proper attention to the implementation problems, not just worry about the purely statistical questions. Important implementation problems at Harley-Davidson were that (1) middle managers were very uncomfortable regarding the operators' use of statistical methods, (2) the operators needed more statistical training than expected, (3) many of the operators needed help in getting the necessary confidence to use these methods, and (4) operators tended to lose interest in these methods if management did not take the corrective action that was called for relatively quickly.

Experts seem to agree that the quality improvement process must begin with a firm's top management. It is very important for top managers to demonstrate a strong commitment to quality improvement. With such a commitment, it frequently is possible to raise quality levels very considerably. Without such a commitment, statistical techniques are likely to have a much more limited effect. Deming's 14 points, which summarize his views concerning the optimal managerial and organizational climate, have had an enormous effect, here and abroad.

Behavioral Objectives

A. You should be able to define the following key concepts in this chapter:

production system	zone A
statistical process	zone B
control	zone C
process	variable data
common causes	attribute data
special causes	$\overline{X}$ chart
assignable causes	R chart
stable process	p chart
unstable process	c chart
statistical control	quality improvement
control chart	Deming's 14 points
centerline	*acceptance number
upper control limit	*rejection number
lower control limit	*acceptable quality level

B. Make sure that you can do each of the following:
1. Determine what measures of quality should be used.
2. Determine how subgroups should be formed.
3. Apply the rules for detecting instability of the process.
4. Construct and interpret an $\overline{X}$ chart.
5. Construct and interpret an R chart.
6. Determine when trial values should become official.
7. Construct and interpret a p chart.
8. Construct and interpret a c chart.
9. Describe the four phases of statistical quality control.
10. Summarize Deming's 14 points.
11. Indicate some of the principal problems in getting statistical techniques applied.
12. Describe some of the ways that firms have solved major problems in getting statistical techniques applied.

---

*These concepts pertain to the appendix of Chapter 16.

The Acidity of Dye Liquor: A Case Study[1]

The acidity of the dye liquor is important in the dyeing of woolen yarns. If the dye liquor is too acidic, the durability of the products made from the yarn is reduced. If it is not acidic enough, the penetration of color is poor. A firm that dyed woolen yarns formulated a control chart for the acidity of the dye liquor; the results were as follows. (Note that low values of the variable on the vertical axis mean that acidity is high, not low.)

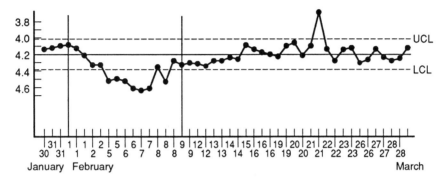

(a) Is there any evidence that the process is unstable? If so, what is it?
(b) On February 1, a new type of wool was subjected to the dyeing process. Can this be regarded as a special cause? Why or why not?
(c) After February 15, is there any evidence that the process is unstable? If so, what is it?
(d) From February 8 to 15, the firm's engineers were trying to adapt the firm's operations to the new type of wool. Does this help to explain the pattern of points from February 8 to 15 in the control chart? Why or why not?

Multiple-Choice Questions

1. Which of the following are dimensions of quality?

   (a) Performance
   (b) Length of life
   (c) Ease of repair
   (d) Reliability
   (e) All of the above

2. A stable process is

   (a) a process where the outcomes depend only on common causes.
   (b) in a state of statistical control.
   (c) a process where the outcomes depend on common and special causes.
   (d) out of statistical control.
   (e) both (a) and (b).

---

1. This case is based on E. Grant and A. Leavenworth, *Statistical Quality Control*, 6th ed. (New York: McGraw-Hill, 1988), p. 91.

3. A sign of instability of the process occurs when

    (a) a point falls above the upper control limit.
    (b) a point falls below the lower control limit.
    (c) nine or more points in a row fall below the centerline.
    (d) two out of three points in a row fall on the same side of the centerline in zone A.
    (e) all of the above.

4. An R chart

    (a) generally is based on 20 or more small samples.
    (b) is generally constructed before an $\overline{X}$ chart is constructed.
    (c) must have a lower control limit.
    (d) all of the above.
    (e) both (a) and (b).

5. Which of the following are based on attribute data?

    (a) $\overline{X}$ chart
    (b) R chart
    (c) p chart
    (d) c chart
    (e) Both (c) and (d)

6. Phases of statistical process control often are

    (a) instability.
    (b) stable, but chronic problems.
    (c) quality improvement.
    (d) ship to customer.
    (e) all of the above.

7. According to W. Edwards Deming, firms should

    (a) award contracts on the basis of price alone.
    (b) maintain barriers between departments.
    (c) stress numerical quotas.
    (d) all of the above.
    (e) none of the above.

8. To improve the quality of its performance, it is important for a firm to

    (a) have its top management strongly committed to the quality improvement process.
    (b) include its major suppliers in the quality improvement process.
    (c) have its middle managers learn from its top managers (and others) that quality improvement is important.
    (d) all of the above.
    (e) none of the above.

9. If the sample size is 5, the value of A_2 is

    (a) 2.115.
    (b) zero.
    (c) 0.577.
    (d) 0.729.
    (e) none of the above.

10. If the sample size is 4, the value of D_4 is

    (a) 2.282.
    (b) zero.
    (c) 2.115.
    (d) 0.577.
    (e) none of the above.

Problems and Problem Sets

1. The Seton Company, a maker of motors, draws a sample of five motors from each shift's output, and measures their lengths. The firm uses an $\overline{X}$ control chart where the upper control limit exceeds the lower control limit by 0.006 inch, and where the centerline is at 14.105 inches.

    (a) If a sample mean equals 14.109 inch, is this an indication that the production process is unstable? Why or why not?

    (b) If two sample means in a row are less than 14.103 inches, is this an indication that the production process is unstable? Why or why not?

(c) Above the centerline, what is zone A? Zone B? Zone C?

(d) Below the centerline, what is zone A? Zone B? Zone C?

2. The Borah Corporation obtains a sample of 5 parts produced each day for 20 consecutive days, and measures the weight of each part. The range of the weights (in ounces) in each sample is as follows:

Day	R	Day	R	Day	R	Day	R
1	3.1	6	2.2	11	4.9	16	3.1
2	1.8	7	4.4	12	3.1	17	2.1
3	4.1	8	1.9	13	2.0	18	3.0
4	2.7	9	2.9	14	0.8	19	3.2
5	6.1	10	2.8	15	4.0	20	4.8

(a) Based on these data, what is the centerline of the R chart for the weight of this part?

(b) What is the upper control limit?

(c) What is the lower control limit?

(d) Plot the control chart in the graph below.

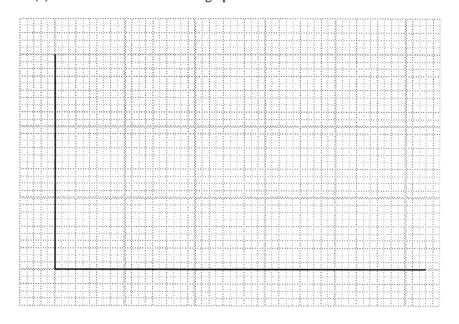

(e) Is there evidence that the process is unstable? Why or why not?

(f) Should the values of the centerline and of the control limits be made official? Why or why not?

3. For the 20 samples (of size 5) described in the previous problem, the sample means of the weights (in ounces) of the part were as follows:

Day	$\overline{X}$	Day	$\overline{X}$	Day	$\overline{X}$	Day	$\overline{X}$
1	12.1	6	11.0	11	13.0	16	13.3
2	11.3	7	12.2	12	12.6	17	12.9
3	12.9	8	13.1	13	12.2	18	14.6
4	11.7	9	11.8	14	13.8	19	15.1
5	11.8	10	11.1	15	15.0	20	13.3

(a) Based on these data, what is the centerline of the $\overline{X}$ chart for the weight of this part?

(b) What is the upper control limit?

(c) What is the lower control limit?

(d) Plot the control chart in the graph below:

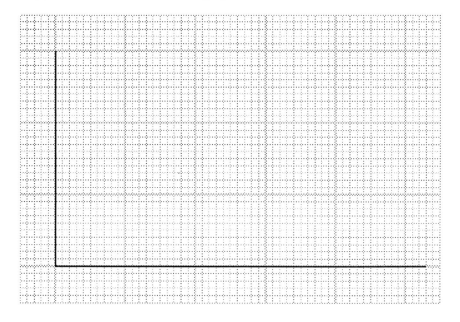

(e) Is there evidence that the process is unstable? Why or why not?

(f) Should the values of the centerline and of the control limits be made official? Why or why not?

4. The Barton Company wants to establish a p chart for the proportion of pens it produces that are defective. It inspects a sample of 200 pens from each day's output. The results for 24 days are as follows:

Day	Proportion defective	Day	Proportion defective	Day	Proportion defective	Day	Proportion defective
1	.015	7	.000	13	.005	19	.005
2	.005	8	.005	14	.005	20	.000
3	.000	9	.000	15	.010	21	.010
4	.010	10	.010	16	.005	22	.015
5	.005	11	.015	17	.005	23	.020
6	.010	12	.010	18	.010	24	.005

(a) Based on these results, what is the upper control limit?

(b) What is the lower control limit?

(c) What is the centerline?

(d) Using the graph below, plot the points on the control chart.

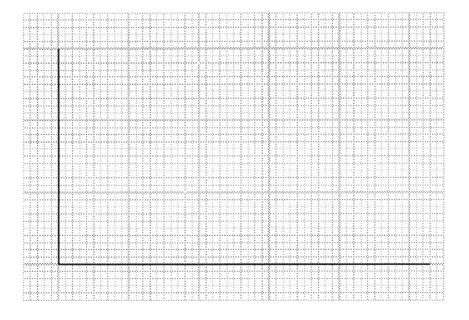

(e) Are any of the points outside the control limits? If so, which points are they?

(f) Is there any evidence that the process is unstable? Why or why not?

(g) Should these values of the centerline and the control limits be made official? Why or why not?

5. The KCH Company wants to establish a c chart for the number of defects per piano that it produces. Data for 28 pianos that it produced are as follows:

Piano	Number of defects	Piano	Number of defects	Piano	Number of defects	Piano	Number of defects
1	1	8	1	15	4	22	1
2	0	9	2	16	2	23	3
3	0	10	1	17	1	24	5
4	1	11	3	18	2	25	2
5	0	12	2	19	2	26	7
6	1	13	1	20	4	27	4
7	2	14	3	21	2	28	4

(a) Based on these results, what is the upper control limit?

(b) What is the lower control limit?

(c) What is the centerline?

(d) Using the graph below, plot the points on the control chart.

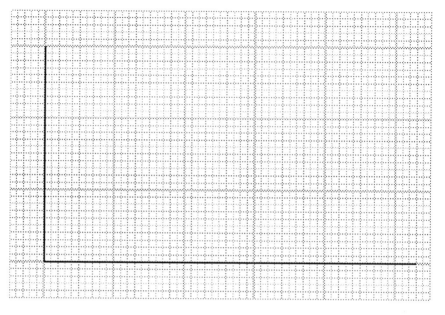

(e) Is there any evidence that the process is unstable? If so, what is it?

(f) Should these values of the centerline and the control limits be made official? Why or why not?

6. The Klosterman Corporation establishes a control chart to monitor and improve the quality of the television sets it produces. Every day, it picks 50 television sets produced at its plant in Tennessee and 50 television sets produced at its plant in Colorado. Then it combines these two subsamples into a sample of 100 television sets and calculates the proportion defective in this combined sample. This sample proportion defective is plotted on the control chart. Comment on the adequacy of the way in which subgroups are chosen by the Klosterman Corporation.

7. The Southeastern Pennsylvania Transit Authority operates trains and buses in Philadelphia and its suburbs. List six major indicators of the quality of its service.

8. (a) Why should an R chart be constructed before the $\overline{X}$ chart is constructed?

    (b) Why does W. Edwards Deming stress that firms should not award business on the basis of price alone?

*9. The TED Corporation receives a shipment of 1,000 radios. It has indicated to the supplier that the acceptable quality level is 2.5 percent.

    (a) Explain what an acceptable quality level of 2.5 percent means.

*This problem pertains to the appendix of Chapter 16.

(b) If the TED Corporation uses the acceptance sampling plan devised by the Department of Defense, how big a sample of these radios should it select?

(c) If the TED Corporation selects a sample of the size required by the Defense Department's acceptance sampling plans and if 7 radios in the sample are defective, should it reject the shipment?

(d) If 4 radios in the sample are defective, should the TED Corporation reject the shipment?

*10. In the previous problem, what is the probability that the TED Corporation, if it uses the Defense Department's acceptance sampling plans and if 4 percent is the acceptable quality level, will accept the shipment:

    (a) if 5 percent of the radios in the shipment are defective?

    (b) if 7.5 percent of the radios in the shipment are defective?

    (c) if 11.9 percent of the radios in the shipment are defective?

*This problem pertains to the appendix of Chapter 16.

Answers

The Acidity of Dye Liquor: A Case Study

(a) Yes. From February 5 to 8, seven points fell below the lower control limit. Subsequently, there was a long run of points below the centerline.

(b) Yes. This new type of wool was not present during the entire period and under all circumstances.

(c) Yes, on February 21, a point fell above the upper control limit. (Since zones A, B, and C are not plotted, it is hard to carry out tests based on these zones.)

(d) Yes. The long run of points below the mean seems to have been due to the fact that it took time to restore the previous mean.

Multiple Choice Questions

1. (e) 2. (e) 3. (e) 4. (e) 5. (e) 6. (e) 7. (e) 8. (d) 9. (c)
10. (a)

Problems

1. (a) Yes. This sample mean is above the upper control limit, which is 14.108 inches.

   (b) Yes. Below the centerline, zone A is from 14.102 to 14.103 inches. Based on Rule 3 in Figure 16.3 of the text, two out of three points in a row in zone A is a signal of instability. Thus, if both points are between 14.102 and 14.103 inches, this is such a signal. And if either point is below 14.102 inches, it falls below the lower control limit, which by itself is a signal of instability.

   (c) Zone A is 14.107 to 14.108 inches, zone B is 14.106 to 14.107 inches, and zone C is 14.105 to 14.106 inches.

   (d) Zone A is 14.102 to 14.103 inches, zone B is 14.103 to 14.104 inches, and zone C is 14.104 to 14.105 inches.

2. (a) $\overline{R} = 63/20 = 3.15$ oz.

   (b) Since $n = 5$, $D_3 = 0$ and $D_4 = 2.115$. Thus, the upper control limit is 6.66 oz.

   (c) There is no lower control limit.

   (d)

   (e) No.

   (f) There seems to be no reason why they should not be made official.

3. (a) $\overline{X} = 254.8/20 = 12.74$.

(b) Since we know from the answer to problem 2 that $\overline{R}$ = 3.15 oz., the upper control limit equals 12.74 + .577(3.15) = 14.56 oz.

(c) 12.74 − .577(3.15) = 10.92 oz.

(d)

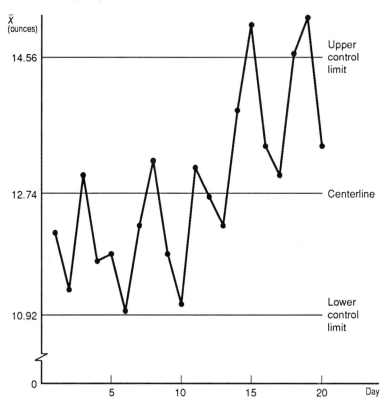

(e) Yes. The points on days 15, 18, and 19 are above the upper control chart. It appears that there is an upward trend in the mean.

(f) No, because the process seems to be unstable.

4. (a) Since $\overline{p}$ = .180/24 = .0075, the upper control limit equals

$$.0075 + 3\sqrt{.0075(.9925)/200} = .0075 + 3\sqrt{.00744375/200} =$$

$$.0075 + 3\sqrt{.00003722} = .0075 + 3(.0061) = .0258.$$

(b) There is no lower control limit.

(c) The centerline is at .0075.

(d)

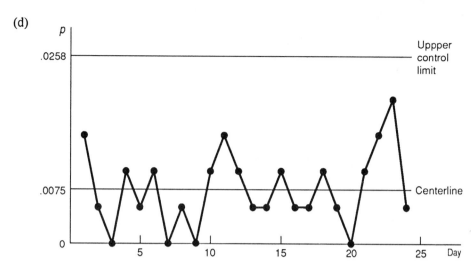

(e) No.

(f) No.

(g) There seems to be no reason why these values should not be made official.

5. (a) Since $\bar{c} = 61/28 = 2.18$, the upper control limit is $2.18 + 3\sqrt{2.18} = 2.18 + 3(1.476) = 6.61$.

(b) Since $\bar{c} - 3\sqrt{\bar{c}} < 0$, there is no lower control limit.

(c) The centerline is at 2.18.

(d)

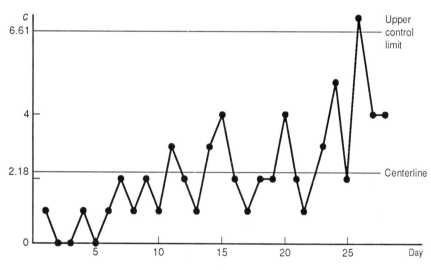

(e) Yes. There is a run of 10 points below the centerline from days 1 to 10, and there is a point above the upper control limit on day 26. Overall, there seems to be an upward trend in the number of defects.

(f) No, because there are indications that the process is unstable.

6. Subgroups should be chosen so that the samples are as homogeneous as possible. Separate samples should be chosen from the Tennessee plant and from the Colorado plant.

7. Examples are the percent of its trains and buses that are on time, the percent that break down, the percent that get into accidents, the number of complaints from customers, the cost of its service, and the price of its service.

8. (a) The R chart should be constructed first because a value of $\overline{R}$ is needed to formulate the $\overline{X}$ chart, and this value of $\overline{R}$ should be based on a period when the process is stable.

   (b) The quality of a product may be as important as its price.

*9. (a) It means that the maximum percentage of radios in the shipment that can be defective, and yet have the shipment acceptable, is 2.5 percent.

   (b) 80.

   (c) Yes.

   (d) No.

*10. (a) .95.

   (b) .75.

   (c) .25.

---

*This question pertains to the chapter appendix.

CHAPTER 17

Statistical Decision Theory

Chapter Profile

Any problem of decision making under uncertainty has two characteristics. First, the decision maker has to make a *choice* (or perhaps a series of choices) among alternative courses of action. Second, this choice (or series of choices) leads to some *consequence,* but the decision maker cannot tell in advance the exact nature of this consequence because it depends on some unpredictable event (or series of events) as well as on his or her choice (or series of choices). A *decision tree* represents such a problem as a series of choices, each of which is depicted by a fork. A *decision fork* is a fork representing a choice where the decision maker is in control; a *chance fork* is a fork where "chance" is in control of the outcome. By the process of *backward induction,* one can work one's way from the right-hand end of a decision tree to the left-hand end in order to solve the problem.

Whether a decision maker wants to maximize expected monetary gain depends on his or her *preferences with regard to risk.* To reflect these attitudes, we can construct a *utility function* for the decision maker if four assumptions described in this chapter are met. The first step in constructing such a utility function is to establish arbitrarily the utilities attached to two monetary values. The second step is to present the decision maker with a choice between a gamble where the possible outcomes are the two monetary values whose utilities were set arbitrarily and the certainty of some third monetary value. After finding the probabilities in this gamble that will make the decision maker indifferent between these two choices, we can calculate the utility of the third monetary value. Next, the latter steps can be repeated again and again to obtain the utilities attached to as many monetary values as we need.

Posterior analysis deals with decisions based both on prior probabilities and on new experimental or sample evidence, whereas *prior analysis* is based on prior probabilities alone. To carry out a posterior analysis, we use Bayes' theorem to compute posterior probabilities, which reflect both the decision maker's prior probabilities and the sample results. As the sample size increases, the posterior probabilities depend more and more on the sample results, and less and less on the prior distribution. Once the posterior probabilities are computed, the optimal choice is the one that maximizes expected monetary value if the decision maker is risk neutral. And we can compute the expected value of perfect information in a posterior analysis as well as in a prior analysis.

An *opportunity loss* is the loss incurred by the decision maker by failing to take the best action possible. For each event that can occur, one can compute the opportunity loss. If the decision maker wants to *maximize* expected monetary value, it can be shown that he or she should choose the action that *minimizes* the expected opportunity loss. This is an alternative way of finding the action that maximizes expected monetary value. It can be applied in either a prior or a posterior analysis. An interesting point concerning this approach is that the expected opportunity loss corresponding to the best action is equal to the expected value of perfect information.

Behavioral Objectives

A. You should be able to define the following key concepts in this chapter:

decision tree
decision fork
chance fork
backward induction
utility function
transitive
independence axiom
expected utility
risk averter
risk lover
risk neutral

prior analysis
posterior analysis
prior expected value
posterior expected value
prior expected value of perfect
  information
posterior expected value of perfect
  information
opportunity loss
expected opportunity loss

B. Make sure that you can do each of the following:
1. Construct a decision tree to represent simple situations involving choice.
2. Use backward induction to find the decision that maximizes expected monetary value.
3. State the assumptions that underlie the construction of a utility function.
4. Specify the steps that must be taken to measure a decision maker's utility function.
5. Use Bayes' theorem to calculate posterior probabilities, given some survey or experimental evidence.
6. Use the posterior probabilities to calculate the posterior expected value, and to find the decision that maximizes the posterior expected value of profit.
7. Calculate the posterior expected value of perfect information.
8. Calculate the opportunity loss associated with each action by the decision maker.
9. Find the decision that minimizes expected opportunity loss.

Drilling for Oil: A Case Study[1]

John Petra, a hypothetical oil prospector who has an option on a particular piece of land, must decide whether to drill on the land before the expiration of the option or give up his rights. If he drills, he believes that the costs will be $200,000. If he finds oil, he expects to receive $1 million; if he does not find oil, he expects to receive nothing.

(a) Construct a decision tree to represent Petra's decision.
(b) Can you tell whether he should drill or not on the basis of the available information? Why, or why not?

Petra believes that the probability of finding oil if he drills on this piece of land is 1/4 and that the probability of not finding oil if he drills here is 3/4.

---

1. This case is a highly simplified example of the sorts of analyses that have sometimes been made in the oil industry. It is similar in spirit to a case presented by John Pratt, Howard Raiffa, and Robert Schlaifer in their book *Introduction to Statistical Decision Theory* (New York: McGraw-Hill, 1965).

(c) Can you tell whether he should drill or not on the basis of the available information? Why, or why not?

(d) Suppose that Petra can be demonstrated to be a risk lover. Should he drill or not? Why?

(e) Suppose that Mr. Petra is risk neutral. Should he drill or not? Why?

Before John Petra has an opportunity to decide whether or not to drill on this piece of land, a geologist friend says that he has carried out some investigations, with favorable results. Petra believes that the probability of obtaining favorable or unfavorable results from these investigations, given alternate states of nature, is as follows:

	Probability	
State of nature	*Favorable results*	*Unfavorable results*
Petra will find oil if he drills	0.6	0.4
Petra will not find oil if he drills	0.4	0.6

(f) Given this new information, what probability should John Petra attach to finding oil if he drills on this piece of land? Why? What is the probability of not finding oil?

(g) If Petra prefers risk, should he drill or not? Why?

(h) If Petra is risk neutral, should he drill or not? Why?

Multiple-Choice Questions

1. A real estate speculator is interested in buying a particular plot of land. If a new shopping center is built near this plot of land, she will gain $1 million if she buys it. If the new shopping center is not built near this plot of land, she will lose $0.5 million if she buys it. If she is risk neutral, the probability that the new shopping center will be built near this plot of land must be at least _____ if she is willing to buy the plot of land.

   (a) 1/5
   (b) 1/4
   (c) 1/3
   (d) 1/2
   (e) none of the above

2. If a decision maker's utility function is such that utility is a linear function of monetary gain, then he or she is

    (a) a risk averter.
    (b) a risk lover.
    (c) risk neutral.
    (d) neither (b) nor (c).
    (e) none of the above.

3. If a decision maker is a risk averter for values of monetary gain above $10,000, then he or she

    (a) must be a risk averter for values of monetary gain below $10,000.
    (b) must be risk neutral for values of monetary gain below $10,000.
    (c) must be a risk lover for values of monetary gain below $10,000.
    (d) must be either (a) or (b).
    (e) must be (a), (b), or (c).

4. If $Y = 2 + 3X$ and if the expected value of X is 10, the expected value of Y must be

    (a) 2.
    (b) 30.
    (c) 32.
    (d) 23.
    (e) none of the above.

5. A plant manager must decide whether or not to install a new process. The manager feels that the chances are 3 to 2 that the new process is better than the old one. To obtain more information, the manager carries out an experiment, the outcomes of which have the following probabilities, given each state of nature:

Outcome of experiment

State of nature	New process seems better	New process does not seem better
New process is better	0.8	0.2
New process is not better	0.3	0.7

If the results of the experiment indicate that the new process is better, the posterior probability that the new process really is better is _____ , and the posterior probability that it is not better is _____ .

    (a) .8; .2
    (b) .7; .3
    (c) .5; .5
    (d) .3; .7
    (e) .2; .8

6. In the previous question, if the results of the experiment indicate that the new process is not better, the posterior probability that the new process really is better is _____ , and the posterior probability that it is not better is

_____ .

    (a) .8; .2
    (b) .7; .3
    (c) .5; .5
    (d) .3; .7
    (e) .2; .8

7. If the plant manager in the previous two questions adopts the new process and it is better, the firm will increase its profit by $1 million. If the manager adopts the new process and it is not better, the firm's profit will be cut by $1 million. If the manager keeps the old process, there will be no effect on the firm's profit. If the manager adopts the new process and if in fact it is superior to the old, the opportunity loss is

    (a) $1 million.
    (b) 0.
    (c) −$1 million.
    (d) $0.5 million.
    (e) none of the above.

8. In the previous question the opportunity loss, if the manager adopts the new process and if in fact it is not superior to the old, is

    (a) $1 million.
    (b) 0.
    (c) −$1 million.
    (d) $0.5 million.
    (e) none of the above.

9. In question 7 the opportunity loss, if the plant manager keeps the old process and if in fact the new is superior, is

    (a) $1 million.
    (b) 0.
    (c) −$1 million.
    (d) $0.5 million.
    (e) none of the above.

10. In question 7 the opportunity loss, if the plant manager keeps the old process and if in fact the new is not superior to the old, is

    (a) $1 million.
    (b) 0.
    (c) −$1 million.
    (d) $0.5 million.
    (e) none of the above.

11. A decision maker's utility function is shown below:

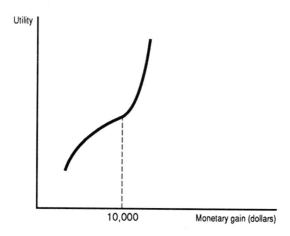

(a) The decision maker is a risk averter at all levels of monetary gain.
(b) The decision maker is a risk averter for monetary gains below $10,000 and a risk lover for larger monetary gains.
(c) The decision maker is a risk lover for monetary gains below $10,000 and a risk averter for larger monetary gains.
(d) The decision maker is a risk lover at all levels of monetary gain.
(e) The decision maker is none of the above.

Problems and Problem Sets

1. According to Caltech's late Nobel prize winning physicist, Richard Feynman,[2] the National Aeronautics and Space Administration (NASA) estimated the probability of a crash of the space shuttle to be 1 in 100,000, whereas it was in fact closer to about .01 to .02. (Recall problem 1 in Chapter 3.) If statistical decision theory had been used to determine whether or not to attempt a launch of the shuttle, what difference, if any, would this have made?

2. *Science,* June 27, 1986, p. 1596.

2. Marcia Madison is indifferent between the certain receipt of $10,000 and a gamble where there is a .5 probability of receiving $30,000 and a .5 probability of receiving nothing.

   (a) If the utility she attaches to receiving nothing is set equal to zero and if the utility she attaches to receiving $30,000 is set equal to one, what is the utility she attaches to receiving $10,000?

   (b) Does she seem to be a risk lover, a risk averter, or risk neutral?

3. A newspaper publisher in a small town must decide whether or not to publish a Sunday edition. The publisher thinks that the probability is .6 that a Sunday edition would be a success and that it is .4 that it would be a failure. If it is a success, the publisher will gain $100,000. If it is a failure, the publisher will lose $80,000.

   (a) Construct the decision tree corresponding to the problem, and use backward induction to solve the problem.

(b) List all forks in the decision tree you constructed, and indicate whether each is a decision fork or a chance fork; state why.

4. The owner of a professional football team must decide whether or not to hire a 36-year-old quarterback who has just had an operation on his elbow. If the operation turns out to be a success, the owner's profits will increase by $200,000 if the player is hired; if the operation turns out to be unsuccessful, the owner's profits will decrease by $150,000 if the player is hired. The owner feels there is a .7 probability that the operation will be a success and a .3 probability that it will not be a success.

   (a) Construct the decision tree corresponding to the owner's problem, and use backward induction to solve the problem.

   (b) Would the decision be altered if the owner of the football team felt that
       (1)   the probability that the operation will be a success is .8, not .7?
       (2)   the probability that the operation will be a success is .6, not .7?

(c) What value of the probability of success of the operation will make the team's owner indifferent between hiring and not hiring the player, if the owner maximizes expected monetary value?

5. Is the decision maker a risk averter or a risk lover if he or she is indifferent between (1) receiving $1,000 for certain, and (2) a gamble where there is a .5 probability of winning $2,000 and a .5 probability of

(a) losing $4,000?

(b) losing $3,000?

(c) losing $1,000?

(d) gaining $500?

6. A decision maker is indifferent between the certainty of receiving $1,000 and a gamble where there is a .5 chance of receiving $2,500 and a .5 chance of receiving nothing. In the graph below, plot three points on the decision maker's utility function.

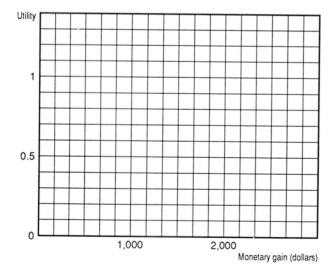

7. The owner of a paint factory is indifferent between the certainty of receiving $7,000 and a gamble where there is a .5 chance of receiving $5,000 and a .5 chance of receiving $10,000. Also, the owner is indifferent between the

certainty of receiving $10,000 and a gamble where there is a .5 chance of receiving $7,500 and a .5 chance of receiving $12,500.

(a) Based on this information, does the owner seem to be a risk averter, a risk lover, or risk neutral? Why?

(b) In the graph below, plot four points on the utility function of the owner of the paint factory.

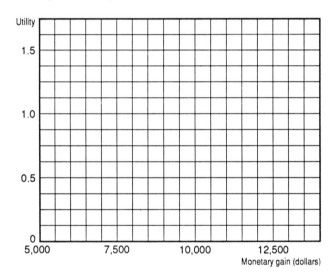

8. A law firm must decide whether or not to offer a young law graduate a job. If the graduate turns out to be a success, the firm will increase its profits by $100,000; if the graduate turns out not to be a success, the law firm's profits will decrease by $80,000. The firm feels that the chances are 50-50 that the graduate will be a success. To get a better idea of how likely this is, the firm asks the graduate to take a battery of tests. The probabilities of various test outcomes, given various states of nature, are shown below.

	Probability	
State of nature	Graduate passes tests	Graduate fails tests
Graduate will be a success	.8	.2
Graduate will not be a success	.1	.9

(a) If the graduate passes the tests, what is the posterior probability distribution of the graduate's success? If the graduate does not pass the tests, what is the posterior probability distribution of the graduate's success?

(b) What was the prior expected value of monetary gain if the firm hired the graduate? If the firm did not hire the graduate?

(c) Suppose that the graduate failed the tests. What was the posterior expected value of monetary gain if the firm hired the graduate? If the firm did not hire the graduate? Compare your answer here with that in (b) and comment on the results of the comparison.

(d) What was the prior expected value of perfect information? Once it was determined that the graduate failed the tests, what was the posterior expected value of perfect information? Why do these two values differ in the way they do?

(e) Calculate the expected opportunity loss (prior to the test results) if the firm does and does not hire the law graduate. Show that the minimization of expected opportunity loss results in the same decision as the maximization of expected profit. Also, show that the expected opportunity loss corresponding to the best action is equal to the expected value of perfect information which you determined in (d).

*9. A firm must decide whether or not to appoint James Milton as vice-president of marketing. If Milton survives for at least three years, there is general agreement that his appointment will mean an additional $1 million in profits for the firm. On the other hand, if he does not survive that long, his appointment would mean an $800,000 decline in the firm's profits due to the problems involved in rapid turnover in a particularly important job. Milton has been in poor health, and the firm's senior executives feel that there is only a 50-50 chance that he will survive for three years or more.

(a) Construct a decision tree to analyze the firm's problem. Given these conditions, what is the firm's optimal strategy? (Assume that the firm is risk neutral.)

*Material pertaining to the chapter appendix.

(b) The firm has the option of having a team of physicians give James Milton a rigorous series of tests on the basis of which the doctors would provide an opinion as to whether or not he would survive for at least three years. The probabilities that they would estimate that he would or would not survive for at least three years, given each state of nature, are as follows:

	Probability that physicians conclude that	
State of nature	Milton will survive for at least three years	Milton will not survive for at least three years
Milton will survive at least three years	.6	.4
Milton will not survive at least three years	.4	.6

Given that the physicians' opinion is that Milton will survive for at least three years, what is the posterior probability that he will in fact survive that long?

(c) Given that the physicians' opinion is that he will not survive at least three years, what is the posterior probability that he will really survive that long?

(d) Construct a decision tree to represent the firm's problem.

(e) What is the probability that the opinion of the physicians will be that Milton will survive for at least three years?

(f) What is the maximum amount that the physicians' opinion is worth to the firm? (Assume that the firm is risk neutral.)

(g) A member of the board of directors of the firm scoffs at this analysis on the grounds that the analysis is no better than the prior probabilities, which he judges to be only rough guesses. Comment on and evaluate his argument.

Answers

Drilling for Oil: A Case Study

(a)

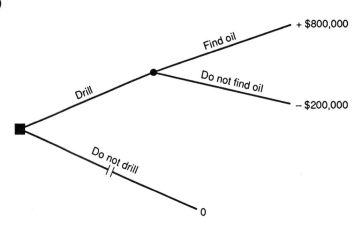

(b) No, because we do not know the probability of finding oil if he drills a well, and we do not know his utility function.

(c) The expected monetary gain, if he drills, is (1/4)($800,000) + (3/4)(–$200,000) = $50,000. If he is a risk lover or risk neutral, he should drill, but if he is sufficiently averse to risk, he should not.

(d) Yes, because the expected monetary gain if he drills ($50,000) exceeds that if he does not drill (0). Since he prefers risk, he would certainly prefer to drill.

(e) Yes, because the expected monetary gain, if he drills, exceeds that if he does not drill.

(f) $Pr\{\text{find oil} \mid \text{favorable results}\} =$

$$\frac{\text{Pr}\{\text{favorable results} \mid \text{find oil}\}\text{Pr}\{\text{find oil}\}}{\text{Pr}\{\text{favorable results} \mid \text{find oil}\}\text{Pr}\{\text{find oil}\} + \text{Pr}\{\text{favorable results} \mid \text{find no oil}\}\text{Pr}\{\text{find no oil}\}}$$

$$= \frac{(0.6)(.25)}{(0.6)(.25) + (0.4)(.75)} = \frac{.15}{.15 + .30} = \frac{1}{3}.$$

$Pr\{\text{find no oil} \mid \text{favorable results}\} =$

$$\frac{\text{Pr}\{\text{favorable results} \mid \text{find no oil}\}\text{Pr}\{\text{find no oil}\}}{\text{Pr}\{\text{favorable results} \mid \text{find oil}\}\text{Pr}\{\text{find oil}\} + \text{Pr}\{\text{favorable results} \mid \text{find no oil}\}\text{Pr}\{\text{find no oil}\}}$$

$$= \frac{(0.4)(.75)}{(0.6)(.25) + (0.4)(.75)} = \frac{.30}{.45} = \frac{2}{3}.$$

(g)   Yes, because the expected monetary gain if he drills equals

$$(1/3)(\$800,000) + (2/3)(-\$200,000) = \frac{\$400,000}{3} = \$133,333.$$

This exceeds the expected monetary gain (0) if he does not drill. Since he prefers risk, he should prefer to drill.

(h)   Yes, because the expected monetary gain if he drills exceeds that if he does not drill.

Multiple-Choice Questions

1. (c)   2. (c)   3. (e)   4. (c)   5. (a)   6. (d)   7. (b)   8. (a)   9. (a)
10. (b)   11. (b)

Problems and Problem Sets

1.   The prior probabilities would have been wrong. The chance of a crash would have been underestimated, and the analysis would have been distorted to favor launching the shuttle.

2.   (a) $U(\$10,000) = 0.5U(0) + 0.5U(\$30,000)$

$$= 0.5(0) + 0.5(1) = 0.5.$$

   (b)   Risk averter.

3.   (a)

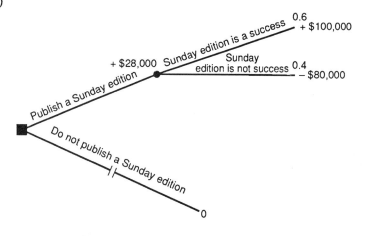

If the publisher wants to maximize expected monetary gain, the publisher should publish the Sunday edition.

(b) There are two forks. The one at the left (whether or not to publish the Sunday edition) is a decision fork. The one at the right (whether or not the edition is a success) is a chance fork.

4. (a)

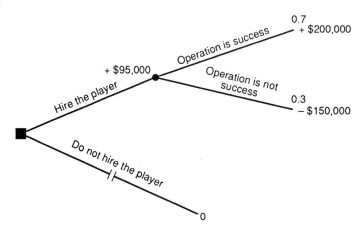

If the owner wants to maximize expected monetary gain, the owner should hire the player.

(b) If the probability of success is .8, the expected monetary gain if the player is hired equals .8($200,000) + .2(–$150,000), or $130,000. Thus, the decision is not altered.

If the probability of success is .6, the expected monetary gain if the player is hired equals .6($200,000) + .4(–$150,000), or $60,000. Thus, the decision is not altered.

(c) If P is this probability, then

$$P(\$200,000) + (1 - P)(-\$150,000) = 0.$$

Thus,
$$P(\$200,000 + \$150,000) = \$150,000.$$
$$P = 150,000 \div 350,000 = 3/7.$$

That is, the probability of success that will make the owner indifferent between hiring and not hiring the player is 3/7.

5. (a) Risk lover.
   (b) Risk lover.
   (c) Risk lover.
   (d) Risk averter.

6. Let $U(0) = 0$ and $U(\$2,500) = 1$. Then,

$$U(\$1,000) = 0.5U(0) + 0.5U(\$2,500) = 0.5.$$

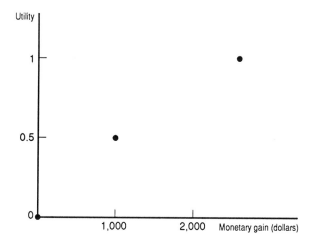

7. (a) The owner seems to be risk neutral, because in both cases the expected value of the gamble equals the certain amount.

   (b) Let $U(\$5,000) = 0$ and $U(\$10,000) = 1$. Then,

   $$U(\$7,500) = 0.5U(\$5,000) + 0.5U(\$10,000) = 0.5.$$

   Further, $U(\$10,000) = .05U(\$7,500) + 0.5U(\$12,500)$, which means that

   $$1 = 0.5(0.5) + 0.5U(\$12,500).$$

   Thus, $U(\$12,500) = .75 \div .5 = 1.5$. The four points are shown below.

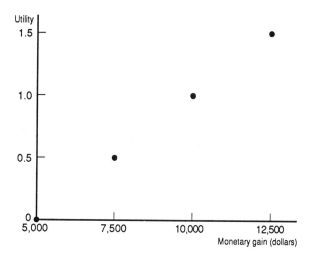

8. (a)

$$\frac{\Pr\{\text{pass test}\,|\,\text{success}\}\Pr\{\text{success}\}}{\Pr\{\text{pass test}\,|\,\text{success}\}\Pr\{\text{success}\} + \Pr\{\text{pass test}\,|\,\text{failure}\}\Pr\{\text{failure}\}}$$

$$= \frac{(.8)(.5)}{(.8)(.5)+(.1)(.5)} = \frac{.4}{.4+.05} = \frac{8}{9}.$$

$$\frac{\Pr\{\text{pass test}\,|\,\text{failure}\}\Pr\{\text{failure}\}}{\Pr\{\text{pass test}\,|\,\text{failure}\}\Pr\{\text{failure}\} + \Pr\{\text{pass test}\,|\,\text{success}\}\Pr\{\text{success}\}}$$

$$= \frac{(.1)(.5)}{(.1)(.5)+(.8)(.5)} = \frac{.05}{.45} = \frac{1}{9}.$$

$$\frac{\Pr\{\text{fail test}\,|\,\text{success}\}\Pr\{\text{success}\}}{\Pr\{\text{fail test}\,|\,\text{success}\}\Pr\{\text{success}\} + \Pr\{\text{fail test}\,|\,\text{failure}\}\Pr\{\text{failure}\}}$$

$$= \frac{(.2)(.5)}{(.2)(.5)+(.9)(.5)} = \frac{.1}{.1+.45} = \frac{2}{11}.$$

$$\frac{\Pr\{\text{fail test}\,|\,\text{failure}\}\Pr\{\text{failure}\}}{\Pr\{\text{fail test}\,|\,\text{failure}\}\Pr\{\text{failure}\} + \Pr\{\text{fail test}\,|\,\text{success}\}\Pr\{\text{success}\}}$$

$$= \frac{(.9)(.5)}{(.9)(.5)+(.2)(.5)} = \frac{.45}{.55} = \frac{9}{11}.$$

(b) If the firm hired the graduate, the prior expected value of monetary gain was .5($100,000) + .5(–$80,000) = $10,000. If the firm did not hire the graduate, the prior expected value of monetary gain was zero.

(c) If the graduate failed the tests, the posterior expected value of monetary gain if the firm hired the graduate was

$$(2/11)(\$100,000) + (9/11)(-\$80,000) = -\$520,000/11 = -\$47,273.$$

If the firm did not hire the graduate, the posterior expected value of monetary gain was zero. Comparing these results with those in (b), it is clear that if the firm maximizes expected monetary value it should reach a different decision after the results of the tests than prior to the results. Whereas before test results were available the firm should have hired the graduate, the opposite decision should have been made after results were available.

(d) The prior expected value of perfect information was

$$.5(\$100,000) + .5(0) - \$10,000 = \$40,000.$$

The posterior expected value of perfect information was

$$(2/11)(\$100,000) + (9/11)(0) - (-\$47,273) = \$65,455.$$

These values differ because the posterior probabilities differ from the prior probabilities, and the posterior expected value of monetary gain differs from the prior expected value of monetary gain.

(e) The opportunity loss for each action, given each possible state of nature, is shown below.

State of nature	Hire graduate	Do not hire graduate
Graduate will be a success	0	$100,000
Graduate will not be a success	$80,000	0

If the firm hires the graduate, the expected opportunity loss is

$$.5(0) + .5(\$80,000) = \$40,000.$$

If the firm does not hire the graduate, the expected opportunity loss is

$$.5(\$100,000) + .5(0) = \$50,000.$$

The best action is to hire the graduate, since this results in the lower expected opportunity loss. The expected opportunity loss corresponding to this action is $40,000, which is equal to the prior expected value of perfect information. See the answer to (d).

9. (a)

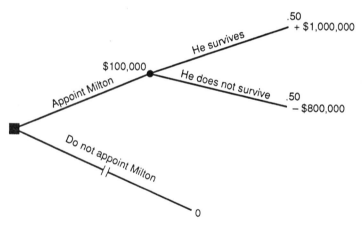

The optimal decision is to appoint Milton.

(b) $Pr\{$survive $|$ opinion is survival$\} =$

$$\frac{Pr\{\text{opinion is survival} \,|\, \text{survive}\} Pr\{\text{survive}\}}{Pr\{\text{opinion is survival} \,|\, \text{survive}\} Pr\{\text{survive}\} + Pr\{\text{opinion is survival} \,|\, \text{death}\} Pr\{\text{death}\}}$$

$$= \frac{(.6)(.5)}{(.6)(.5) + (.4)(.5)} = \frac{.30}{.50} = .60.$$

(c) $Pr\{$survive $|$ opinion is death$\} =$

$$\frac{Pr\{\text{opinion is death} \,|\, \text{survive}\} Pr\{\text{survive}\}}{Pr\{\text{opinion is death} \,|\, \text{survive}\} Pr\{\text{survive}\} + Pr\{\text{opinion is death} \,|\, \text{death}\} Pr\{\text{death}\}}$$

$$= \frac{(.4)(.5)}{(.4)(.5) + (.6)(.5)} = \frac{.20}{.50} = .40.$$

(d)

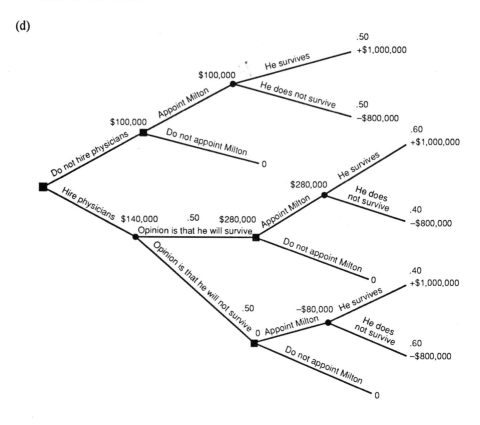

(e) *Pr*{opinion is survival} = *Pr*{opinion is survival | survive}*Pr*{survive} + *Pr*{opinion is survival | death}*Pr*{death} = (.6)(.5) + (.4)(.5) = .5.

(f) $140,000 – $100,000, or $40,000, since this is the expected value of the sample information.

(g) It certainly is true that if analyses of this sort are based on distorted, unreliable values of the prior probabilities, the results are likely to be wrong and misleading. However, the results may not be sensitive to small errors in them. One can, of course, see how changes in these prior probabilities affect the results.